The Culture War in the Civil Rights Movement

UNIVERSITY PRESS OF FLORIDA

Florida A&M University, Tallahassee
Florida Atlantic University, Boca Raton
Florida Gulf Coast University, Ft. Myers
Florida International University, Miami
Florida State University, Tallahassee
New College of Florida, Sarasota
University of Central Florida, Orlando
University of Florida, Gainesville
University of North Florida, Jacksonville
University of South Florida, Tampa
University of West Florida, Pensacola

The Culture War in the

University Press of Florida
Gainesville
Tallahassee
Tampa
Boca Raton
Pensacola
Orlando
Miami
Jacksonville
Ft. Myers
Sarasota

Civil Rights Movement

Joe Street

22 21 20 19 18 17   6 5 4 3 2 1

First cloth printing, 2007
First paperback printing, 2017

Library of Congress Cataloging-in-Publication Data
Street, Joe.
The culture war in the Civil Rights Movement / Joe Street.
p. cm.
Includes bibliographical references and index.
ISBN 978-0-8130-3196-5 (cloth: alk. paper)
ISBN 978-0-8130-5487-2 (pbk.)
1. African Americans—Civil rights—History—20th century.
2. Civil rights movements—United States—History—20th century.
3. African Americans in popular culture—History—20th century.
4. African Americans—Race identity. 5. Popular culture—United
States—History—20th century. 6. United States—Race relations—
History—20th century. I. Title.
E185.61.S9144 2007
323.1196'073—dc22   2007027541

The University Press of Florida is the scholarly publishing agency
for the State University System of Florida, comprising Florida
A&M University, Florida Atlantic University, Florida Gulf
Coast University, Florida International University, Florida State
University, New College of Florida, University of Central Florida,
University of Florida, University of North Florida, University of
South Florida, and University of West Florida.

University Press of Florida
15 Northwest 15th Street
Gainesville, FL 32611-2079
http://upress.ufl.edu

For Ruth,
. . . And all I possess, I give to you

Contents

Figures

Abbreviations

AAA	Afro-American Association
BARTS	Black Arts Repertory Theater/School
BPP	Black Panther Party
CEP	Citizenship Education Program
CIO	Congress of Industrial Organizations
COFO	Council of Federated Organizations
CORE	Congress of Racial Equality
FPCC	Fair Play for Cuba Committee
FST	Free Southern Theater
NAACP	National Association for the Advancement of Colored People
OAAU	Organization of Afro-American Unity
OYM	Organization of Young Men
PPC	Poor People's Campaign
SCLC	Southern Christian Leadership Conference
SFCRP	Southern Folk Cultural Revival Project
SGCV	Southeast Georgia Crusade for Voters
SNCC	Student Nonviolent Coordinating Committee
SSOC	Southern Student Organizing Committee
VEP	Voter Education Project

Acknowledgments

Many people have contributed to the production of this book. They all deserve more than a mere mention in these pages. First of all, Robert Cook has been an inspirational, encouraging, and hugely supportive supervisor, colleague, and friend. It is with immense pride that I am able to say that I was—and in numerous ways always will be—his student.

My family has been incredibly supportive. My fab sister, Jenny, told me years ago that I would write a book. I hope that this one is adequate. Eddy (Dad) and Anna have always provided a loving and supportive environment. Barbara—Mum—inspires me daily. Tesni is, as she always says, fine. Col is a true friend. My grandparents, Eddie and Laura, support everything I do. The Mynotts keep me on the straight and narrow and the McGroarys are as welcoming a family as anyone could have.

My great friend Kris Holl and her parents, Steven and Kathy, fed, clothed, and housed me during three(!) research trips. Words cannot express my gratitude for their kindness and friendship. Suffice to say that the Holls occupy a special place in my heart. Jon Wallace and Anne Langley offered me a room and friendship in Chapel Hill. Elizabeth Eagleson, Alan, Delia, and Stuey have always been available to pour oil on troubled waters. I treasure their friendship. Jim, Christine, and Alice Pawley kindly offered me the top floor of their house and their friendship. I shall never forget their generosity and support. Jordi Getman and Patrick Michelson entertained me for many evenings. Finally, my cousin Randi Herman and her husband Steve, took me into their home. They have my enduring love and gratitude.

At home, I could not ask for better friends than Matt Garlick, Kevin Watson, and Simon Hall, better known as The Mo. Matt keeps me laughing and regularly punctures my delusions. Kev is always ready for a frothy beer, a bad movie, and random conversation. With good humor, The Mo has fielded many phone calls related to this book. Most recently, he cast an editorial eye over the introduction with only seven cups of tea, a roast pork sandwich, one egg custard, and half a Twix for sustenance, and says that he deserves full credit for paragraph nine, sentence four. His visits always provide moments of great comedy, often of a slapstick nature. My friends Graham Macklin, Peter Webster, Colin Howley, Rosie Wild, Sid Lowe, Tracey Wire, Alun Burge, and fellow Albion fans Andy Jones and Chris Gripton are excellent company and lent great support. Thanks, guys. I also wish to thank my colleagues at Sheffield and Kent for their companionship and support over the last few years.

The staff at all the institutions at which my research was conducted were patient, efficient, and gave good advice freely. Many thanks to those in the Manuscripts Departments at the Library of Congress, the State Historical Society of Wisconsin, Stanford University, the Bancroft Library, and UNC (particularly Laura Brown and Amy Davis); JoEllen El Bashir and her terrific colleagues at the Moorland-Spingarn Research Center; Clayborne Carson and the staff at the Martin Luther King, Jr. Papers Project; Brenda Square and the staff of the Amistad Research Center. Emory Douglas kindly gave an afternoon to talk about his life. Thank you to the funding sources, including the Streets, BAAS, UNC, the RHS, and Sheffield University. Many, many thanks to Meredith Morris-Babb and Eli Bortz at UPF for their sterling support and hard work on my behalf.

Among the genuinely friendly and supportive community of American historians, the bearded wonder Hugh Wilford, Richard Carwardine, and Dom Sandbrook offered advice, inspiration, and comradeship. Adam Fairclough gave trenchant criticism and sage advice. Bill Van Deburg offered an excellent critique of the manuscript and much support. Thank you, Bill. Brian Ward, Peter Ling, Tim Tyson, Geneva Smitherman, Erika Doss, John Rickford, Nick Salvatore, Howard Zinn, Cleveland Sellers, Stephen Tuck, John Dittmer, and Robert Cassanello gave helpful advice along the way. The footnotes attest to the debt that I owe generations of scholars. I should say that the faults in the book are mine alone, but I am sure that The Mo contributed to them, somehow.

Above all of this, Ruth has been the most important person in my life for some time now. Her enthusiasm for and faith in my work are unwavering sources of inspiration, and her love brings me an inexpressible amount of happiness. She is the love of my life, and this book is for her.

Finally, without Ann and Claude Mynott, none of this would have happened. My only regret is that they are not here to see it completed. This book is also dedicated, with much love, to Grandma and Grandad.

Introduction

On the opening night of the Southern Christian Leadership Conference's (SCLC) tenth anniversary convention held in Atlanta, Georgia, during August 1967, the delegates gathered for a gala banquet. Aretha Franklin sang for her supper and was given a special award to acknowledge her contribution to the civil rights movement. Franklin had not been a frontline demonstrator for civil rights; nor was she prone to outspoken political statements. She was, however, known in movement circles for her generosity toward civil rights workers. More important, her songs were huge Billboard chart hits, and were considered by many to be expressions of racial pride that related strongly to the ongoing movement. Five months after the banquet, Franklin was the recipient of another honor. Her hometown of Detroit declared that, as part of Black History Week, 16 February 1968 was to be "Aretha Franklin Day." The highlight was a homecoming performance by Franklin at Cobo Hall. That evening, an ecstatic crowd cheered Franklin's set and went even wilder when she introduced a secret guest. Visibly exhausted from his strenuous efforts on behalf of the civil rights movement, Martin Luther King Jr. entered from the wings. Laryngitis robbed the audience of King's sonorous tones, but his presentation of the SCLC's Drum Beat Award to Franklin spoke volumes about the relationship between the civil rights movement and African American culture.[1]

For two weeks in June 1967, "Respect," Franklin's second Atlantic Records single, sat at the number one spot on Billboard's "Hot 100" chart. Her previous single, the top ten hit "I Never Loved a Man (The Way I Love You)," dramatized the helplessness of her love for a "no good heartbreaker." When sung by its writer, Otis Redding, "Respect" continued this domestic theme, being a call for domestic respect and conjugal rights. By its very nature, Franklin's interpretation flipped this clichéd gender relationship on its head.

Meanwhile, the song's audience imposed its own interpretations and meanings onto the song. While musical texts may have one particular intention, their interaction with their audience in the public arena often reveals further meanings, as was the case with "Respect." In the charged atmosphere of 1967, "Respect" assumed a weighty political message. Many took the song to be a metaphor for the message of the entire civil rights movement. Redding's claim to his rights thus became a call for (domestic) gender and (public) racial equality. For *Ebony* magazine, the song effectively became the "new Negro national anthem." The SCLC's very public alignment with Franklin should be interpreted within this context of these shifting messages and meanings of popular culture.[2]

From a certain perspective, it appears that King was simply cashing in on Aretha Franklin's popularity. Following his condemnation of the Vietnam War, he found himself increasingly alienated from the federal government. As evinced by his exhaustion, he was struggling to build bridges in the northern black community after the failure of the SCLC's 1966 Chicago campaign. King and the SCLC needed to reestablish their national standing at a time when the nonviolent movement seemed to be at the mercy of the Black Panther Party's guns and Kwame Ture's furious oratory.[3] Franklin's popularity in northern urban centers represented a ripe opportunity for the SCLC to attract much-needed youth appeal and illustrate its national program. In this manner, the relationship with Franklin reflects the SCLC's attempt to capture the zeitgeist and underline its radical credentials.

Franklin's award must also be understood within the context of the role that celebrities play in modern culture. The civil rights movement often attempted to use the fame of certain individuals in order to boost its own popularity: the comedian Dick Gregory and the writer James Baldwin, among many others, made appearances at civil rights protests. Civil rights organizations competed with each other for funds, publicity, prominence, and even a form of radical chic. That Franklin was known to hand out concert tickets to Student Nonviolent Coordinating Committee (SNCC) activists rather than SCLC workers adds another layer of meaning onto King's public association with her. SNCC was a more youthful, radical, and, by the mid-1960s, less Christian organization than the SCLC. Although it was in terminal decline by the time of Aretha Franklin Day, it retained an almost mythical aura in movement circles, due to its earlier involvement at the radical edge of the civil rights movement. The patronage of the most popular African American singer in the country, one whose popularity transcended many racial divides, was appealing to the SCLC, and through the relationship with

Franklin, the SCLC could continue to press its claim to preeminence within the movement. Moreover, Franklin's approval could offer the organization a direct link with youth culture and, perhaps, a more radical constituency. If the historian Craig Werner is right to situate "Respect" as the moment that indicated the civil rights movement's shift from King's interracial coalition to the more radical polemic of the Black Power generation, then King's move could be interpreted as an attempt to bridge a widening generational and political divide. In light of her popularity, Franklin's bandwagon was certainly one worth chasing. Thus the award should be linked to the SCLC's continuing campaign to place itself as the most visible and successful civil rights pressure group.[4]

Symbolically, the meeting also represented a passing of the civil rights baton. King's mass demonstrations were a declining force for change. His faltering popularity in urban America contrasted with the national success of Franklin's records. The epochal nature of Franklin's entry onto the popular music scene placed soul music in the center of the national consciousness. As Bob Rolontz, the head of promotion at Atlantic Records, recalled, "Aretha came, Aretha conquered and made that soul trend happen." Her records paved the way for more explicitly political soul music such as Sly and the Family Stone's "Don't Call Me Nigger, Whitey" and Marvin Gaye's 1971 opus, *What's Going On*. White acceptance of the new African American mood seemed to be confined to the pop charts, far from the physical realities of housing, schooling, and employment. King's meeting with Franklin thus appears at a moment when the vanguard of the African American freedom struggle transformed from mass political demonstrations into cultural articulations of racial identity. Franklin's identity also poses questions about the gendered relationship between politics and culture. King's interaction with Franklin might suggest that the SCLC was upholding a gender relationship that associated men with politics and women with less explicitly political actions. But the political nature of this mass culture was coming to the fore, and women had been advancing to leadership positions in the movement. In a sense, King was deferring to Franklin's more potent leadership potential. This moment confirms that leadership was not an exclusively male right and that culture/politics and male/female demarcations were more fluid than rigid.[5]

Adding to the complexity of King's meeting with the Queen of Soul is the fact that the SCLC president was a good friend of Franklin's preacher father, the Reverend C. L. Franklin. His preaching at the New Bethel Baptist Church in Detroit was considered so unearthly that two nurses were always on hand to tend to overwhelmed parishioners. He was not averse to politicizing the Word, not least because his church was only four blocks from Albert Cleage's Shrine of the Black Madonna and one mile away from the Nation of Islam's Mosque Number 1, where Malcolm X often spoke. Rev. Franklin's daughter was a devout Christian who had traversed the country numerous times with his gospel caravan. Her childhood had been spent in the musical, and occasionally physical, company of legendary gospel singers such as Clara Ward and Mahalia Jackson. She was candid about her musical influences, telling *Time* magazine in 1968, "My heart is still there in gospel music. It never left." Indeed, in commenting on *Amazing Grace*, her 1972 gospel album, Franklin identifies gospel as "the original source of my musical inspiration. . . . Church is as much as me as the air I breathe." Although ostensibly a secular song, "Respect" reflects many gospel characteristics: Franklin's vocals are punctuated by exclamations from her backing singers, much like gospel singers are backed up by their choir; the interplay between Franklin and her backing singers reflects call-and-response gestures, in similar fashion to the interplay between Franklin's message and her public's interpretation of the song. After the middle eight, Franklin stops the music to spell out her message ("R-E-S-P-E-C-T/Find out what it means to me"), much like preachers stopped their sermons to speak a few impromptu words to the congregation before returning to their text. Franklin's vocal also reflects the close relationship between the mundane and the transcendental. Within this context, the meeting between King and Franklin takes on a more religious air and illustrates the centrality of Christianity to the movement. King's approval, therefore, is an example of the SCLC's continuing insistence that Christianity was central to African American life.[6]

Even while the African American community was being atomized and subordinated under slavery and later segregation, it was able to forge a certain level of autonomy through, for example, the church and music. This cultural autonomy was one of the means through which African Americans were able to express themselves to each other and continue a tradition of accommodation and resistance, one exploited by the civil rights movement.[7] Franklin's music, for example, was an extension of the songs sung by slaves in the antebellum period. Call-and-response dynamics emerged in the work songs that field slaves sang to give their work rhythm and to take their thoughts away from the mindless drudgery of their work. The psychological importance of the songs developed from their lyrical content. They might have expressed the singers' sorrow, but they also spoke of the joy of life and, crucially, to a future without slavery. Thus, the spirituals and work songs offered psychological freedom to physically enslaved African Americans. The reactions of many African Americans to Aretha Franklin's work suggest that the promise of this psychological freedom remained of vital importance. "Miss Ree saved some of us," stated one black solider who fought in Vietnam. "After one of those suicide missions . . . we put on that tape, 'Chain of Fools.' . . . We danced [to that record] until we puked our guts out and laughed and cried. . . . If we hadn't have done it, I might have lost my mind." In this sense, Franklin was tapping into a centuries-long tradition of song. The SCLC, too, was doing so by association.[8]

Franklin's music represents the many regional tributaries of African American culture and an undeniable cross-racial influence. Born in Memphis, Tennessee, to Mississippian parents, Franklin was raised in Detroit. Her frequent singing tours opened her ears and eyes to many different regional cultures. Her singing reflected both the gospel songs of her childhood and the urban sounds emanating from the Hitsville studio of the Motown record label in Detroit. She united the smoothness of Sam Cooke with the rambunctiousness of Ray Charles, the spirituality of her idol Clara Ward with the carnality of Jackie Wilson. Her first Atlantic recordings were made in the Deep South, at Fame Studios in Muscle Shoals, Alabama, with the all-white house band that specialized in a hybrid music that equally reflected soul and country-and-western influences. Toward the end of her first session at Fame, tensions between the musicians and Franklin's husband boiled over, leading to Franklin's departure from the studio. She and the band later completed the sessions in New York City, with the assistance of the African American saxophonist King Curtis and Franklin's sisters, Carolyn and Erma. "I Never Loved a Man" and "Respect," the two most famous records from these sessions, were, respectively, written by a northerner and a southerner. Although she never returned to Alabama to record, the Muscle Shoals musicians continued to play on her records; the distinctive sound that they generated typified Franklin's work in the late 1960s.[9] Franklin's music combined northern and southern black and white influences, reflecting the fact that there is not an exclusive homogenous African American culture. It highlights the importance of regional identities and cultures within the black American population and the interaction between the local and the national, the North and the South.[10]

King's appearance with Franklin, then, suggests much about the relationship between the civil rights movement in the 1960s and African American culture. It begs questions relating to when, why, and how the SCLC concluded that an association with Franklin was worthwhile, and how the organization conceived of the relationship between African American cultural expressions and civil rights action. It suggests that the moderate movement was cognizant of the power of cultural forms and their utility as political weapons, an issue that historians have generally overlooked. Throughout the decade of the 1960s, cultural politics was contested terrain within the movement.[11] King's relationship with Franklin also poses numerous questions about the influence of gender, geography, urbanization, and generational change on the civil rights movement and how they helped shape the movement's deployment of cultural forms as political weapons. Few histories of the civil rights movement have engaged with these questions, which are crucial for an understanding of the wide parameters and profound implications of the civil rights movement.

What, though, is "culture," and how should it be interpreted in relation to the civil rights movement? Culture is best understood as a collection of customs, artistic expressions, and public expressions of learning and identity that define a way of life and afford insight into the core values of a society. Civil rights movement activists and supporters can be viewed as a society with certain shared values that focus on achieving rights and respect for black Americans. The key issue that the King-Franklin relationship raises surrounds the use of this culture for political ends: how African American cultural forms (referring to genre, such as jazz or theater) or expressions (such as an individual song or theatrical play) were manipulated to make a political point, to bolster a political argument in a public arena, or, as in Franklin's case, to boost the civil rights movement's appeal among certain constituencies.[12] These issues can be explored through an evaluation of the symbolic dimensions of certain cultural forms—secular and religious music, linguistic and visual arts, education, aspects of history and folklore—and a semiotic interpretation of the role of "high" cultural forms such as literature and theater. These public forms were more likely to be used as organizing tools or political weapons than generally private expressions, which were designed primarily to energize existing participants.[13] The freedom songs, for example, were central to the movement experience, particularly for early 1960s activists. Certain cultural workers such as James Baldwin and Dick Gregory used their art as a political weapon, addressing it to the concerns of the movement. Education was fundamental to the movement's quest to redefine the United States. The fight for better schools for black children lay at the heart of the civil rights struggle; some activists took it upon themselves to create these schools and offer education to adults and children alike in an attempt to transform the self-image of black southerners and the political culture of the South itself. Plays were performed for local people during movement campaigns such as the 1964 Mississippi Summer Project, and were often accompanied by workshops, which enabled audiences to interact with the players. Furthermore, many such plays contained elements of audience participation in an attempt to erase the bond between spectator and performer. This new audience-performer relationship mirrored the personal relationship that many movement activists hoped to generate between themselves and the local people that they encountered during their organizing efforts. Movement participants frequently used these cultural forms to broaden both the parameters of the movement and the movement's appeal to ordinary Americans. Movement activists engaged with and used these cultural productions at a local level, where white hegemony was most easily challenged. At this level, participants and observers were encouraged to develop an individual, personal relationship with the movement and to espy the close links between cultural forms and political action. While movement activists were not able to control the discourse completely, they were able to use it to demonstrate the validity of political action.[14] Certain cultural expressions are emblematic of the relationship between the movement and African American culture. Amiri Baraka's journalism and plays, for example, reflect the growth of black nationalism in the 1960s. Baraka suggests that some roots of Black Power lay in the Cuban Revolution and that the black nationalist critique emerged outside the nonviolent movement. Yet his relationship with militant black activist Robert F. Williams also confirms that there were strong links between Black Power and the southern movement.

By making the civil rights movement part of people's lives, civil rights activism transcended the boundary between the personal and the political, thereby widening participation in the movement itself. In a similar fashion, the organizing efforts that manipulated certain cultural forms often attempted to blur the distinctions between politics and culture: the act of reading a book could be a political act; watching a play could inspire political action; a piece of music was part of a political struggle. The transformative power of these cultural forms at the individual level between movement participants is the central issue. The examples of civil rights activists deliberately constructing or manipulating cultural forms or expressions for their own devices offer useful insights into the movement's engagement with the wider culture (in the anthropological sense) and into the development of the movement itself. The attempt to control these forms represented a battleground for self-definition within the movement and helped to place the issue of racial identity at its center. Crucially, the fact that movement activists or organizations constructed and attempted to define the terms under which cultural forms were used for political purposes situates these forms as an arena in which discourse concerning the movement's development could occur.

The use of cultural forms and expressions as organizing and political tools might be called "cultural organizing." The term is used to indicate when activists made an explicit attempt to use cultural forms or expressions as an integral, perhaps even dominant, part of the political struggle and when, during this process, attention was drawn to the intrinsic political meaning of the cultural activity. The role of theater in SNCC's 1964 Mississippi Summer Project, for example, is termed cultural organizing. Here theater was employed to reinforce the project's political message, to unite audience members behind that message—and that of the wider civil rights movement—and to develop bonds between the audience, the actors, and the activists. The Summer Project built on the methodology practiced in citizenship education by activists linked to the Highlander Folk School, where the lived experience of black southerners became a tool to teach literacy, numeracy, and other skills necessary for participation in American political life. Elsewhere, Baraka used theater as a conduit through which he could develop community organizations in Harlem and later Newark, and to broaden the appeal of black nationalism among young African Americans. He deliberately constructed his plays to force his audiences to confront their own political realities, both as individuals and as a group. Theater, in his view, "should force change." His was "a political theatre, a weapon" in the struggle for black freedom.[15] Dick Gregory's presence in the local campaign in Greenwood, Mississippi similarly emboldened and inspired the local community. His national renown as a comedian and his comedy routines themselves became important weapons in the local struggle. The Black Panther Party (BPP) even employed an artist to transmit its political message.

This is not to suggest that the forms under consideration here comprised the totality of African American culture during the period of the civil rights movement, or to deny the importance of the movement's engagement with other elements in the wider American culture. Religion, of course, was fundamental to the movement's ability to motivate and organize black Americans. The SCLC was also well aware of the importance of media imagery to the success of its direct action campaigns, and made sure that its demonstrations received adequate media coverage. The eruption of violence by white segregationists provided powerful images that resonated far beyond the immediate surroundings of the campaigns and placed the civil rights movement in the national and international spotlight. Elsewhere, radio was a crucial site for discussion of both movement campaigns and wider issues pertaining to black identity and integration, and complex links existed between movement activities and cultural production in Detroit.[16] These were undeniably important to the movement. The discussion at hand, however, focuses on the (mostly secular) forms that were integral to the organizing style of certain important initiatives: freedom songs were central to Highlander's praxis and to the conduct of civil rights demonstrations in Albany, Georgia; theater work was, according to SNCC, one of the two or three most important aspects of the 1964 Summer Project; Baraka's plays were geared toward developing black nationalist sentiment among his audience, and he insisted that black music was inherently political; for many supporters and members of the BPP, Emory Douglas's artwork was the most significant element of the party's newspapers.[17] Taken together, they illustrate how African American cultural identity became an important aspect of the civil rights movement's campaign during the early 1960s, and how this focus informed the development of black militancy later in the decade. They demonstrate how civil rights activists tried to meld politics with culture, how the focus on black culture offered psychological and spiritual benefits but also hindered the movement's ability to appeal to a multiracial constituency.

While there should be no reification of divisions between "high" and "low" culture, distinctions are necessary for easy reference. "Popular" culture denotes cultural forms that attract and are to an extent reliant upon a mass audience, such as recorded pop or soul music. While literature and theater are certainly popular forms, not least because books and plays need an audience for their continued relevance, their position within our understanding of the European cultural model means that they can be termed *high* culture. Folk cultural forms are performed in a more organic fashion than the other types and are characterized by interaction between performers and audience, and between different generations of performers. There is less reliance on popularity with a mass audience for their perpetuation and perhaps a closer relationship between the content and the form. The elements of communality and connection between performers, audiences, and the works performed are greater within the folk culture sphere than in the popular and high culture spheres, although this is not to suggest that there is no such interaction in popular and high culture. Folk culture also tends to be more fluid and more reliant upon oral transmission than popular culture, which in recent times has become largely dependant upon either written or recorded documentation for its longevity. Thus gospel music, which developed over centuries within the black community, is regarded as a folk cultural form, despite its popular audience. This is not to divide popular from folk culture, since many popular forms retain strong roots in "the folk," and of course some folk forms reach a popular audience. Most obviously, soul music is clearly rooted in gospel, black spirituals, jazz, and to some extent country music. Similarly, many forms of folk culture rely to some degree on a popular audience: certainly, the popularity of folk music among white activists in the civil rights movement must not be divorced from the contemporaneous folk music revival in the popular music charts.[18] Nor is this discussion concerned with the transformation from "folk" to "popular" or with judging the relative artistic and/or political value of each to the individual and to society. Merely for purposes of simplification, forms of culture that rely on popular exposure will be referred to as "popular"; those more closely identified with a more intimate, personal interaction will be termed *folk*.

Folk culture was of great importance to the civil rights movement and formed one of its most important backbones. The songs of the movement emerged out of the confluence of white folk music, slave songs, and the black gospel tradition. Through these songs and through engaging with this biracial singing tradition, the movement helped to forge a cultural form of its own. The songs gave spiritual uplift to participants, engendered a spirit of unity, inspired and mobilized thousands, and embedded the movement in the psyche of many more. They even provided the opportunity for civil rights organizations to generate funds through concert performances and album sales. Without song, the movement would have been a very different phenomenon. But the movement also engaged with folk culture in a subtler manner. As Antonio Gramsci suggests, education is used in the construction of a popular hegemony. It therefore follows that counterhegemonic practices can be revised to include education.[19] Through the educational programs of the Citizenship Education Program (CEP) and SNCC's 1964 Mississippi Summer Project, African American adults and children learned to take pride in their own culture. Educators learned that African American culture could be a powerful educational tool. Indeed, singing was a fundamental component of these programs: lessons began and ended with the communal singing of freedom songs. More important, folk culture was an important pedagogic element of the movement. Through it, the movement was able to involve many people who might otherwise have been left to continue their lives without access to the American political system. Without the protection of literacy, many southern blacks were unable to register to vote. Prior to (and indeed, following) the passage of the 1965 Voting Rights Act, the educational policy of the civil rights movement played a vital role in creating a new political culture in the South. This education policy also sheds light on the relationship between movement organizations and the local community. The Highlander Folk School was central to the development of the link between education and freedom. Highlander laid much of the groundwork for the civil rights movement, training generations of activists for social protest and contributing in no small way to the transformation of southern politics. Its fusion of the indigenous culture of black and white Americans drew influence from religious and secular thought to form a culture of protest. The success of the CEP was a result of its grounding in the communities of the rural South and its application of local experience and culture as an educational tool. Highlander's staff believed that oppressed people were cognizant of the most effective strategies through which to overcome oppression and that it was the task of organizers and activists to facilitate the transformation of these ideas into action. This conviction was tremendously influential on SNCC and helped to define SNCC's conception of the civil rights struggle. Highlander also maintained that folk culture, such as song and dance, was of vital importance in solidifying bonds between people and in creating a sense of community. Without Highlander, the so-called culture of the civil rights movement would have developed an entirely different character.

Another concern of the movement was the reclamation of black history from white America. Most scholars of Black Power acknowledge that Black Power activists sought to reject the dominant white interpretation of history and white control of black education. The response to William Styron's *The Confessions of Nat Turner* and the furor over Black Studies are pertinent examples of this in action. For Malcolm X, as for Frederick Douglass, W. E. B. Du Bois, and others, reclaiming black history was a vital concern. Malcolm insisted that the lack of knowledge about history was one of the black community's key failings and stressed that to become free, African Americans had to be awakened to their history. Similarly, history was a prime concern of SNCC's 1964 Mississippi Summer Project. This initiative established a network of independent "freedom schools," where children and adults received education in a variety of subjects. One of the most important achievements of the summer of 1964, the freedom schools have been underappreciated by historians concerned more with the effect of the project on voter registration or on the white students who assisted in the registration campaign and taught in the freedom schools. The SNCC schools placed particular emphasis on instruction in black history, which further illuminates how cultural forms were manipulated to stimulate political action. The Summer Project represents a confluence of a number of the intellectual and cultural concerns debated in the integrationist phase of the civil rights movement, including the rise of black nationalism, the impact of class, and the influence of Highlander.[20]

Certain African American literary texts were used as educational tools in movement activities, but the work of Amiri Baraka was of more significance to the 1960s generation of black artists and activists. He initially refused to engage with the movement, but events compelled him to embroil himself in the struggle. In a series of polemical articles and his landmark study of black music, *Blues People*, Baraka demonstrated that African American art was inextricably linked with African American political life. He insisted that the innovative jazz music played by African American musicians in the early 1960s was central to the redefinition of black identity. This thesis was promoted further through his theatrical work, most notably in two plays from 1964, *Dutchman* and *The Slave*. During the late 1960s, his interpretation of the relationship between jazz and the political struggle grew even more strident, reaching its apex in his 1967 play, *Slave Ship*, which triumphantly unites black cultural expressions with the liberation struggle and draws together a number of themes in his theater and journalism.[21]

In 1969, the Free Southern Theater (FST) toured *Slave Ship*. The theater group emerged from SNCC in 1964 and then established itself as an independent organization. It played a central role in SNCC's 1964 Mississippi Summer Project before relocating to New Orleans and embracing black nationalism. This philosophical development came about largely as a result of the FST's experience of working in the South; consequently, the FST's history is another significant indicator of how the movement itself generated black nationalist sentiment. After its relocation, the FST searched for a play that accurately reflected the African American experience. The search concluded with *Slave Ship*. The FST's longevity suggests that the union of culture and politics could succeed at a local level, that the emergence of Black Power was linked to southern organizing initiatives, and that Black Power activism was not limited to northern urban centers. The FST also reveals Black Power's financial paradox: its reliance on white foundation support amid general black middle-class indifference.

Elsewhere, cultural figures and forms aided movement campaigns and contributed to the development of movement ideology. The 1961 civil rights campaign in Albany, Georgia, was one of the turning points of the civil rights movement, notably because it revealed the profound impact that the singing culture of Highlander could have on civil rights activism, not least when it was fused with black choral traditions. The relationship that developed between SNCC activists in Albany and the local population also became an influential testing ground for SNCC's later organizing style. Another result of the Albany movement was the formation of SNCC's Freedom Singers, who toured the nation in an effort to raise funds for and consciousness about the movement. Dick Gregory was one celebrity who was drawn into the movement by his conscience and who defined the terms under which he protested. While Gregory's union of comedy and politics was not replicated elsewhere, it remains highly suggestive of the many links between African American politics and culture at the time. Robert F. Williams's radio broadcasts from Cuba electrified thousands of listeners during the movement's peak through his innovative mix of political invective and provocative music. For Williams, as for Baraka, African American culture was both a central battleground for black liberation and a bond to unite the black community.

The relationship between the BPP and African American art reveals that the cultural impulse permeated most African American protest organizations during the 1960s. The dispute between the BPP and US, the latter organization led by the cultural nationalist Maulana Ron Karenga, reveals the extent to which the BPP acknowledged how important cultural forms could be to the liberation struggle and suggests that the party's conception of cultural nationalism was more nuanced than its rhetoric suggests. Contrary to most historical evaluations, this was no battle over the validity of using cultural forms as political weapons. Rather, this dispute concerned the importance of African culture (as opposed to African American culture) to African American political organizing.

As Black Power became an influential force within the civil rights movement, many moderates within the movement were forced to grapple with the notion that black culture and identity were key battlegrounds. Their reaction to the insistence that culture was the key to liberation was a contributing factor in the movement's dissolution, and their belated attempts to jump on the cultural bandwagon contributed to this decline. The SCLC desired simultaneously to Christianize Black Power culture, uphold the "black is beautiful" message, and help create a multiracial army of the poor—a confused, even paradoxical response to Black Power. Hoping to reunite the people of the South with their biracial folk traditions, Anne Romaine and Bernice Reagon established an organization, the Southern Folk Cultural Revival Project, to promote the singing culture that both had experienced at Highlander. Their experience illuminates how Black Power worked to undermine interracial organizing efforts. The problems that Romaine encountered are indicative of wider trends among white organizers, and echo the problems that Guy Carawan experienced in the black community.

Throughout the 1960s, cultural organizing broadened the parameters of black protest and deepened the movement's relationship with the African American community. Assessing cultural organizing, and personal and group responses to it, affords new insights into the internal workings of the civil rights movement: how different organizations related to each other; how class, race, and gender interacted; how activists related to individuals and communities; and how and why the movement succeeded and failed. Such an assessment demonstrates that the assertion of the value and legitimacy of African American heritage and culture was central to the freedom struggle. The debate over heritage and culture proved to be a battleground not only between black and white America, but also within black America during the peak years of the struggle for civil rights. African American cultural organizing did not solve the problem of racial inequality and white supremacy. Yet to understand it more fully is to extend the parameters through which we study the experiences of African Americans and to come to terms with the massive impact and legacy of the civil rights movement for black communities in the United States.

1

Singing for Freedom

The 1932 founding of the Highlander Folk School in Monteagle, Tennessee, is one of the most important moments in the history of the American Left. Myles Horton, a Christian activist and educator from Tennessee, previously discovered that the encroachment of industry into rural Appalachia robbed many local people of their livelihoods and culture. He devoted his work to reengaging the people with their culture by offering them opportunities to discuss their common experiences with other rural people. Horton found that the discussions flowed more freely if the meetings began with a communal song. Inspired by the radical Christian Marxist Reinhold Niebuhr, Horton founded Highlander with Don West, a Georgian Christian who shared the vision of establishing a folk school that would encourage people to challenge the South's moral and political shortcomings and that would resist authoritarian dogma, whether it be religious or political. West and Horton did not want to use books to teach but instead wanted to use the culture, heritage, history, and social structure of Grundy County (where Highlander was located) and the wider South as teaching tools. Highlander's ethos was not simply community development but, as Horton stressed, *"people* development," upholding individual and group bonds with the working-class values and heritage that Highlander associated with Appalachia. It was based around the idea that the solutions to social problems would be found through the lessons of history and the pooling of individual experiences and knowledge.[1]

During the 1950s and 1960s, Highlander became the great meeting place for those in the civil rights movement. Many activists spent numerous hours discussing methods of protest with Highlander's staff and volunteers before applying these techniques elsewhere. Through its workshops, Highlander helped to mold a new generation of activists who spread the Highlander ethos throughout the South. Folk songs were fundamental to Highlander's operation. Visitors were encouraged to join in singing, dancing, and making music. These activities, Highlander staff reasoned, would develop community bonds and create indigenous leaders in southern black communities, aiding the struggle for black civil rights.

Staff and students at Highlander swapped songs regularly. Staff sang new compositions at subsequent workshops to judge the response. If groups responded well, the songs would be kept and used again.[2] Through this method, Highlander staff compiled a collection of songs that visitors identified with both musically and politically. By the late 1950s, Highlander's repertoire had coalesced around an amalgam of African American spirituals, secular union songs, and original compositions that were an explicit attempt to portray the message of the African American freedom movement through song. The freedom songs remain as a powerful reminder of the civil rights movement and illustrate perfectly how the movement engaged with a tradition of cultural and political protest. To understand the legacy and meaning of these songs fully, it is necessary to examine the influence of Highlander's two music directors: Zilphia Horton and her successor, Guy Carawan. Their experiences illustrate how Highlander staff fused white and black American protest culture and why they were so keen to utilize folk culture in the creation of protest movements. Furthermore, Carawan's experience as a traveling singer in the early 1960s raises important questions about the black community's relationship with its culture and heritage. While Carawan might have made mistakes in his assessment of this issue, his conclusions pose important questions about the role of the civil rights movement and of white people within it.

The influence of Highlander is also illustrated by the Citizenship Education Program (CEP), which created a network of over 900 informal citizenship schools in many areas of the rural South and led to the registration of hundreds of thousands of African American voters. The CEP played a critical role in ensuring the ongoing success of the civil rights movement. Although the primary goal of these schools was to increase black enfranchisement, underneath this exterior was a complex program designed to perpetuate black cultural traditions and instill a commitment to democratic protest in southern communities. The freedom songs played a central role in the curriculum. In fact, the CEP curriculum was explicitly designed to reflect the indigenous culture of the black South. In doing so, its designers ensured that the CEP did not become an alienating experience for students and helped to preserve many important cultural traditions. By 1960, the

CEP had been passed over to the direction of the Southern Christian Leadership Conference (SCLC). Although the essence of the program remained, the SCLC attempted to make subtle changes in the program in order to fuse it with an overtly Christian message. These events illustrate how the SCLC engaged with black and white folk culture while it simultaneously emphasized the middle-class and respectable aura of black protest in the early 1960s.

Cultural Policy at Highlander

The attendance of movement activists such as Rosa Parks and John Lewis at Highlander and the profound impact it had on their lives are well documented. Less attention, however, has been given to the importance of cultural organizing to Highlander's educational policy.[3] Yet Highlander's plans extended far beyond simple education. For Myles Horton, the simple process of literacy was no protection against corruption, since people could "learn to write for the purpose of forging a check." He wanted Highlander to spread "the concept of what *ought to be*—human brotherhood, dignity and democracy."[4] Highlander's relationship with local communities and local people became a leitmotif that characterized the work of those who trained at the school throughout the 1960s. This influence can easily be detected in the Student Nonviolent Coordinating Committee's (SNCC) grassroots organizing work and SNCC's belief that local people should lead local organizations. The creation of this new political culture was based on the knowledge that most black southerners were not registered to vote and were not educated to a level at which they were aware of their potential political power. Highlander's work revealed that this situation could be altered through encouraging these southerners to understand their political rights and responsibilities. Once they realized the power that they could wield, they would be able to make their own decisions about their lives and start to exercise their rights. The promise of Reconstruction could then be fulfilled, and black southerners would be able to participate fully in civic life. An additional effect of these schools proved to be a huge change in self-awareness among southern blacks, notably around their own self-image. The Highlander program emphasized that their heritage was valid and that their culture was viable and legitimate.

Highlander's early programs explored the problems experienced by local workers in their relationships with employers and unions. With the arrival of Zilphia Johnson in early 1935, cultural activities became more prominent.

A Spanish-Indian native of Arkansas, Johnson was inspired to embrace left-ist politics by radical Presbyterian minister Claude Williams, who urged her to visit Highlander. Within three months of her arrival, she had married Myles Horton and become Highlander's music director. She brought song to the center of Highlander's ethos, believing that music should be at the heart of all things: "of situations, beliefs, of struggle, of ideas, of life itself." She argued that people's lives could be enriched through song, especially through songs of other cultures. For her, songs that spoke of people's everyday lives, and particularly folk songs from rural areas, were a vital conduit for the development of personal dignity and pride in cultural heritage. Zilphia Horton collected well over 1,000 songs from the unions, from other leftist groups, and from black and white folk traditions. These she disseminated to the thousands of people who passed through Highlander or participated in picket lines at which she sang.[5] Horton was adept at transforming the message of folk songs into something that related directly to the experience of her audience. She overhauled "Old MacDonald's Farm" into a song celebrating the leader of the Congress of Industrial Organizations (CIO): "John L. Lewis Had a Plan" (C-I-, C-I-O). The stoical Pentecostal hymn "I Shall Not Be Moved" was developed into the more inclusive "We Shall Not Be Moved." Previously an expression of the individual's relationship with God, the song was transformed into a declaration of group solidarity. The original presents the individual being assailed by the tempest; faith renders the individual as firmly rooted as a tree. The second version transforms this solidity into the conviction that the group will not be swayed from attaining its goal, a message that was taken to heart by the unions and later the civil rights movement.[6]

Group singing, for Zilphia Horton, was important in the development of group solidarity and in ensuring that the masses and their leaders did not become alienated from each other. She believed that leaders had to emerge organically from the people and needed to retain a close bond with those being led. Song played a central role in preserving this organic relationship. This understanding of the role and duties of leadership was central to the Highlander ethos. Horton interpreted folk song as an international language of brotherhood and sisterhood. Well aware of the slave and share-cropper tradition of singing while working, Horton detected similarities with the union movement. For her, these twin traditions of song cut across racial lines. She was not alone in considering song a fundamental weapon against oppression: her husband considered music and singing to be part of the school's original concept. Song lyrics could inspire people to become activists, tell stories that illiterate people might not otherwise read, and, importantly, involve the whole community. Through its activism and example, Highlander reconnected vast numbers of southerners, black and white, with their common heritage and insisted that their culture was a valid expression of their lives and their politics.[7]

Highlander's work focused on weeklong residential workshops at which groups of people from a variety of southern communities would be encouraged to discuss their community problems and how to solve them. This pooling of intellectual resources often led visitors to recognize the common obstacles that they faced and the common bonds that united them, leading them to conclude that group political action was a viable means through which they could challenge oppression. Highlander's staff limited themselves to supervisory roles, facilitating rather than leading the discussions, acting as an additional resource should the workshop request it. Visitors were encouraged to speak freely throughout their stay at Highlander, with discussions often lasting through mealtimes and long into the night. Zilphia Horton integrated Highlander's cultural program with the more formal curriculum, thus designating music and folk dancing as a mixture of education and entertainment. Groups would be encouraged to sing together during the day. These activities instilled solidarity, cultural pride, inspiration, and hope in communities and contributed to the development of leadership. Furthermore, if people could come together as an impromptu choir, then why not as a political organization? Highlander's official policy asserted that democracy meant more than simply freedom of thought and religion, and more than equal rights to a livelihood, education, and health; it also meant an equal opportunity "to participate in the cultural life of the community." For Highlander's staff, the cultural programs, especially those involving group singing and collective improvisation, exemplified the spirit of the community that the school hoped to create. These activities helped to forge bonds between individuals in a group by breaking down personal barriers and opening up channels of communication. Once people had sung songs together, they became less reticent to speak in front of the group. These groups bonded with each other over their shared heritage and learned of the different traditions within the larger shared history of the South. More than simply a means to create bonds of friendship, the democratic practice of communal singing was also a device for transmitting ideological and pedagogical messages. For the staff of Highlander, cultural programs had a dual purpose: they helped to develop group cohesion, and they highlighted how culture and politics existed in symbiosis. Thus the cultural work fed into and informed the political work, as well as making a political point itself.[8]

Zilphia Horton insisted that the word content of the song was vital to its resonance, ensuring that the audience received both information and inspiration. The responsibility of the leader of the group was to make certain that the songs sung at a meeting related to the group's interests and goals. Zilphia Horton had seen this theory work in practice on numerous occasions. In 1948, for example, she and Myles conducted an educational meeting for rural blacks in a barn in western Tennessee. They began by singing songs with a small group of interested people, which soon grew into a large gathering as others heard the music and became drawn to this seemingly impromptu revival meeting. The group sang old spirituals and songs familiar to the local people. The Hortons encouraged them to add new words about the Cooperative Union that the locals had recently established, thus linking their political present with their cultural heritage. The first round of songs was augmented by a long political discussion of the role of the co-op before the group returned to song after two local people fetched a fiddle and banjo. The hootenanny–cum–political meeting eventually exhausted itself late in the night. For Zilphia Horton, music had provided a means to bring the community together. It was now the job of the community leader to direct the community in a creative direction. By using the folk culture of the group, the leader could enliven political meetings and prevent them from becoming dull and unappealing to the local populace. Not only could song bring people together, it could provoke thought and even transmit ideology. For the Hortons and Highlander, it was an invaluable tool.[9]

Highlander successfully used these methods within the union movement during the early 1940s, but Zilphia Horton, who viewed song as a multiracial working-class organizing tool, became particularly frustrated at the pace of racial change within the unions. By the late 1940s, Highlander had become critical of the CIO's attitude toward race and was concerned about the lack of progress being made in educating workers about the value of a biracial approach to organizing. The school had developed a large dependence on the funds accruing from the workshops that it conducted for a number of southern CIO-affiliated unions. Despite the fact that several of these unions bristled at Highlander's rejection of segregation and occasionally refused to integrate, Highlander was instrumental in devising the curriculum for the CIO's worker education programs. Aware that some CIO unions were establishing their own education programs, Highlander decided to broaden its program outside the CIO, with the obvious benefit that Highlander no longer had to squabble with the less progressive unions over the race issue and was less reliant on their money. Horton was also dismayed at the failure of the CIO's southern organizing drive, Operation Dixie, to transcend racial antagonism in the South between 1946 and 1948. In an atmosphere that was increasingly tainted with anti-Communism, the CIO abandoned its commitment to racial solidarity and grew ever more wary of offending the sensibilities of white workers. Highlander's refusal to engage in Red-baiting exacerbated the divisions between it and the CIO. By 1947, the CIO's new direction included the withdrawal of funds for Highlander. This was a galling slight for the Highlander staff who drew great pride from their challenge to the CIO's attitudes to race and segregation and who placed particular emphasis on the role of the working class in forming the vanguard of the struggles against racial discrimination.[10]

Throughout her working life at Highlander, Zilphia Horton insisted that folk culture was fundamental to enacting change in the southern working-class community. This culture not only spread democratic ideology through the lyrics of folk song, but it also spread democratic practice through uniting leaders and the masses in a common vocality. Moreover, her ideas, even her personality, were central to Highlander's work in the South.

Guy Carawan and the Freedom Songs

Following Zilphia Horton's tragic accidental death from uremic poisoning in 1956, the Highlander music program entered a fallow period that lasted until the appointment of Guy Carawan in 1959. Arriving at Highlander on the recommendation of Pete Seeger, Carawan soon revived the school's musical traditions, contributing a fundamental component of the growing freedom movement among African American students in the South. That he was able to do so in such a short time underscores the importance of the cultural program to Highlander.[11]

Born in Los Angeles to southern parents, Carawan learned guitar at college from records and visits by folksingers such as Woody Guthrie, Lead Belly (Huddie Ledbetter), and Seeger. Carawan first visited the South in 1953 after earning a master's degree in sociology, visiting Highlander, and finding solace and inspiration in the school's amalgamation of Popular Front radicalism and folk song. From the very beginning of his work at Highlander, Carawan emphasized the role of folk culture in the burgeoning black freedom movement. He thought that the potential for a singing movement to become part of the African American freedom struggle was far greater than in the union movement. Combining the religious nature of African American folk song (most notably, spirituals and gospel songs) with the politicized folk songs from the white American tradition was a potentially powerful means through which the civil rights movement could be integrated culturally as well as socially. Carawan noted that this task was perfectly suited to his skills, knowledge, and beliefs.[12]

The seeds of the singing civil rights movement were sown during three meetings during 1960. In April, Highlander presented its annual college workshop, which attracted eighty-two students, most of whom had been active in the sit-in demonstrations. Group singing punctuated the discussions. Two weeks later, Carawan attended the founding conference of SNCC and introduced the students to "We Shall Overcome." Less than four months later, Carawan directed a "Sing for Freedom" workshop for seventy-five singers, activists, and teachers. The songs sung at these meetings formed the bedrock of the repertoire of freedom songs that were sung throughout the civil rights movement.[13]

Somewhat surprisingly, Carawan was frustrated at the inertia of many African Americans when it came to using songs in their movement, arguing that there was a degree of "cultural resistance" to the songs. His subtle understanding of the multiform nature of American racism is revealed in his reasoning. Carawan thought that college-educated African Americans had become dissociated from their folk culture. Educated blacks, he claimed, rejected the revivalist tone of the new freedom songs, with their improvisational, communal aura, because of its association with the African American past. Many educated blacks wanted to present themselves as "cultured," sophisticated, and modern in that they appreciated so-called high culture and rejected so-called low culture. The culture of the folk—the primitive songs of the slaves, the free and often spontaneous expression of emotion during black church services, and the expressly primitive nature of white folk music—was incompatible with this desire. According to Carawan, modernization and white acculturation played an insidious role in this process. In alienating educated blacks from their heritage, white society was atomizing the black community through developing a cultural as well as a political hegemony, preventing African Americans from uniting with one another. Thus class played a crucial role in perpetuating inequality. It is commonly appreciated that African Americans who attended white schools faced severe psychological and cultural impediments. That Carawan was already aware of this cultural displacement is a testament to his sensitivity to the polymorphism of racism.[14]

Despite this perspicacity, Carawan had one major blind spot: his own role within this process. He was a white man interpreting black culture, adopting a role in which he taught blacks how to relate to their own culture. He was therefore performing a white version of a black culture. Many of the black students at the Highlander workshops were either practicing Christians or had been brought up in Christian families. They would have heard many of the spirituals that Carawan performed, but in a slightly different form. In performing the updated (white) versions, Carawan was unwittingly reinforcing a paternalist ideology that implied that only white people, or even white men, could preserve and transmit black culture. Furthermore, his performance suggested that whites had the right to determine the message of this culture, thus presupposing that white cultural influence was more powerful than black cultural traditions.

A useful example of this acculturation process in operation is in the history of the song "We Shall Overcome" at Highlander. Zilphia Horton first heard the song sung as "We Will Overcome" by black food and tobacco workers in the 1940s as an adaptation of the church song "I'll Overcome Someday." She passed it on to Pete Seeger, who, unconvinced by the grammar and the alliteration, substituted the (grammatically correct) auxiliary verb "shall" for "will" and added a number of new verses. Through successive verses, the song establishes the mood of hopeful commitment in stanzas such as "we are not alone," "the truth will set us free," and "we'll walk hand in hand." Once the tone had been set, more specific verses could be added, including "black and white together." Thus a universal-local pattern was established, which guaranteed the song's longevity and relevance.[15] Seeger's ideas concerning the song neatly encapsulate the Highlander approach to folk culture, namely, that it is in a constant state of flux, always adapting itself—or being adapted—to suit the particular context in which it is presented. By 1959, Carawan was spreading Seeger's version to the new generation of activists. On 31 July 1959, the Tennessee police, as part of the state's attempt to discredit and close down the school, raided Highlander. While the police were searching the premises to find illegal alcohol, the students and volunteers, led by Mary Ethel Dozier, a black high school student, began to sing "We Shall Overcome." Dozier added a new verse, "we are not afraid," which was instantly adopted by the other singers. Meanwhile, the song continued to be featured as a religious hymn in the black church.

During the Albany, Georgia, campaign in December 1961, singers led by Bernice Johnson Reagon pushed the song through another transformation. The Highlander version had been sung firmly in the white folk and southern ballad traditions, with all singers following the same melody. At Albany, students who had attended Highlander helped to spread this interpretation of the song. Other protesters moved the song up to a different key and fused it with black choral traditions, bringing in elements of call-and-response, new accents, and improvisations.[16] Adding a further level to the competing influences, in 1960 Carawan, Seeger, and Myles Horton copyrighted the song in order to prevent less scrupulous individuals profiting from its popularity. In 1965, the We Shall Overcome Fund was signed over to the administration of Highlander. In 1966, the We Shall Overcome board agreed to grant funds only for proposals relating to African American folk culture with the emphasis on music.[17]

Initially an African American song, "We Shall Overcome" was interpreted and modified by white singers who passed it on to a younger generation of predominantly black activists who reclaimed it as an African American song. White institutionalization of the song was then used to benefit black cultural organizing. While there is no suggestion that whites such as Zilphia Horton were deliberately trying to denude black culture of its distinctiveness, "We Shall Overcome" illustrates how black and white culture interacted in the twentieth century. That the song was transmitted in white circles as a folk song while the same song was simultaneously being preserved in a black cultural tradition through the church serves as an example of how white culture accommodated and, to an extent, subverted black culture. That men often "owned" the song in the white tradition and women led the transformations in the black community indicates that cultural "ownership" of the song also had gender ramifications. Carawan's statement of frustration at the African American relationship to black culture therefore does not reveal the entire story. His audiences might only have been responding to a white man interpreting their culture, thinking that this was another example of the accommodation and dilution of their heritage.

Carawan's viewpoint highlights the importance of biracial cultural engagement and dialogue in creating a culture of resistance to oppression. The song's parallel lives reveals why some of Carawan's students struggled to relate to the song. They were effectively being introduced to a new song from a different tradition. The apparent segregation of "We Shall Overcome" also speaks to the separation of the races in the Jim Crow South. The reaction to slavery and freedom defined the contours of black culture and consciousness throughout the nineteenth century. The formal separation of the races in certain areas of the South allowed the development of distinct black and white folk traditions. While biracial interaction might have made Carawan's job easier, segregation perhaps rendered the church version of "We Shall Overcome" a purer reflection of an African American folk culture than a hybrid version. Although some in the black community had become alienated from their heritage, more isolated groups had been able to insulate many aspects of black culture from white influence and preserve their own folk heritage. The fact that this isolation formed a barrier against modernization also helped to maintain this heritage. Furthermore, the black church, perhaps the most important social structure among black southerners, perpetuated many cultural traditions, ensuring that many black Americans remained in contact with their heritage. Carawan's pessimism, then, was somewhat shortsighted.[18]

In December 1959 and again during the following winter, Carawan visited the South Carolina Sea Islands to augment the local citizenship schools that the community had established. He took his repertoire of freedom songs to the Sea Islands, hoping to teach them to the locals and learn new songs. On his first visit in 1959, he was taught a local version of "Keep Your Hand on the Plow," a song that he had learned during the 1950s. Alice Wine, a student at the citizenship school, sang a different version: "Keep Your Eyes on the Prize," which Carawan took back with him and introduced to the students who attended Highlander the following year. Carawan hoped to train new song leaders, but very few were willing to grasp the leadership baton that he was passing to them. He reported to Highlander that he had failed to train new leaders and that somebody with better educational skills should conduct such work. Carawan failed to appreciate the racial implications of his presence on the Sea Islands. The physical isolation of the Sea Islands sequestered the black community; most local blacks rarely encountered whites who were not authority figures. They would quite probably have struggled to come to terms with Carawan's presence and his modus operandi. An African American song leader would have been a more appropriate figure. Despite this blind spot, Carawan arrived at a fitting conclusion. Instead of teaching songs to everybody with whom he came in contact, he would only tutor song leaders and encourage them to spread the gospel. This guaranteed that Carawan would be able to maximize the number of people who would come into contact with the songs without placing too heavy a burden on his shoulders and without perpetuating the paternalist cycle that had led many African Americans to reject their own heritage.[19]

Carawan's experience in the Sea Islands citizenship schools ultimately convinced him that he needed to alter the nature of his work and suggests that there was a fine line between pedagogy and paternalism. By the end of 1961, when he left the Sea Islands after loaning one of the citizenship school students $100 for a new set of teeth, he was coming to the conclusion that his instrumental work was actually hindering the effectiveness of the songs. His white folk style, which relied on guitar or banjo accompaniment, did not integrate well with the a cappella style that developed from the black church, since it imposed a rhythm that prevented the full emergence of the cadences and improvisations that characterized the latter style. He decided to redirect his attention to documenting the songs of the freedom struggle in recorded and written formats, and only to engage with the actual teaching when people did not know a particular song. Carawan appeared at mass meetings, conferences, and freedom rides, singing, playing guitar, and handing out mimeographed sheets of songs, helping to spread the gospel of the freedom song. He often revisited Johns Island, living there with his wife, Candie, and their son permanently between 1963 and 1965. He also worked extensively with SNCC, documenting the Greenwood, Mississippi, movement and organizing numerous song festivals while maintaining his Highlander commitments.[20]

It is likely that witnessing the vibrancy of black culture on the Sea Islands emphasized to Carawan his whiteness, spurring him to withdraw into a role as primarily a folklorist, as opposed to an interpreter of black culture. Although he thought that "a folksong in a book is like a photograph of a bird in flight" and stressed the importance of improvisation to the folk tradition, Carawan understood that templates had to be set down in print to record a particular moment in the development of American folk song. Sheet music could also help preserve the various singing styles that he encountered. It is significant that Carawan began to abandon nominally black cultural traditions (namely, the oral transmission of culture) for white cultural norms (documentation and written transmission) at this point. Perhaps he belatedly came to appreciate his limitations as a white "possessor" of black culture and realized the inherent flaw of spreading white cultural traditions within a movement dedicated to ending white supremacy. His sensitivity to this issue predates the decision of many black civil rights activists to encourage their white comrades to organize only in the white community and reminds us of the visionary genius of those who worked at Highlander during the middle decades of the twentieth century.[21]

Citizenship Education

It would be simplistic to restrict Highlander's influence on the culture of the civil rights movement to the spreading of the freedom songs. Its legacy ran far deeper and was rooted in the school's pedagogic techniques and its attitude toward the local community. Highlander was committed to democracy and aimed to create new leaders from the working class. Its stated purpose was to broaden the scope of democracy to include all peoples. Beyond this, it sought to deepen the concept in order that individuals could embrace democratic relationships in all aspects of their lives. By doing this, Highlander asserted, "the army of democracy would be so vast and so determined that nothing undemocratic could stand in its path."[22]

Myles Horton led abortive attempts at community development in parts of rural Tennessee during the 1950s. He sought the formation of local community organizations that would address the issues pertinent to local people's problems, be they schooling, farming, voting rights, or merely the creation of local leaders. For Horton, the failure of these programs was not due to the lack of commitment on the part of the Highlander staff, nor was it due to programmatic inadequacies, despite the inexperience of the staff and the fact that Highlander was still experimenting with its methodology. Rather, Horton believed, the crucial factor was simply that the communities had not requested Highlander to come to help them. The staff had not spent the time developing bonds with the community, and as a result, they often fell into leadership roles, which led to a reliance on Highlander staff and prevented the organic development of indigenous leadership. The experience convinced Horton that the key to the long-term success and stability of such programs was that the initial impetus came from the local people. This belief, then, led to a trust in the needs and desires of the students who attended the school, and was the root of Highlander's policy of allowing the specific education program of any workshop to be determined by the needs of the students, which again emphasized the importance of organic leadership. Horton's particular genius was not necessarily in the discovery of the right answers but in asking the right questions.[23]

Highlander's lack of didacticism profoundly influenced Septima Clark and Esau Jenkins, both of whom first visited Highlander in 1954. Within a year, the two had established citizenship classes on Johns Island, South Carolina, and Clark had been invited to join Highlander's staff. The freewheeling Highlander style had taken over their classes. "Everything is discussed," Myles Horton wrote of them. "It had been almost three weeks since the last meeting and people were still discussing . . . the last meeting." The participants were not expected to consider citizenship as an end in itself, but as part of a process that allowed for greater interaction between the individual, the locality, and the wider world.[24] The Sea Islands project became the prototype for the citizenship schools that proliferated in the South under the administration of the SCLC. By 1960, citizenship schools were running in Tennessee, Georgia, Alabama, and South Carolina. Between September and December 1960 alone, some 9,000 African Americans were registered to vote in Savannah, Georgia, through the citizenship schools. Between July 1962 and early 1964, eighty citizenship schools operated in South Carolina. During this period, the number of black voters in the state increased from 57,000 to 150,000. It is not an exaggeration to assert that the citizenship schools were the most important single program that Highlander ever developed.[25]

Septima Clark's role in the civil rights movement is well documented, but little attention has been paid to her teaching style and her entrenchment in the culture of the South.[26] Clark defined the style of the citizenship schools and did much to spread them throughout the South. Although the primary aims of the citizenship schools were to increase the number of black voters and develop people's ability to use their voting power effectively, there was a corollary, but no less important, aim of community development. Clark's cousin, Bernice Robinson, led the classes and asked the question of her students that was the key to the success of the whole program: "What do you want to learn?" This interactivity challenged the boundaries that traditionally emerge between "teacher" and "students" while developing stronger bonds within the group. Sensing that material from elementary schools would not be appropriate for teaching adults, Robinson set about creating a new curriculum. The cornerstone of this Highlander-influenced syllabus was Johns Island culture. She copied a money order form in enough numbers for each student to practice filling one out. Election laws and copies of the Constitution were used in reading and spelling exercises. The students would discuss their everyday lives and use each other's stories as the basis for writing exercises. Reading books would include sections on health services available in the locality, directions on how to address public officials in writing, a résumé of local political parties, and so on. Singing was a vital part of the curriculum. It added spirit to the work, livening up the meetings and helping people forget their temporal surroundings. More pertinent, the songs offered the students the opportunity to focus on working together as a group, concentrating their attention on each other. The words of the songs also focused them on the goals toward which the school was striving.[27]

Myles Horton was particularly impressed at the integration of the educational and cultural programs on Johns Island. Literacy went hand in hand with reaffirming the value of their own culture; their values, traditions, heritage, and songs were thus given a key role in the assertion of their democratic rights. The motivation, Horton noted, "was for an achievable goal *rooted in their culture.*" Highlander staff also observed the change in attitude toward learning that this approach engendered. The appropriate materials notwithstanding, the citizenship schools demonstrated that education had a purpose and that the process of learning itself was beneficial. No whites would be staring over students' shoulders, taking notes on who was present. The teachers could be trusted, since they were members of the same community. It is no surprise that Highlander reported that this new approach accelerated the educational process and that previously unqualified local people could understand, address, and work toward solving the community's problems within a mere three months, at the paltry cost of $8 per person. By legitimating the folk culture of the Sea Islands—the songs, the heritage, and the lived experience of the residents—the citizenship schools were developing a new political culture within the local black community.[28]

Because of their success, the citizenship schools were exported back to Highlander for dissemination to other areas in the South. Such success, however, had its drawbacks. The work that Highlander conducted was best suited to small-scale programs, and the school's funding restricted the number of projects that could be undertaken at any one time. Committing Highlander staff and funds to the spread of the citizenship schools would erode the school's other projects and spread its staff too thinly. Once the citizenship schools were established, Highlander envisaged passing them on to another organization. This was related to Highlander's central purpose of nurturing local leaders in an organic fashion rather than reinforcing the local community's reliance on outsiders. The citizenship schools would therefore become a breeding ground for successive generations of local leaders, where a community development program would evolve naturally with the local community. Highlander preferred its role to be one of teaching teachers. Trainees would visit Highlander to be trained before returning to their communities to establish community groups that would address the particular concerns of the local people. Just like Guy Carawan, Highlander staff realized that their energies were best reserved for developing the skills of a small number of people who would then pass on their expertise to the wider community. Thus the strain would be removed from Highlander's resources without the program being too diluted. Another advantage to this approach was that the interaction between individuals at Highlander developed bonds between (as well as within) communities, which would help create a vast network of community organizers in the South. After potential leaders returned home from Highlander, Septima Clark and Bernice Robinson would assist the establishment of their schools and then let the local leaders take charge. Schools would run for three months of the year, with classes meeting twice weekly for two hours in the evening. Classes typically had between twenty-five and thirty-five students, who were encouraged to bring friends and relatives to the meetings. The spread of the program would extend the local organizing network of the civil rights movement, bringing more and more people into the front line of the freedom struggle.[29]

The basic purpose of the CEP, as the initiative became known, was to educate black rural southerners in the skills needed to become full citizens in Jim Crow (and post–Jim Crow) society. Initially, the CEP focused on such requirements as basic literacy and passing the rigorous tests that prevented many black southerners from being able to vote. Clark's experiences, particularly at Highlander, taught her that education was not a linear progression toward gaining certain skills, but was a holistic process. Thus the CEP's curriculum naturally broadened to encompass concepts that were pertinent to rural southerners. Examples of this practical attitude abound in the CEP's citizenship workbooks, which were produced to accompany the training program. In addition to the more traditional sound charts that feature such objects as boats, pigs, saws, churches, and goats, the CEP included a word sheet, with instructions to construct sentences and stories from the various words, arranged according to their initial letter. These word sheets were much more appropriate to the lived experience of adults than were traditional schoolbooks. "A," for example, featured "alderman" and "attorney." "R" included "rebellion," "registration," and "representatives." The CEP employed other clearly identifiable teaching tools, such as in arithmetic, where amounts of fertilizer and numbers of cucumber seeds were used in exercises. This devotion to utilizing materials relevant to the audience was central to the CEP's operation and was a calculated attempt to ground its work in the culture of the South. These exercises also complemented the Highlander ethos of questioning everything. A new reader finding out how to spell the word *rebellion* (a word that Sea Islanders might not have heard in context) would be encouraged to discuss and explore its meanings. As a result, the newly educated voters would become confident enough to discuss politics and start to question the political system in the South. This concept of education reflected Myles Horton's insistence that education was a holistic process, rather than an end in itself, since people could learn to write in order to forge a check and not necessarily to address inequality.[30] The workbooks were intended to develop reading and analytical skills, asking questions about the extracts to stimulate debates, such as "Why do you think Sojourner Truth spoke against slavery?" The workbooks also featured the freedom songs, which were sung at all meetings, and a large section on historical African American figures. Profiles of heroic African Americans such as Crispus Attucks and Benjamin Banneker illustrated concepts of slavery, freedom, and education, and parallels were drawn between the historical tales and the present. Mary McLeod Bethune's story stressed the value of education, directly linking her childhood devotion to reading with her later success as an adviser to President Franklin Delano Roosevelt. These extracts grounded the students in their history and challenged the assumption that there were no African American historical heroes. The inclusion of figures such as Sojourner Truth also contested gender stereotypes, adding another oppositional element to the curriculum and acting as extra inspiration for black women.[31]

In incorporating these exercises into the curriculum, the CEP made certain that history became a weapon in the freedom struggle. Where white schools emphasized the primacy of white history and asserted that black people comprised a subordinate race, the citizenship schools taught that African Americans played a central role in the creation of the American nation. This notion was further emphasized by the singing of freedom songs, just as schoolchildren sang the national anthem at the beginning of the school day. Questions about the continuities and changes in African American life could be brought into a reading exercise, which then led to wider-ranging discussions on how to effect change, which itself could lead to a discussion on the need for voting. While adults were learning to read in order to be able to vote, they were also learning about their history, culture, and heritage, and how they could use their vote to bring about change. The citizenship schools also challenged gender assumptions within the black community. Many citizenship schoolteachers were women. If that merely reinforced typical gender demarcations, the fact that these women were explicitly engaging in *political* education suggests that they were also challenging the concept that politics was a male sphere. In adopting leadership roles, such women were also becoming role models for local women.

Their very being insisted that ordinary people were able to overcome any obstacles placed before them simply by getting together and talking. The CEP deliberately looked for potential leaders in the community to train. A person's educational background did not matter. As Clark pointed out, "we didn't need anyone with a high school education, nor did we need anyone with a college education. We just wanted to have a community person, so that the illiterates would feel comfortable and happy."[32] All the trained citizenship school leaders used the CEP citizenship workbooks. Likewise, they learned how to lead the singing of freedom songs and were encouraged to make music an integral part of the curriculum. Meetings began and ended with communal singing of freedom songs in order to develop a sense of community, to further the school's focus on literacy, and to emphasize the links between the civil rights movement and the CEP. Students would use the songs as a reading aid, facilitating the (oral) transmission and (written) preservation of a vital element of African American culture. Music, history, and folk culture remained at the center of the citizenship schools, even in an informal setting.

Concerned that Highlander was fomenting dissent against segregation, white authorities in Tennessee initiated a campaign to shut the school down. In 1960, a kangaroo court revoked Highlander's charter, forcing the school to close in September 1961. Horton expected this outcome and had already taken steps to reopen the school in Knoxville. Aware that Highlander could not cope with the plan to extend the CEP to reach 90,000 potential voters, Horton had opened discussions with the SCLC for the transfer of the administration of the program.[33] The SCLC was initially skeptical of the value of Septima Clark's work with the CEP. It is possible that, for the SCLC, her work with mostly illiterate and barely literate people did not project the correct image to mainstream America. The SCLC was busy promoting the humanity and decency of African Americans; its program was designed to illustrate that black Southerners were as human as whites. Clark's work suggested that many African Americans were unaware of much outside their immediate surroundings, since they needed education in the duties and responsibilities of citizenship. Moreover, her work placed particular emphasis on developing the independence of a group that the SCLC preferred to think of as followers, rather than as potential leaders. This engagement with working-class blacks, coupled with an informality that blurred the boundaries between leaders and followers, was not enticing to the SCLC's leadership cadre. The lack of whites in the citizenship schools also clashed with the SCLC's commitment to integration. The vast majority of citizenship school students were African American—indeed, there is no evidence to suggest that any whites regularly attended citizenship schools—and it was a deliberate tactic to use only black teachers. While this did not constitute an acceptance of black nationalist tenets but instead was designed to break the cycle of white dominance and black dependence, it suggested that African American progress was not dependent on white involvement, a proposition that the SCLC preferred not to acknowledge.

Clark, though, was a persuasive individual. The SCLC was won over by her insistence that its program for redeeming the soul of America had not yet led to many concrete results. She, on the other hand, was easily able to demonstrate the success of the citizenship schools simply by producing lists of the number of blacks who had successfully registered to vote after attending classes. Martin Luther King Jr. and the SCLC's executive director, Wyatt T. Walker, became attracted to the new dimension that Clark's methods would add to the SCLC's program, believing that Clark could educate voter registration workers while the SCLC's leadership motivated the rest of the community. It would also help to cement the SCLC in many southern black communities, which could provide a crucial support base for future campaigns.[34] By late 1960, the SCLC's public relations director, James R. Wood, was arguing that Highlander's plan met the SCLC's need for a grassroots leadership development program. The success of the student sit-ins and their implicit rejection of King's leadership had taken the SCLC by surprise. With little finances and no field staff, the SCLC was still in its infancy. It had not yet decided to embark on mass nonviolent direct action but was concentrating its energies on voter registration. For Wood, the CEP constituted an opportunity for the SCLC to develop its own networks and expand its influence at the local level. King became similarly convinced.[35] It made perfect sense for Septima Clark to follow her program to the SCLC, where she became director of workshops and the conscience of the organization, not to mention a feminist thorn in the side of the organization's notoriously masculine central clique. The CEP proved to be one of the SCLC's most extensive, effective, and enduring grassroots initiatives. Between July 1962 and November 1963, the CEP influenced over 27,000 people to register to vote. Given that voter registration was entirely under the control of local white authorities in the South, this constitutes quite a success.[36] Citizenship school teacher and local activist Victoria Gray reported to the SCLC in 1966 on CEP activities in Mississippi, arguing that it was vital that the battle for "the minds of the masses" be won. For Gray, unless the CEP encouraged people to understand what freedom, political representation, economic opportunity, and self-determination meant in terms of lived experience, the movement would be letting history, most pertinently the failure of Reconstruction, repeat itself.[37]

Gray's observations illustrate that Highlander's understanding of the relationship between experience and theory had become hugely influential within the movement. Highlander's genius was to bring abstract philosophical and economic concepts to local people and encourage them to relate to such concepts as realities. The CEP reported that the curriculum was expanding its commitment to African American history in response to student demands, noting also that "self realization" was among the most valuable results of the program. Unsurprisingly, Septima Clark had a hand in this, pointing out that the CEP was encountering problems that were not easily solved through basic reading and writing instruction. A more extensive program would be needed in order to facilitate the spread of the CEP into other southern states such as Alabama and Louisiana. Yet arguably the CEP had already succeeded in transforming the political culture of the South. By 1965, nearly 900 citizenship schools were operating. The SCLC estimated that 25,000 people had attended citizenship classes since 1961, with at least 50,000 new voters being registered as a result. Every SCLC trainee produced between thirty-five and sixty-seven new voters, a fine return on the investment. Just as important, these voters had received a holistic education in a citizen's duties and in the contributions of African Americans to the United States.[38]

That, however, is not the entire story. It is highly significant that most of these new voters had been instructed in African American history by fellow black Americans and had been encouraged to develop a questioning attitude toward their lives and the system around them. In doing so, their own culture was legitimized and utilized to service their personal development, and the foundations of the most ambitious of the civil rights movement's programs had been laid. To overlook the value of the teaching style and the role that indigenous culture played in the education of these people would be to underestimate severely their impact on the movement. The empowerment felt by citizenship schoolteachers cannot be underestimated, nor can the impetus that their example gave their students. Simply seeing a black person in a position of authority was an inspiring lesson to those without formal qualifications or the "correct" skin color. It revealed that everyone could participate fully in the freedom movement and that this movement was more than simply a series of marches; it was a holistic challenge to oppression. Although it was not given as much priority as direct action, the

SCLC's sponsorship of the CEP suggests that the organization held a commitment to the black underclass in the South and that it appreciated the wider perspective of the freedom struggle. Indeed, King asserted in 1962 that the CEP was "the sole effort to deal with the problem of cultural lag due to racial deprivation on a South-wide level."[39]

The contrast between the CEP's educational practice and that of another SCLC-sponsored project reveals the different attitudes toward education and the different interpretations of the role of African American culture in the movement within the SCLC. In August 1962, after the National Association for the Advancement of Colored People (NAACP) withdrew its financial support, the Chatham County Crusade for Voters changed its allegiance to the SCLC. Hosea Williams, a fiery and energetic local organizer, led it and its partner organization, the Southeast Georgia Crusade for Voters (SGCV).[40] The mere names of the organizations give an indication of the overtly missionary nature of their quest. The two shared office space, Williams's evangelical zeal, and a slightly paternalist interpretation of their commitment to voter education. Both limited themselves to teaching their students the minimum requirements for voting. Voter registration activists in southeast Georgia relied heavily on Williams for making and implementing policy decisions. In Georgia, the vote was restricted to those who were literate or those who could answer twenty of thirty questions set by the registrar. Williams's organizations set about teaching people the answers to the questions before moving on to other matters. Williams himself was the guiding light behind this policy.[41]

For Williams, the organization would use "every possible means" to improve every citizen's "moral, social, economic and educational stature." The outcome would be "a large intelligent Negro vote." Where Highlander believed that ordinary people would discover solutions to their own problems with minimal guidance, Williams was convinced that a large proportion of black Americans were ignorant and needed clear instruction on their citizenship duties, lest their votes be wasted. This attitude had troubling echoes of the white control of black voting prior to the implementation of the secret ballot. Williams also suggested that the African American population was in need of some moral guidance from its leadership caste and suggested that anybody without an education was unintelligent, a particularly offensive suggestion to those who had been denied an education by their state authorities or by economic necessity. Where Myles Horton let people come to their own decisions about who to vote for, Williams had no qualms in telling his charges which ballot to punch. Where the CEP was careful to attune its teaching materials to the lives and experiences of its students, Williams was prepared to use Sunday school material as a teaching aid. On one level, Williams's decision reinforced a paternalist agenda that implicitly prevented the SGCV students from being treated as adults. At another level, it reinforced his belief that education was also to offer moral, spiritual, and religious guidance. This paternalist attitude points to Williams's egotistical view of his work, reinforced by his tendency to draw parallels between his work and that of one of his Christian predecessors: "As Jesus Christ said, 'I did not come to destroy, but to fulfill.'"[42]

The shortcomings of such an approach became apparent by 1963. While the CEP was quietly and efficiently expanding the voter rolls, the SGCV was struggling to develop indigenous leaders. Jack Minnis, a Voter Education Project (VEP) observer, speculated that SGCV's problems might have been due to the focus on educating people, rather than merely encouraging them to register to vote, but this criticism seems wide of the mark. What differentiated the SGCV operation from the more successful CEP (which continued to receive large amounts of VEP funding) was Williams's overbearing presence and domination of the curriculum. The difference in emphasis between Williams and the Highlander staff had been brought into sharp focus during a January 1961 workshop at Highlander. In the course of a heated discussion, Septima Clark and Williams revealed their respective ideas about the purpose of citizenship education. For Williams, voter registration was the sole focus of the citizenship schools. Thus he advocated teaching people the minimum level of literacy in order that they could pass the registration tests set by registrars. This maximized efficiency, registering the largest possible number of people in the quickest time and with the minimum level of financial commitment from the schools: the students were merely required to learn the questions that the Georgia registrar was likely to ask them. Williams exhibited a paternalist attitude toward ordinary black southerners and a ruthless streak that did not gel with the Highlander ethos. Clark had already witnessed the limitations of this approach in the early days of organizing on Johns Island, and had moved her citizenship schools toward a more holistic method of educating. For her, the concept of citizenship was central to the operation of the schools. Literacy was vital to the development of independent thought; political involvement developed from there. The individual, under this system, was in control of her or his destiny and, through the local organizations that the citizenship schools encouraged, would be able to act politically from a position of strength. Where Williams insisted that the only difference between his program and the CEP was marketing, Clark patiently pointed out that the CEP was interested in the whole person rather than merely the ballot box. And where Williams saw the means and the end as indivisible, Clark refused to countenance the idea that there was an end: as Highlander had taught her, education was a never-ending process.[43]

Both Williams and Clark drew on their Christian heritage to inform their work but afforded religion different emphases in the educational process. Clark rarely used her religion as a tool for teaching, whereas Christianity was the backbone of Williams's program. The difference between Clark and Williams does much to highlight the attitude toward the use of cultural expressions within the SCLC. For the SCLC, African American culture was often considered synonymous with religion, although Williams embodied a more rigid Christian doctrine than that held by many in his organization. Williams's use of Sunday school materials as teaching aids suggests two crucial differences between his approach and that of Highlander. First, he made explicit the use of Christianity as a teaching supplement, something that was never on the agenda at Highlander. Second, the use of materials designed for children's education implies that Williams did not understand that the materials had to be age appropriate. He thus suggested that those attending his schools were effectively children. Williams passed up the opportunity to apply the students' education to everyday life. Georgian voters needed to fill out state tax-exemption forms on an annual basis. Not only did Williams fail to incorporate this ideal teaching tool into the curriculum, but his students were not even aware of the need to fill out these forms annually. Williams was consequently ignoring the opportunity to tailor the education process to the specific problems that faced black Georgians and was implicitly denying that any secular black culture existed in the South. While many Highlander staff, from Myles Horton down, were Christian, Highlander's true religion was democracy.[44]

By ensuring that both the material and those disseminating it related to the local community, and that locals felt comfortable with both, Highlander guaranteed that the CEP became an integral part of the 1960s freedom struggle. Highlander's contribution to the civil rights movement's ideology was a crucial step in acknowledging the protest value of African American culture. The freedom songs spread from the school throughout the movement. Indeed, they are as central to the narrative of the civil rights movement as the March on Washington and possibly Martin Luther King Jr. himself. They not only provided a soundtrack to the movement's marches and demonstrations but also offered significant psychological armor for its participants. Jailed protesters did not simply sing to while away the time: the songs were both release from temporal surroundings and a message to the white authorities that their prisoners were not afraid. Furthermore, the songs provided a crucial link between the 1960s struggle and its antecedents. The fusion of white and black cultural traditions gelled perfectly with the integrationist message of the mature civil rights movement. The freedom songs used the historical memory of slavery and freedom to invoke African American culture as a movement weapon. In legitimizing and popularizing this culture, Highlander ensured that movement culture drew on and integrated itself with a wider tradition of oppositional culture.

Guy Carawan made a huge contribution to the civil rights movement. It is likely that the movement would have developed its own singing culture without his input, but had this been the case, this singing culture would have been very different. Thanks to Carawan and the Highlander staff, the leftist tradition of song continued to influence American protest movements. Carawan's role reveals that one of the major successes of Highlander's program and the civil rights movement was the union of black and white, religious and secular cultures. As a result of the interaction of these elements, participants received a multiracial, multicultural message. The common desire for freedom unified the potentially disparate groups within the civil rights movement and provided for a vibrant, media-friendly united front. Carawan also exemplifies the tension that existed beneath the surface. His work spreading white cultural traditions to the African American community could only go so far, as he experienced on his early trips to Johns Island. The tension between the written tradition of white folk music and the generally oral nature of African American culture is revealed by the adaptation of Carawan's version of "We Shall Overcome" to one based more centrally in the African American church. This transformation is also revealing of the limitations of Highlander's avowedly secular praxis when faced with the religiosity of African American society. Nonetheless, Carawan's success in bringing folk culture to the center of the civil rights movement indicates the value of placing such culture at the center of a protest movement. Carawan's example suggests that the folkways that went back into the nineteenth century remained viable means through which protest could be articulated, revealing the vital role of shared memory in the twentieth-century African American experience. Without song, the civil rights movement would have had an entirely different aura. And, as Zilphia Horton's example attests, without song, many organizing initiatives would have struggled to survive.

Highlander also made certain that, away from the mass marches, the movement educated African Americans to become full citizens and helped them to rediscover their historical memory. Citizenship education involved much more than simply providing an education to vote: it legitimized a culture of opposition that ran through African American history, and it fed on a southern culture within the black community that had been dismissed by white society. Septima Clark's and Bernice Robinson's pedagogical concepts guaranteed that the CEP spoke directly to black southerners and that cultural traditions such as storytelling remained valid. Highlander also convinced many SNCC activists that grassroots work was vital. Its model for voter registration and education became central to SNCC's operations and differentiated the organization from its peers. Behind Highlander's liberating atmosphere lay a determined and focused attempt to perpetuate African American cultural traditions in tandem with a commitment to ending oppressive practice.

2

Cultural Organizing in the Integrationist Movement, 1961–1964

Highlander's methods were best put into practice by the Student Nonviolent Coordinating Committee's (SNCC) southern organizers. Drawing from Highlander's fusion of music and politics, SNCC entered numerous communities with the intention not only of forging a political movement but also of developing the community's consciousness in wider terms. Thus it embraced Highlander's idea that, regardless of the terms under which a group is organized, a political discussion could emerge. In Albany, Georgia, SNCC used these methods to organize the local black community and to generate a new generation of community leaders. While the traditional narrative of the civil rights movement labels the campaign in Albany a failure, SNCC drew numerous positive lessons from the experience. The Freedom Singers, an a capella singing group, was founded shortly after the town's movement peaked. Within weeks, the group was performing across the nation, providing crucial new revenue streams and confirming the close relationship between African American musical culture and the political movement. SNCC activists also discovered how to boost the organization's profile in the local community by building up levels of trust among the people and by inviting them into SNCC's fold not simply through talking politics but through more informal means.

SNCC's largely informal nature attracted many young people to the organization. It also allowed organizers and fellow travelers the opportunity to redefine the nature of political protest in the South. When Dick Gregory was invited to help SNCC's operations in Greenwood, Mississippi, the comedian was given considerable latitude to develop his own methodology. His union of direct action and satirical comedy gave great succor to the local movement, not least because, through his comedy routines and his very presence, he highlighted the absurdity of segregation. This offered his audiences and fellow protesters a vital opportunity for psychological relief and uplift, in part because he was fully aware of the impact that his fame had on the local movement and its foes. Knowing that his arrest would inevitably become front-page news, he deliberately provoked and taunted the local police. Were Gregory's taunts to have come from the mouth of a SNCC activist or local protester, they would most likely have been met with swift arrest and a brutal beating. That they came from a nationally renowned comedian, however, rendered the law authorities powerless, adding to their subversive value.

Albany and the Freedom Songs

Since the Montgomery Bus Boycott, Martin Luther King Jr. had been aware of the power of the singing culture that was developing among the civil rights protesters. In November 1961, he asserted that "We Shall Overcome" was an expression of hope and faith in progress, even in the face of hostility and violence, and acknowledged that it provided a similar backbone to the students' strength that Christianity did for the leaders of the SCLC.[1] The song dovetailed neatly with King's Hegelian conception of history as a story of progress toward a world where justice, rather than oppression, ruled. In practice, the campaigns of the early 1960s illustrated to the Southern Christian Leadership Conference (SCLC) that the freedom songs were a vital component of the civil rights movement, even though few in the organization were able to discern exactly how the singing benefited the movement. As Andrew Young revealed in July 1964, "[M]usic has been the backbone of the Freedom Movement. . . . [F]reedom songs have done as much for inspiring our students as all the teaching and preaching. There is a liberating effect that comes from shouting and clapping to songs which express the long suppressed desire for freedom within the Negro."[2]

As Highlander's experience had proved, though, singing went far deeper than this. For Young, Albany seemed to be a place where the black community had successfully insulated itself from white cultural interference.[3] For a time, King and the SCLC were able to exploit the fervor that erupted from the mass meetings through song, and it was precisely this rapture that the organization tried to replicate in Birmingham, Alabama, and subsequent campaigns. The mass meetings, and especially the songs that were sung therein, expressed the new spirit of the movement. Here was what one black minister called "the true church," a place where black politics, protest, and culture melded into one irresistible force that was channeled through group song. As the historian-activist Staughton Lynd watched a mass meeting evolve into a march while the participants sang "We Shall Overcome," he was swept up in the emotion of the moment, believing that it was nearly impossible not to believe them. Many other participants assert that the songs acted to create bonds between the singers, offered spiritual guidance and reassurance in the face of hostility and brutality, and provided a sense of purpose. Lynd's optimism for success in Albany was a fleeting moment, however. Outwitted by Chief of Police Laurie Pritchett, the SCLC was forced to leave Albany without extracting any concrete desegregation agreements from the local authorities.[4]

While the political failure was perhaps the most important lesson for the SCLC, the singing culture of the Albany protests exerted an even more powerful influence on the local SNCC workers. Although many of the songs had been introduced to SNCC in 1960, at Albany they were transformed. This was the first time that Bernice Reagon, a local student activist, became fully aware of the unique power of the freedom songs, an epiphany that revealed the close relationship between culture and politics. Songs were so integral to the Albany movement that she was compelled to define it as a singing movement. For her, the songs had acted to bind the protesters together, erasing their class, cultural, and political differences and emphasizing that which bound them together. For James Forman, a long-term activist who had recently been appointed SNCC's executive secretary, they were the most important factor in creating the spirit of the campaign. Local activist Goldie Jackson thought that two things held activists together: prayer and song. Charles Sherrod must be partially credited with the emphasis on song: when setting down a list of priorities for the mobilization of the local movement, he placed teaching the freedom songs at the top.[5]

When SNCC moved into a community, its first task was to register voters who could already pass the local requirements. A single activist could conduct this work. More activists, either as a result of other interested staff, a successful initial program, or through funding from SNCC, would then develop this work. Charles Sherrod and Cordell Reagon arrived in Albany during autumn 1961 to establish a voter registration office and start the process of registering voters.[6] Their work provided the backbone for SNCC's operations in the locality. By refusing to focus their organizing activity on any particular segment of the black community, Sherrod and Reagon tried to emphasize the benefits of cross-class interaction. Working in pool halls, churches, nightclubs, and lunchrooms, as well as on the streets—even playing basketball in local high schools—the SNCC workers moved beyond the SCLC's and the National Association for the Advancement of Colored People's (NAACP) suggestion that community leaders such as preachers, teachers, and business leaders were most essential to the success of a local movement. Instead, Reagon and Sherrod attracted relatively large numbers of young people from local schools and colleges and from the ranks of the unemployed or the underemployed. As the movement developed in the community, they asked local schools and churches to provide space for the development of a community center, eventually establishing a base in a non-descript building owned by C. W. King, a local builder and real estate broker. Thus SNCC relied to a certain extent on the support of middle-class blacks, even though it did not privilege their personal contribution. By November 1961, the Albany movement had been formed, which combined SNCC activists with the local NAACP, a number of ministers, and other local groups. The community center became the focus of the local movement, providing a valuable space for political meetings and cultural activities. Here, as in other SNCC campaigns around the South, the community center did not limit its function to political meetings, also organizing film presentations, reading groups, and quilt-making sessions. SNCC did not make clear distinctions between such activities and the political meetings, blurring the boundaries between politics and culture.[7]

On 25 November, local blacks met at Mount Zion Baptist Church to discuss a recent student protest and the inevitable arrest of the protesters by the local police. Albany's first mass meeting overflowed with bodies and emotion. The SNCC workers had arranged for a capella singing, led by Cordell Reagon and two local young women, Bernice Reagon and Rutha Harris, to be a central feature of the meeting. As the singing swelled, the SNCC activists noticed that even the most introverted members of the group joined the singing and that the fearful became emboldened. They concluded that a true feeling of community emerged from the glorious noise. The singers were able to channel this energy into the songs and hence into the political movement. At the meeting's close, after Bertha Gober's emotional testimony of her arrest, the entire gathering sang "We Shall Overcome"—introduced to the locals by Cordell Reagon, who learned the song at Highlander—in a state of exhilaration. "Nobody could imagine what kept the church on four corners," recalled Sherrod. King's arrival in Albany on 16 December was met with similarly euphoric singing from packed meetings at both Shiloh and Mount Zion churches. Amending the lyrics of the traditional song "Amen" to "Freedom," the singers swiftly acknowledged their titular leader's arrival with a chorus of "Martin King says freedom!" before Rutha Harris's solo changed the tune to "Woke Up This Morning with My Mind on Freedom." After singing the first four words, Harris did not need to complete the stanza since the fervent crowd responded with such volume that she would never have been heard.[8]

SNCC's song leaders were able to manipulate mass meetings. Bernice Reagon and other SNCC activists transformed religious songs into explicitly political songs. Their secularization of old spirituals and Christian hymns metaphorically erased the many decades between the protest culture of the Albany movement and the antebellum period, linking the protesters with their ancestors through song. New verses were inserted into "Ain't Gonna Let Nobody Turn Me Around," giving notice that Mayor Asa Kelly was not going to turn the protesters around. The song's religious imagery became a cry of defiance against Chief of Police Laurie Pritchett personally and the institution of segregation in a wider sense. Similarly, Bernice Reagon substituted "freedom" for "trouble" in the spiritual "Over My Head (I See Trouble in the Air)." Reagon transformed the spiritual's sense of foreboding into an expression of destiny that was filtered through the political message of the Albany movement. This singing continued even when the protesters were jailed, helping to raise spirits and maintain communication between cells. So powerful were the songs that Pritchett and his colleagues often pleaded with demonstrators to stop singing, aware of the curious shift in the power (im)balance that the singing caused. It seemed incongruous to be arresting people while they sang songs of joy and empowerment. That the songs seemed to insulate the protesters from temporal suffering further irked Pritchett and the local police, not least because the singers' conviction confronted them with the suggestion that they were fighting a higher force.[9]

Deepening its interaction with the local community, SNCC encouraged its workers to respect local traditions and differences in order to ensure that local people did not find themselves feeling inferior to the more cosmopolitan and educated SNCC activists. The community centers established as a bridgehead for SNCC in the community helped to reinforce this mutually supportive relationship and are a direct reflection of Highlander's influence on SNCC. These institutions were designed with Highlander's structure in mind, where the expertise of certain individuals would be used to preserve local cultures, spread organizational techniques, and cultivate the community's political awareness. Local individuals could use the community centers to develop their own skills, talk politics, and forge links with fellow community members. Through this organizing structure, SNCC hoped that indigenous leaders would develop, freeing the local community from reliance on outside organizers, and potentially from its own middle-class leaders whose position was often compromised by economic proximity to the white community. To accentuate this bond, many SNCC activists, including Bob Moses, adopted working clothes as an unofficial uniform. In contrast with most national civil rights leaders, many SNCC workers eschewed starched shirts and sober suits in favor of workers' shirts and dungarees. This had a twofold purpose. First, it reflected the fact that SNCC was working in the community, rather than attempting to lead the community. Working clothes were intended to demonstrate SNCC activists' belief that they could and should operate at the same level as local people, rather than imposing leadership from above. In wearing the same clothes as the average person, SNCC workers tried to emphasize that they were working alongside black southerners. Second, the actions of adopting everyday clothes and simply by being present everyday reinforced SNCC's insistence that it was different from the other civil rights organizations and that it did not consider mass marches to be the focal point of the civil rights movement. This minimization of the sartorial difference between civil rights workers and local people bespoke of SNCC's close identification with working-class black southerners and its rejection of traditional uplift ideology. It also reinforced the self-image of local people, insisting that they should not consider themselves inadequate or inferior to the outside agitators. In this sense, locals were discouraged from mimicking the outsiders and following their leadership. Instead, they were implicitly encouraged to consider themselves as leaders, that their decisions, their actions, and their appearance could not easily be dismissed. This working-class culture, SNCC believed, was more in tune with the lived experience of the people with whom the organization worked and was thus more likely to break down barriers between inside and outside agitators.

SNCC's leadership in Albany raises a number of pertinent issues regarding the organization's relationship with local communities and their leadership, the black church, and generational change, as well as the relationship between religion and activism. Most obviously, SNCC's use of the location of the church for the Albany meetings indicates its understanding of the importance of African American Christianity to the local community in terms of its spiritual meaning, its putative leadership of the community, and its physical presence. Churches were safe havens from interfering whites and were ideal locations for mass meetings, being large enough to contain large numbers of people, familiar enough for local people to be comfortable attending the meetings, and independent enough to avoid white economic intimidation. SNCC thus tapped into the same well of faith that benefited the SCLC. The structure of the meetings mirrored that of church services; speeches (sermons) from activists were punctuated by group singing and praying, reinforcing the Christian atmosphere of the mass meeting. SNCC was therefore acknowledging that Christianity was at the center of the African American community and its culture. Yet SNCC's secularization of religious hymns hints at an ambivalent attitude toward the role of the church. While confirming the importance of these songs in terms of their cultural meaning (that the songs were a central link between the present generation and previous generations), the activists suggested that the political meaning (or message) of these songs was inadequate for the present day. In a sense, the transformations that the SNCC activists wrought on the spirituals imposed modernity onto a cultural form from the past. This attitude toward the words also suggests that SNCC's acceptance of the importance of Christianity had its limits: secular action, rather than merely religious faith, would sustain the movement. Thus Reagon's substitution of "freedom" for "trouble" ("in the air") transforms the spiritual into an expression of expectation, although singers and listeners would also have noted that this new version did not completely erase the anxiety inherent in the original lyrics. They might have seen freedom in the air, but knew they would encounter trouble beforehand. Yet much like Highlander's transformation of "I Shall Not Be Moved," the new lyrics placed the singers in a metaphorical position of control. Through their activism, they were able to see freedom beyond the present troubles. Moreover, through their activism, this freedom would be attained.

In taking control of the meetings, SNCC's local supporters and activists were supplanting a local leadership caste. While SNCC was usually respected and tried to develop a new generation of local leaders, its actions in Albany suggest some frustration with the work of certain leaders, a frustration that also reflects class tensions within the black community. Historically, middle-class blacks assumed leadership roles, and quite naturally, their leadership was often compromised by their own fragile status between the black and white communities.[10] Their position as unofficial ambassadors for African Americans blurred the color line for these community leaders. Their visibility ensured that the white community would scrutinize their actions; any rabble-rousing would inevitably arouse the suspicions of local white segregationists. While they were able to mitigate the white community's hostility toward their black neighbors, they were also required to temper the potential militancy of their black friends. This often led to them urging other blacks to work slowly and patiently in their opposition to segregation and oppression, a pose that some younger blacks took to be a form of Uncle Tomism. The black clergy, as a particularly visible social group, were to some younger African Americans fully implicated in this state of affairs. SNCC's field activists, including Charles Sherrod, often came from more working-class backgrounds, adding a further layer of class tension. Bernice Reagon's role in Albany adds a gendered dimension to SNCC's actions as well, suggesting that young working-class women were moving toward vanguard positions in the fight for equality. So, although it maintained a largely respectful pose toward the church and the clergy's position in the community, SNCC was suggesting that this leadership caste needed unseating.

In October 1963, Robert Mants expressed frustration at the pace of change in Americus, Georgia. Like many other SNCC activists, Mants believed that if physical oppression were to be beaten, it was important to address the issue of psychological freedom. He contended that it was not enough merely to tell black people that whites were not always right. In order to bring about psychological freedom, SNCC had to inculcate self-awareness within the local community, knowledge of their identity as individuals and as a race. Local people also needed an understanding of the contributions of blacks to world civilization.[11] The issue of psychological freedom is crucial for an understanding of SNCC's attitude toward the relationship between the movement and African American culture during the early 1960s. Psychological freedom was arguably as important to SNCC as physical and social freedom. This freedom was best brought about through action on a local level in black communities throughout the South. SNCC workers were fiercely defensive of the rights of the individual and dedicated their work to developing local leaders. In doing so, the organization aimed to develop rather than impose leadership, thus breaking the black community's reliance on outside leaders. More pertinently, it also freed southern black communities from reliance on middle-class leaders. In attempting to develop local working-class leadership, SNCC continued the abortive work of the Congress of Industrial Organizations (CIO) and Highlander in deconstructing class divisions within many southern communities. SNCC's staff was comprised of a mixture of middle- and working-class blacks, from the sharecropper Fannie Lou Hamer to the well-connected Morehouse student Julian Bond and the Harvard-educated Bob Moses. Its loose organizational structure ensured that the leadership cadre reflected the class identities within the organization; in contrast to the other major national civil rights organizations, SNCC's leadership was not dominated by its middle-class members. It hoped that the local leadership it was nurturing would similarly not emerge solely from the middle class.

SNCC's Georgian campaign not only confirmed the importance of community centers to local movements, but it also provided the foundations for the organization's most successful attempt to harness the power of the freedom songs as a fund- and consciousness-raising tool. Formed by Cordell Reagon while campaigning in Albany during 1962, the SNCC Freedom Singers featured Bernice Reagon, Rutha Harris, and Charles Neblett, and made their official debut on 11 November 1962 in concert with Pete Seeger. They performed for movement participants wherever SNCC operated: in churches, meeting halls, streets, and even jail cells, providing a spiritual and psychological boost to jailed activists. More important, from the perspective of SNCC's public relations, the Freedom Singers traveled far beyond the region in which SNCC was active, visiting college campuses throughout the nation to raise awareness of and funds for the southern movement. Bernice Reagon claims that northern movement sympathizers in the early 1960s struggled to give full expression to their philosophical and political commitment to racial equality. The Freedom Singers were able to exploit the distance between northern campuses and the movement by pricking the consciences of students and liberal sympathizers. Although the group could not bring the emotional intensity of southern mass meetings to northern concert halls, the music was able to convey the drama, emotion, and meaning of the civil rights struggle to those who might only have seen it on television. The success of these tours generated national exposure and funds for SNCC, and led to an appearance by the group at the 1963 Newport Folk Festival. It also allowed SNCC to develop personal links with campus organizers throughout the nation, certainly aiding the recruitment drive for the 1964 Mississippi Summer Project. Using music as the primary medium for their message, the Freedom Singers aimed to compel liberal whites to offer a financial contribution to the movement in lieu of a physical commitment. Large concerts were a useful fund-raising tool and a means through which SNCC's real story could be spread. For the participants, this was a crucial way of circumventing the news agencies that did not necessarily offer a friendly interpretation of the movement.[12]

Bernice Reagon later confirmed that the Freedom Singers intended to exploit the orality of southern black culture. This the group did before largely white audiences, although Freedom Singers' concerts were far from neo-minstrelsy. Influenced by Highlander, their concerts integrated education and entertainment. The a cappella renditions of freedom songs were accompanied by a commentary on the creation of the songs, which stressed the links between the civil rights movement and the African American tradition of resistance and explained the meaning and significance of each song to the local movements in the South. The singers also talked about recent events in the movement to add further context and enrich their audiences' understanding of the relationship between the freedom songs and the freedom movement. Through this, SNCC was able to propagandize its work to northern audiences.[13]

The Freedom Singers were happy to acknowledge the entertainment value of their work, but the serious message behind the songs was of prime importance. They linked the present struggle with previous struggles for freedom, reaffirming the value of cultural forms to sustaining a political and social movement. Audiences were encouraged to understand the political and cultural roots of the southern movement, including its relationship with black Christianity; to empathize with those singing the songs (both in the hall and in the jails); and to come to terms with the political significance of the movement. SNCC used freedom songs to deepen bonds with local people when its activists arrived in a community, and these songs were also an important unifying force. When in front of the white audiences, the Freedom Singers emphasized that this performance, indeed the act of paying for a ticket, was a political act, bringing the southern movement closer to the North.

The audiences most receptive to the Freedom Singers were on the campuses of northern universities. In the early 1960s, many northern students found themselves without an outlet for their interest in the southern movement. Attending such concerts and listening to movement activists provided a psychological release and certainly revealed to northern students the urgency of the southern movement, opening a vital channel of communication between the movement and its northern supporters. Although the entertainment value of the concerts was important, the Freedom Singers were insistent that the political message at the heart of their work was paramount. They made a considerable contribution to SNCC's campaigns, doing much to cement the organization's status on campuses and insisting that African American cultural forms were central to the freedom struggle.[14]

Dick Gregory and Performative Protest

SNCC's union of black expressive culture and political organizing went further than the Freedom Singers' work. When a SNCC representative invited Dick Gregory to donate to a 1963 food drive for the black residents of Leflore County, Mississippi, the intention was to utilize Gregory's celebrity status to highlight the county's withdrawal from a federal program that supplied surplus food to those who were deprived. Like the other civil rights organizations, SNCC generally used celebrities to boost its status in the public eye. James Forman suggested that the vicarious relationship between such personalities and the black population brought the many thousands of black Americans who identified with the personalities into the movement. Naturally, the fund-raising and public relations power of an individual like Harry Belafonte offered other benefits. SNCC fund-raisers featured personal appearances from luminaries such as Lorraine Hansberry, Thelonious Monk, Charles Mingus, and James Baldwin. At these fund-raisers, audience participation tended to be limited to the act of paying for a ticket or sponsoring the performance.[15] Crucially, the celebrities were allowed to decide their level of involvement. Bob Dylan, for example, aided SNCC's efforts in the South, helping to load food trucks as well as singing songs. By contrast, in 1963 Josephine Baker brought a $250,000 wardrobe to a joint benefit for SNCC, the Congress of Racial Equality (CORE), the SCLC, and the NAACP, staying at the Hilton Hotel at their expense and even invoicing the no doubt regretful groups for the $581 import duty.[16]

Gregory's contribution, however, was different. He not only brought the national media to Greenwood but also illustrated how the civil rights movement entwined with African American expressive culture. Gregory first became aware of the civil rights issue at school in St. Louis during the early 1950s, after having his athletics records not listed in the school's record books due to his color. The youthful Gregory, who by then was a minor media figure in St. Louis, was so incensed that he joined a Parent-Teacher Association (PTA) march. That the march was about overcrowding in black schools and Gregory was protesting his own treatment was not the point. He did not march again until the 1960s, by which time he had become rich through his success on the comedy circuit.[17]

At first, Gregory's act was generally apolitical, but civil rights issues began to find their way into his routine alongside a deprecatory admission of his own reticence to become involved in the movement. "They asked me to buy a lifetime membership in the NAACP, but I told them I'd pay a week at a time. Hell of a thing to buy a lifetime membership, wake up one morning and find the country's been integrated," Gregory cracked to his black Chicago audience. He frequently offered a doubly satirical bon mot to white crowds: "Wouldn't it be a hell of a thing if all this was burnt cork and you people were being tolerant for nothing?" Gregory's initial target was the self-satisfied liberal attitude of his audience. Underneath the suggestion that Gregory might be a white man in disguise lay more troubling connotations: was Gregory himself adopting a mask to perform? Gregory knew that he was acting out a predefined role on stage, performing for his paying masters. While doing so, was he laughing at them and their simplistic, even racist, notions of black humor? Who was in control of the situation: the paymasters or the performing clown? In citing the mask of performance, Gregory confirmed that African American identity was partially a response to white expectations; in deconstructing it, he offered a more dangerous suggestion that whites no longer held the upper hand.[18]

By 1960, Gregory had honed his race material to a fine point. "Good evening, ladies and gentlemen," he would begin,

> I understand there are a good many Southerners in the room tonight. I know the South very well. I spent twenty years there one night.... Last time I was down South, I walked into this restaurant. This white waitress came up to me and said, "We don't serve colored people in here." I said, "That's all right, I don't eat colored people, no way! Bring me a whole fried chicken."[19]

Aside from his fondness for fried chicken, Gregory's eating habits had an impact on his relationship with the sit-in movement: "I spent six months, once, sitting at an Alabama lunch counter. And when they finally served me, they didn't have what I wanted!"[20]

Gregory first arrived in Mississippi at the invitation of local NAACP organizer Medgar Evers in 1962. At an NAACP rally, Gregory heard the testimony of an old man whose wife died on the night that he was jailed for leading a voter registration drive. It was the couple's first night apart in sixty years of marriage. The man's tearful admission proved to be a turning point in Gregory's life. In response to this tragic story, Gregory chose to devote his life to the movement.[21]

After returning to Greenwood in March 1963, Gregory gave a series of benefit concerts for local people, working closely with SNCC's local campaign. These performances became a vital part of the local campaign, offering much needed relief from segregation and the pressures of daily harassment and encouraging audiences to take a slightly detached view of life in the South. His comedy became an interface between African American vernacular culture and the civil rights movement, continuing the long tradition of using humor as a relief from oppression. It is notable that Gregory's quips were met with applause rather than laughter, as if the brutality of Mississippian segregation had stripped the audience of their ability to laugh. In Chicago, his act focused on the absurdity of a life that the audience might not have known personally. Although discrimination was very real in Chicago, white harassment was generally less likely to be life threatening. Certainly Gregory's white audiences would not have experienced the discrimination that the comic cited. In Greenwood, he was revealing truths to his audience and was confirming that freedom had not yet been achieved. His comedy offered only temporary relief, suggesting that its illocutionary force changed dramatically in the South. Locals understood what Gregory meant when he said that he had spent twenty years in the South one night. They also knew the absurdity of the situation when Gregory noted that "if [the white man] . . . really believes we was [sic] really inferior to him, he would integrate his schools tomorrow and we would flunk out by noon." They responded with a metaphorical nod when Gregory asserted that "here's a man that didn't have enough intelligence to know that if you want to segregate someone and really keep 'em down, you put 'em up front! He made the great mistake of putting us in the back. So for 300 years, we've been watching *him*." This was not material that confirmed comfortable liberal sentiments about blacks but instead was a challenge to the local audience to take control of their own situation. Gregory went on to dissect black violence, observing that whites "have accused us of having the number one crime rate in America, and I wonder if you ever stopped and asked yourself, have we? . . . [W]e ain't never lynched nobody, man!"[22]

In concluding his monologues, Gregory abandoned comedy for explicit political comment. "Keep me a second class citizen if you must," he said, "but please baby, don't make me pay first class taxes! Send me to the worst schools in Mississippi if you must, but please baby, when I go to take my voter test, don't give me the same test you gave that white boy. Give me the dirtiest, stinkinest [sic] job in the field, if you must, but please don't go out to tell people I stink."[23]

If laughter represents freedom from fear and the weak defeating the mighty, Gregory's act confirmed that the Mississippi movement still faced an indomitable foe.[24] As if to acknowledge the limitations of comedy alone,

Gregory took the relationship between humor and freedom, art and activism, to a deeper level, using his position as a comedian to engage humor in actively pushing for (as opposed to commenting on) freedom. Rather than merely lending his name to campaigns and making the occasional appearance in high-profile demonstrations, Gregory insisted on playing a central role in civil rights work, telling anybody, "If it's an organization I can work with, I'll work."[25]

It is likely that this desire to define these terms lies behind Gregory's decision to work more closely with SNCC than with the local NAACP. His performative and highly confrontational role in Greenwood was more akin to SNCC's desire for "freedom now!" and its activists' boldness when faced with white violence than was the NAACP's more gradualist stance. Furthermore, his frank admission that he might not be able to remain nonviolent comprised a tacit agreement with many local SNCC activists that nonviolence was a tactic rather than a philosophy. He headed marches, inspired the locals, and brought his comedy act into the heart of the movement. The historian Charles Payne credits Gregory with forcing Greenwood ministers to sign a petition endorsing the freedom movement after months of equivocation. His arrival in Greenwood also brought scores of Justice Department officials to the town. They were there to prevent Gregory from being killed in Mississippi, an event that would have had national repercussions, not least because he had brought the national media with him: his first arrest was front-page news in the *New York Times*, which also faithfully reported Gregory openly taunting the chief of police. Subsequently, local officials feared the national publicity that assaulting or arresting Gregory would bring. With the presence of Justice Department officials, this gave Gregory an aura of untouchability. Aware of this, and experiencing another epiphany, Gregory upped the ante for the local police, inviting his wife and newborn son to join in the activities. He transformed each demonstration into a confrontational performance described as "so daring as to be touched by madness or sublime inspiration."[26]

He took full advantage of his fame, thumbing his nose literally and metaphorically to any officer who came near him, and offering small amounts of money to those who escorted him from demonstrations, quipping to the press that he always tipped his chauffeurs. Where most southern blacks had learned not to respond to racial epithets, Gregory's response was vitriolic. After the chief of police racially abused him, Gregory exploded, telling the startled racist, "I could take you to Chicago today and let you walk through my home then come back here and walk through your home, and out of the two of us, you'd know which one was the nigger." He clearly understood that race and class were muddled, even mutable terms.[27]

SNCC benefited from the psychological relief that Gregory's presence and material brought. His guerrilla street theater provided light entertainment and a crucial underlying message: African Americans should not be pushed around. Gregory's appearance pressured Greenwood officials to refrain from harassing black citizens who tried to register to vote, to quash the convictions of eight SNCC workers who had tried to facilitate voter registration, and to provide police protection at the registration office. As Charles Payne has noted, Gregory provided SNCC with a perfect opportunity to motivate people. By giving them public recognition and a shared platform with a national celebrity such as Gregory, SNCC was able to push previously reticent people into the limelight, bringing out their leadership qualities and thereby stimulating the local people to more action by their example. Gregory's example became a beacon of hope and inspiration for the local people, proving that a black man could become a success, demand respect from whites, and, more important, receive it.[28]

Gregory's professional routine was irrevocably changed by his experiences in the movement, and eventually he decided to abandon his comedy in favor of full-time activism. Following the Greenwood campaign, Gregory helped the SCLC in Birmingham, receiving his first "butt kicking" in the bargain and incorporating local commissioner of public safety Eugene "Bull" Connor into his act. Even the death of his son only temporarily pulled Gregory away from the front line.[29] His involvement continued through 1964, with the activist-comedian appearing at numerous demonstrations, conducting a thirty-day tour for SNCC, and canceling so many paid performances in favor of action that he soon found himself heavily in debt. This parlous financial state was exacerbated by his willingness to perform for free wherever and whenever his hosts wanted him to tell the truth rather than jokes. The former was his preferred gig because, he shrugged, "if the South integrated tomorrow, I'd have more places to work." Near the end of the year, Gregory published his first autobiography, simply and pointedly entitled *Nigger. Jet* magazine reported that some black leaders hated the title, which surprised Gregory, who in characteristic fashion quipped, "Wherever you hear the name nigger. . . . you know they are advertising my book."[30]

In Greenwood, Gregory cast himself as a classic artist-activist. The experience of the many deaths involved with the movement convinced Gregory of his calling in life: "My career was interfering with my demonstrating."

Throughout his time with the civil rights movement, however, Gregory was aware of his function: he could use his celebrity to bring national attention to local initiatives and quite possibly action from the Justice Department. His oral talents could give succor and catharsis to those on the front lines. He never shirked from placing himself on the firing line at the expense of his personal safety and professional gain, and movement histories abound with references to his appearances at the head of various marches and his commentary on the various stages of the movement. His guerrilla street theater also provided light entertainment and a crucial underlying message, namely, that African Americans should not be pushed around.[31]

In addition to establishing how SNCC linked cultural forms to the freedom movement, Gregory and the Freedom Singers reveal the importance of individual dedication to SNCC. Staff members were paid subsistence (sometimes sub-subsistence) wages, and no membership fees were imposed. The profits from benefit concerts were channeled straight into SNCC's finances. The influence of the so-called floaters who supported Bob Moses and the concept of the "freedom high" pushed SNCC toward an even greater reliance on individual conscience. These floaters believed that the civil rights movement was defined by the dedication of its activists and that organizations had no right to dictate policy or duties to its volunteers. Many in SNCC believed that contributions should not be determined by the organization but should be according to the skills of the individual: Gregory's case is a perfect example. SNCC welcomed support from anybody regardless of their political leanings and rarely attempted to guide people toward what the organization wanted. After observing SNCC activities in Albany, Students for a Democratic Society activist Tom Hayden noted the ramifications of SNCC's lack of didacticism. According to Hayden, SNCC staff members made no attempts to control the local movement or to direct its participants, choosing instead to work cooperatively in full consultation with their supporters. This attitude was particularly visible in SNCC's local community operations in southwest Georgia. SNCC's work there has been described as one of the two most important testing grounds for the organization's approach to community organizing. It is also an excellent example of how local organizing, voter registration, and SNCC's philosophy entwined with cultural organizing.[32]

The Albany campaign was a learning process for the movement, although where the SCLC interpreted its mistakes largely within an organizational-strategic framework, SNCC became further cognizant of the cultural dimension of the freedom struggle. The Freedom Singers were the most obvious manifestation of this interest in using African American cultural forms as political weapons. Dick Gregory's role in Greenwood also points to the various methods of protest that were employed during the civil rights movement. While his use of comedy to comment on the movement was not the first union of humor and oppositional politics, his role in the Greenwood protests, where he brought comedy into the front line of the local movement, was almost unique and is testament to the comedian's bravery, to his commitment to the civil rights movement, and to his peculiar brand of genius.

3

Jazz and Radical Politics, 1960–1964

Most historians acknowledge that the promotion of African American culture was a fundamental component of late 1960s Black Power protest. For
many Black Power activists, theorists, and rhetoricians, cultural freedom—
namely the right to express one's racial identity through cultural forms—was
vital to achieving the psychological freedom that the integrationist civil rights
movement did not offer. Amiri Baraka's experiments in theater, journalism,
and political and cultural activism were of great importance to the Black
Arts Movement. He serves as a perfect example of how African American
artists involved themselves directly in the Black Power movement. Prior to
1964, he concentrated his political energies on Cuba and Robert F. Williams's
struggle in North Carolina. Baraka's experiences in this period laid the foundations for his later attempts to unite cultural forms such as jazz and theater
with the fight against white oppression. His work in these fields prior to his
conversion to black nationalism helps to establish how African American
identity became a central issue to the Black Power generation, and how the
Black Arts Movement conceived the role of art in the black freedom struggle.

Baraka was a forbidding critic of white liberalism: his jazz writing from
this period included various swipes at white liberal jazz fans, and *Dutchman* and *The Slave*, the two most important plays that Baraka wrote before adopting black nationalism, offer damning indictments of liberalism.
Moreover, Baraka considered his writing to be intrinsically political. After
witnessing the revolutionary pageant of the July 26 Celebration in Cuba,
Baraka became convinced that he had to make his writing part of the black
political struggle.[1] *Dutchman* is also usefully contrasted with James Baldwin's *Blues for Mister Charlie*, which ran on Broadway during *Dutchman's*
first run. *Mister Charlie* was no artistic triumph, and despite his distrust of
white liberalism, Baldwin was forced to rely on white liberals to prolong the

play's life. Baraka was unconcerned about the liberal response to his plays and more interested in exploring the notion of a common black identity that might be used as a weapon in the liberation struggle, an issue that unites his cultural productions of the 1960s. Given that both authors acknowledged their own role in the developing civil rights struggle, their work is worthy of consideration as a contribution to the cultural front of the civil rights movement.

A number of late 1960s black nationalists took great influence from Robert F. Williams's fierce response to white supremacy. Many Black Power activists used his 1962 text, *Negroes with Guns*, as a handbook for independent black organizing and as proof of the efficacy of armed self-defense. Williams's pamphlet, the *Crusader*, also brought his conception of the struggle to thousands of southern activists during the 1960s. The National Association for the Advancement of Colored People (NAACP) convinced him of the value of propaganda, and his interest in black music led him to conclude that music could be a powerful propaganda tool.[2] He developed a radio program that educated and challenged his listeners through a startling mix of incendiary oratory and music. Williams combined the sounds of progressive black music with his own rhetoric, believing that each would reinforce the other. He focused on the underlying political message of much black music, particularly the experimental postbop jazz that Baraka was championing. Williams insisted that the freedom of the "free" jazz players could be replicated in the physical world, that black people could be inspired to challenge the status quo by drawing lessons from the postbop players' refusal to follow the "rules" of jazz. Williams was also fond of irritating and provoking people, a characteristic that he had in common with much of the free jazz of the time. In mixing this music with the more explicit political message of freedom and protest songs, he made the message of this music more apparent; in mixing it with his own impassioned rhetoric, he confirmed the urgency of his appeal and the African American situation. Where Baraka's work demonstrates that late 1960s black nationalism emerged as a critique of the southern movement, Williams suggests that important strands of this critique emerged within the movement itself. Crucially, both establish how black militants saw African American culture as a tool of the freedom struggle; importantly, the blind spots within their vision of African American culture were repeated in the outlook of their successors and indicate the limitations of Black Power cultural activism, notably in its reification of an homogenous black culture.

Jazz, Theater, and Radical Politics in the Work of Amiri Baraka

The civil rights movement fatally compromised the art of Amiri Baraka but in doing so demonstrated how art and politics could usefully be combined. Prior to his involvement with the freedom struggle, Baraka had been an acclaimed Beat poet convinced that his only duty was to his art. The turning point in his intellectual development was a July 1960 trip to Cuba. Afterward, Baraka's art became subsumed within his commitment to the black freedom struggle. By the end of the decade, it had entered an irreversible decline. Yet his actions are illustrative of the role of the artist within the movement.[3]

Under the auspices of the Fair Play for Cuba Committee (FPCC), Baraka was invited to visit revolutionary Cuba along with Julian Mayfield, Harold Cruse, and Robert F. Williams.[4] During the trip, Baraka was stung by the barbs of a number of Cubans who denounced him as a "cowardly bourgeois individualist." While in Havana, he visited the Casa de Las Americas, Cuba's new literary and cultural center. Here, Cuban culture was promoted as an integral part of the revolution, and adult education classes were offered, where Cubans could learn about and discuss Cuban culture. This experience profoundly affected Baraka's interpretation of the value of cultural forms to revolutionary movements. Wanting to experience the revolution at a deeper level, he took a long train ride to the July 26 Celebration at Sierra Maestra. Fidel Castro's characteristically protracted speech was followed by a concert that included choral singing, ballet, calypso dancing, and Mexican singing and dancing, climaxing with a Mexican Mardi Gras procession. The celebration had a major impact on Baraka. While he was impressed with the Cubans' political fervor, it is clear that the Cuban understanding that the cultural was political was just as pertinent. The "strange mixture" of cultural forms also had an impact. The Cubans saw no artistic distinction between a ballet and a folk song: neither was intrinsically more valuable as art, and both were equally efficient at conveying a political message. The content was far more important to the revolution than the form.[5]

Baraka later remarked that Cuba turned him *completely* around." He had never previously considered engaging with the political world. Cuba opened his eyes to the worldwide anticolonial struggle and convinced him of the need to address art to the black freedom struggle. Soon after his return to the United States, he withdrew from his Beat friends, berating them for their apolitical stance. He joined the New York City chapter of the FPCC and established the Organization of Young Men (OYM), a group that he hoped could build political consciousness in downtown New York.[6]

Baraka's work also began to change, a process signaled by the account of his visit to Cuba, "Cuba Libre." Following the success of his Cuban reportage, Baraka embarked on writing a new prose piece, which was published as *The System of Dante's Hell*. Baraka's prose fizzed and crackled with his energy and his zealous commitment to his new political vision. In the long term, this union of a Kerouacian writing style with impulsive political action led to Baraka's literary style becoming more attuned to the black freedom struggle. His black nationalist works often give the impression of being unedited first drafts: a combination, perhaps, of Beat spontaneity and black nationalist (later, Marxist) dogmatism.

During the early 1960s, Baraka became increasingly inspired by the growing radical black culture in New York City and channeled his energy through critical writing on jazz music. Immersed in the Greenwich Village jazz scene, by March 1962 he was writing a regular column in *Down Beat*, a jazz periodical largely skeptical of the jazz avant-garde. This new wave of jazz emerged in the late 1950s through the work of a young generation of musicians that included Eric Dolphy, Archie Shepp, and John Coltrane, most of whom played frequently in the jazz clubs of Manhattan. The music of these players abandoned many previous norms associated with the form of jazz: sixteen- and thirty-two-bar structures, Western harmonic melodies and chord structures, even standard rhythms. In doing so, the avant-garde players concentrated the focus of the group on the individual skill of and interplay between the players, opening up the possibilities for collective and individual improvisation. To the lazy ear, much of this free jazz appeared simply cacophonous, but most groups followed certain prearranged themes or riffs and had a number of set points at which the players would begin (and sometimes end) improvisations, navigating the music between conformity and chaos.[7]

A great fan of the music, Baraka was convinced that this new wave of "free" jazz was as valid a political statement as the southern civil rights protests. For Baraka, feeling rather than technical virtuosity and adherence to European melodic restrictions was the key to this new music. More pertinent, Baraka insisted that this music was a cultural front in the war against white supremacy. That avant-garde jazz was largely written and performed by African American musicians who rejected the gentrification and bleaching of the music was further evidence that this music was part of a black revolution. That white critics and audiences were regularly appalled or alienated by this music was of even more comfort. That a number of its musicians consciously addressed their music to the civil rights movement was conclusive proof of its political qualities.[8]

While *Down Beat*'s white writers urged the musicians to abandon their musical freedom and militant politics, Baraka castigated the critical establishment for its middlebrow tendencies. "Jazz and the White Critic" further alienated him from *Down Beat*, but offered a number of pertinent observations concerning the relationship between jazz and its listeners. The article explores the refusal of the cultural establishment to note the sociocultural background that informed the best of black jazz and that firmly rooted the music in the politics of its day. Baraka explained why he so detested the middlebrow inclinations of jazz critics, arguing that "real" intellectuals dismissed jazz as an artistic expression, leaving petit bourgeois hobbyists who feared innovation to debase critical standards. Furthermore, while most innovative jazz musicians were black, the critical establishment was, almost to a man, white. These white hobbyist critics failed to appreciate hard bop when it arrived in the 1940s, and the music was forced to gain acceptance in the urban black clubs, a process that was repeating itself with free jazz. Of course, this allowed Baraka to remind readers that white racism forced black musicians underground and that an African American music was being subjected to inappropriate European American critical standards. Furthermore, it afforded Baraka the opportunity to argue that the supposedly working-class players who worked in the clubs represented jazz's vanguard and that the middle-class big band players (whom the hobbyists revered) were merely following the whims of their white middle-class conservative audience. Not long afterward, Malcolm X was to echo these sentiments. At the Savoy Ballroom in early 1940s Harlem, he had witnessed the desperation of whites to experience black culture firsthand in the belief that it was somehow more carefree. They "were just mad for Negro 'atmosphere,' especially [in] some of the places which had what you might call Negro *soul*," he sneered in his autobiography. While Baraka had not at this point fallen under Malcolm X's influence, they clearly shared the sentiment that whites, in searching for a transgressive or dangerous cultural experience, were diluting black culture. Conveniently, Baraka's contention that feeling was more important than technical skill allowed him to impose a political interpretation on free jazz and to suggest that orality was at the center of black culture. This art not only reflected black life, it *was* black life. To criticize it was to criticize the musicians' lives and therefore the African American community itself, a statement that tied *Down Beat*'s white critics in knots for a number of years.

"The notes *mean something*," he fumed, "and the something is, regardless of its stylistic considerations, part of the black psyche as it dictates the various forms of Negro culture." To transcribe the music was to miss its point: the moment of creation was the most important point of the music.[9]

Baraka's argument concerning the preservation of black music placed him in a curious alliance with Guy Carawan over the relative merits of performance and transcription. Both were skeptical of the value of written documentation of their music. While modern jazz was also best experienced "live" in clubs and concerts, it depended on studio (and live) recordings for its preservation, which entailed reliance on an industry that was funded mainly by white benefactors and consumers. Indeed, even when Baraka documented his contribution to the new wave of jazz in his 1965 fund-raising concert for the Black Arts Repertory Theater/School (BARTS), it was released on the white-owned Impulse record label, suggesting that there were limits to Baraka's exclusion of whites from the jazz community. Baraka's occasional contributions of liner notes to albums on Impulse by artists such as Archie Shepp and John Coltrane offers further evidence of the flexibility of his racial attitudes. His opinion of the music's relationship with an elemental black spirit also disregarded the extent to which the free jazz players relied on their own structures for their playing. Their "freedom" was built on foundations of technical virtuosity that could only be erected on the solid ground of training and countless hours of practice.[10]

Baraka's forays into jazz criticism led to the production of a full-length social history of African American music. *Blues People* remains a landmark in jazz criticism. In it, Baraka imposes a class analysis on listeners' preferences that deepened his criticism of the white critics, and extends this analysis to the creation of jazz music. Influenced by E. Franklin Frazier's *The Black Bourgeoisie, Blues People* questions the assimilationist tendencies of the black middle class, asserting that jazz was the music of the field slaves and their descendants alone. Middle-class blacks began to reject the music in the early twentieth century because of its associations with their past. Baraka's interpretation is rather simplistic—in asserting that these people were aiming to disappear into white America, he underestimates the extent to which class aspirations influenced this process—but it suits his wider political point about the impact of whiteness on the black psyche. *Blues People* is not merely a history of jazz music; it is a highly personal cultural history of African Americans and of the relationship between politics and music. In the context of the 1960s, it was also a profound statement about the African heritage of black Americans and the cultural debts that black

Americans owed to Africa and white Americans owed to black Americans. Despite his atheism, Baraka did not ignore the impact of Christianity on black Americans; even so, he insisted that African Americans transformed the religion into an Afro-Christianity that was peppered with African influences, including the ring shout and remnants of voodoo practices and beliefs. Critics delighted (and still delight) in debunking the inaccuracies and prejudices that are apparent in *Blues People*. Yet it remains an ambitious and pioneering attempt to construct a social history of African American music and a forceful articulation of Baraka's belief that jazz was a truly black political music.[11]

Baraka's insistence that jazz was the only true art of black Americans led him to dismiss almost the entire canon of African American literature as a body of stultifying, mediocre work. His resentment of his middle-class background lay at the core of this criticism. For him, most black writers were in thrall to middle-class ideology and desires, and were consequently unrepresentative of African American people. Moreover, their aspiration to create "art" resulted in their work failing almost by definition. For Baraka, black literature was too self-conscious, formalized, and wedded to white cultural mores to be a true reflection of African American life. Ingenuously, Baraka suggested that jazz was the creation solely of working-class blacks and that its musicians unselfconsciously and almost accidentally created art in their desire to express their innate political sensibilities. This analysis comes close to an exoticist celebration of the primitive. In this, and in the insistence that feeling was more important than skill, there is a suggestion that Baraka reveled in a certain lack of sophistication among working-class jazz players that did not actually exist. Herein lies one of the reasons for the decline in Baraka's writing during the late 1960s. Convinced of the self-consciousness of black literature, Baraka attempted to re-create the improvisational flow of free jazz in his writing, believing that the moment of creation was also the moment of clarity. The inconsistency in this argument—as Josef Jarab puts it, that there was "white black literature" and a "black black music"—was of little concern to Baraka, since he firmly believed that his "jazz literature" was solving this so-called paradox.[12]

Baraka was not alone in noting the relevance of jazz music to black nationalist politics. Malcolm X was a jazz enthusiast, although he detested the close association between the musicians and degenerate behavior. His reflections on his hustling days emphasize the role of drugs in the jazz scene: "at least half of the musicians smoked reefers." In those earlier days, prior to his conversion to Islam, much of his regular income came from musicians visiting Harlem who needed a fix. Given that Islam forbade any form of drug taking, it is unsurprising that Malcolm X later publicly rejected the transformative power of jazz, associating it with drugs and degeneracy.[13] One further factor prevented him expressing his interest in the music: the fact that many jazz bands were racially integrated. Even while some musicians made inflammatory comments about white racism, a number performed alongside whites. Malcolm X understood that jazz was African American music, but he maintained his distance from the music and its players for two of its associations—drugs and integration—not the music itself.[14]

At the founding of the Organization of Afro-American Unity (OAAU) in June 1964, Malcolm X reiterated the need for a cultural element to the freedom struggle. Until African Americans used their own talent, took pride in their history and culture, and affirmed their selfhood and identity, he argued, they would forever be subordinate. He knew that the African American population's roots lay in Africa, and were being expressed daily: "The soul of Africa is still reflected in the music played by black men." Indeed, during 1964 Malcolm X explicitly linked jazz to political organizing, noting the similarities between improvisational jazz and the black (indeed, his own) search for new forms of politics and philosophy. While this might suggest that he was making things up as he went along, it more accurately illustrates his understanding that a close relationship existed between African American politics and culture, and he was doing in politics what the free jazz players were doing in music.[15]

Although it took Malcolm X's assassination to convert Baraka to black nationalism, as early as 1962 he was advocating a form of black nationalism as the solution to the racial crisis. This can be linked to his jazz criticism: Baraka, after all, was determined to emphasize the value of black musicians working together to ensure the end of white domination of jazz criticism and white control of jazz economics. Aware of the struggles of black musicians to gain acceptance and earn a living in an industry that was controlled by whites, Baraka harbored a brooding resentment of whites who muscled in on the scene. In *Blues People*, he reserved particular disdain for white musicians, whom he believed exploited jazz for economic gain without truly understanding the music's roots. Thus black unity in jazz was a key to ensuring the success of black musicians and in perpetuating the music's symbiotic relationship with African American society. In Baraka's mind, the same could be said for the civil rights movement, which was the message of his 1962 essay, "'Black' Is a Country."[16]

In 1964, a quartet of plays pushed Baraka into the theatrical limelight. *Dutchman* and *The Slave* remain the most important of the 1964 plays and are closely linked through their pessimistic view of integration and through their central characters' understanding of the black response to white liberalism.[17]

Dutchman, the winner of the 1964 award for the best off-Broadway play, is about black-white relations. On its opening, *Jet* magazine considered it to be an apocalyptic vision of the deterioration of race relations, hailing it as "frighteningly frank and roaringly realistic." The play suggests that, at heart, we are all savages. Those who mask savagery with civility (middle-class blacks in Baraka's interpretation) are doomed to death at the hands of those who conceal their savagery more subtly (whites). The play undercuts the white assumption that blackness could be equated with hipness.

The play's setting is a subway train—which serves as a metaphor for the civil rights movement—on which a black middle-class man, Clay, is traveling to a party. Clay is approached by a white woman, Lula, who acts as a personification of white Americans, notably their patronizing attitude toward blacks and their dangerous, even murderous, tendencies. She taunts Clay by mocking his facial hair and fondness for drinking tea, and by suggesting that he lives with his parents. Aroused by Lula's uninhibited attitude, embodied in her freedom to say and do as she pleases, Clay begins to flirt with her. Toying with his emotions, Lula begins to taunt him for wearing a suit and tie, clothes that she considers to be unreflective of African American traditions. Seeing through his attempt at respectability, Lula taunts Clay for his ambivalent relationship with his race. Act 1 concludes with Lula labeling Clay a murderer and satirically suggesting that he pretend that he is no longer visible—no longer of color—and free of his own history; that he literally becomes Ralph Ellison's Invisible Man.[18]

Act 2 begins with Lula promising to take Clay back to her apartment after the party. Continuing the fantasy, Lula allows Clay to imagine himself in love with her (which also prompts him to complain about the slow speed of the train). Lula then ridicules Clay's ignorance of his own history when he talks of life on slave plantations and the birth of blues music. Deriding his race even further, Lula satirizes African American dance by offering to "rub bellies" and do "the nasty . . . the gritty grind . . . the navel scratcher" on the train. After emasculating him, Lula then deracinates him, in a voice audible to all of those on the subway car, "You ain't no nigger, you're just a dirty white man." Aroused further by being called an Uncle Tom and forced to confront his own racial identity, Clay physically restrains Lula. A drunk passenger attempts to intervene, and Clay wrestles him to the ground. Telling Lula that his descent into violence is being prevented only by his suit, Clay threatens to kill her. Aware that the rest of the passengers are watching him, he threatens to kill them as well before launching into an impassioned speech about white fetishizing of black culture. Rejecting his earlier interpretation of black music, Clay claims that the root of the music is hatred of whites, satirizing white jazz fans for idolizing musicians such as Charlie Parker who "would've played not a note of music if he just walked up to East Sixty-seventh Street and killed the first ten white people he saw." Clay then slips into Baraka's persona: "I'm the great would-be poet. . . . Some kind of bastard literature . . . all it needs is a simple knife thrust. Just let me bleed you, you loud whore, and one poem vanished." Clay's radical sentiments are uncovered by Lula's relentless taunting of his attempt to pass as white. His revelation that black behavior is a mask for hatred of whites is a profoundly shocking statement. This is underscored by its apparent contradiction of the earlier argument that black culture evolved from the celebration of life under slavery and reaches a peak in Clay's prediction that a race war will ensue. Lula's actions have forced him to remove his own mask—and that of the entire African American population. "Murder," Clay concludes, "[w]ould make us all sane." Lula seems to concur. After Clay recovers his composure and apologizes for ruining the evening, she kills him and enlists the other whites on the subway to dump the body. Clay's refusal to take on the mantle of the revolutionary by fulfilling his threat leads to his final emasculation. The play's conclusion is designed to energize the black audience, to provoke them to act on their political impulses, and to force whites to confront their own prejudices.[19]

The Slave also explores interracial love and operates as a companion piece to Dutchman. More verbose than Dutchman, The Slave is also a more violent play set near the conclusion of a racial apocalypse where a black revolutionary army is about to lay waste to a white city. It has a powerful sexual undercurrent. The central character is an overeducated black revolutionary leader and poet, Walker Vessels, whose name recalls black nationalist icons David Walker and Denmark Vesey and whose vocations combine Baraka's private dreams and public identity. Walker Vessels offers an alternative resolution to the dilemma facing Clay. Rather than letting his civilized mind dominate, Vessels acts on his black instincts. He is first seen in a prologue as an old man dressed as a field slave, delivering a rambling speech before lapsing into inarticulacy. The play then leaps in time to the race war threatened by

Clay, where a young Vessels returns to his white ex-wife's home. Grace has married Bradford Easley, a liberal professor of literature who once taught Vessels. Both whites are disgusted at the actions of the revolutionary blacks and at Vessels in particular. In a reversal of Lula's manipulation of Clay, Vessels ridicules Grace's liberalism and her husband's physical inferiority. So emasculated is Easley that he is only able to denounce Vessels's limitations as a poet. The three trade literary allusions as insults before Vessels reveals that he has come to reclaim his daughters for the black race, to allow them to reject double consciousness. Echoing Clay, Vessels tells Easley and Grace that his creative impulses have been replaced by "murderous philosophies." Act 1 ends with Vessels indicting Western liberalism as a tool of white supremacy and apparently falling asleep under the influence of alcohol. Act 2 begins with Easley attempting to wrestle Vessels, who shoots him dead. When Grace accuses him of being out of his mind, Vessels declares that this is the only state of mind that is fully justifiable. Plagued with ambivalence, Vessels finds himself unable to erase his integrationist past by killing Grace. An apocalyptic barrage of explosions around the house instead leaves her mortally wounded. The play concludes with Vessels telling Grace that the children are dead. Since the only time that Vessels actually visits their room is at the start of the play, Grace and the audience suspect that he killed them. A child's voice is heard screaming as Vessels exits the stage, although the play does not reveal whether the voice belongs to one of Vessels and Grace's daughters or whether it is a metaphor for the loss of innocence in the racial struggle. As he walks out of the door, Vessels's appearance reverts to the old man of the prologue. The play concludes with the suggestion that Vessels is still a slave, not because of his racial essentialism but because he has failed to overcome his attraction to a white world: Easley and Grace might be dead, but he remains enslaved to double consciousness. The prolonged barrage at the play's conclusion offers more ambiguity for the audience, forcing it to question whether a racial war is taking place outside the theater, making the entire play a metaphor for the audience's relationship with the black freedom struggle. Vessels spends time in the Easleys' house, just as the audience spends an evening at the theater. Both represent a temporary distraction: the Easleys' from the fictional black rebellion, and the audience's from the real racial struggle.[20]

Baraka's impending conversion to racial essentialism, not to mention his misogyny, is tangible in these two plays. His strident nationalism could not be reconciled with his marriage to a white Jewish woman, Hettie Cohen. Both plays, particularly *The Slave*, can be interpreted as a reflection of his

frustration at his domestic situation and as a foreshadowing of his separation from Cohen, which occurred in 1965. Although Vessels confesses that
he loves Grace, his duty to his race impels him to reject her and to reclaim
his daughters, but it is significant that he does not kill her. Yet his final act
of violence is to leave her thinking that he has killed their children. This
interracial relationship has corrupted Vessels almost completely. Part of his
disgust with Grace is that she can never understand his relationship with his
race, that during their relationship she believed that he could be hers alone
and not also married to his blackness. Baraka suggests that no such choice
existed; Vessels's entire identity is constructed by his race.

Baraka's image of masculinity grows more rigid and strident in the plays.
In June 1964, Baraka declared that the rise of the boxer Muhammad Ali represented the emergence of a new generation of black men. His dramatic productions further helped to define this new generation of overtly masculine
black males. While there is no indication that the name of the *Dutchman's*
protagonist was inspired by the boxer, Clay's downfall echoes Ali's rejection of his slave name (a symbolic murder of his former identity), perhaps
acting as a warning to those African Americans who remained wedded to
a hybrid identity. More important, arguably the greatest failure of Baraka's
Clay and Vessels is their refusal to kill the women at the center of their lives.
Their spite toward these women does not receive physical expression and
possibly contributes to their downfall. This misogynist understanding of
the male psyche, which received further clarification in the plays that followed *Dutchman* and *The Slave*, proved extremely influential upon the new
generation of black militants. The macho posturing of men such as Huey P.
Newton and Eldridge Cleaver is not distant from Baraka's suggestion that
the black male had to reject white *and* female dominance.[21]

The white educational structure is also fully implicated in Baraka's damning critique of race relations. In *Dutchman*, Clay's emasculation is a direct
result of his being educated in white establishments and his consequent
desire to abandon his racial identity. In *The Slave*, Walker Vessels returns
to slay his white teacher both physically and metaphorically. The veneer of
civilized values provided by an education at white establishments—his version of Clay's suit—has elevated him from the black masses but ultimately
cannot prevent his descent into violence. Baraka suggests that violence in
the United States is inevitable: if African Americans maintain civility, whites
will kill them. The question, therefore, is when the facade will crumble. The
plays conclude that the future of the races lies with separation: the funda-

mental distance between black and white individuals or the demands of the black race at large result in integration being an elusive and pointless goal.

The plays are also a useful barometer of Baraka's escalating interest in black nationalism. In contrast to his later plays, white characters are in the majority; Clay and Vessels are forced to interact with them. Clay's double consciousness leads to his death, but his failure to identify with his race (rather than his individuality) is his Achilles heel. In standing by his liberal principles in refusing to kill Lula, he allows the mendacious whites literally to get away with murder. Despite his apparent freedom, Vessels is still enslaved: as Baraka has pointed out, had he really been free, he would not have felt the need to return to Grace's house and would not have suffered Easley's cant. *The Slave* suggests that essentialism is the route to black freedom, that Vessels should not have entered the white house but instead let the cannons do their work. Vessels realizes the threats of Clay's final speech. Ultimately, those who accept integration are doomed, a message that characterized all of Baraka's drama until his conversion to Marxism-Leninism in the 1970s.[22]

During 1964, Baraka also complained that African American artists "must carry the weight of white America's social and cultural stupidity, as well as the ordinary burdens of art's responsibilities." Baraka was painfully aware that white Americans would only see him as a representative of his race: "an advertisement for the NAACP," he claimed, "but very rarely as a man." He encountered this in the responses to *Dutchman*, when critics wondered what racial characteristics Lula and Clay exhibited. For Baraka, this white attitude toward black Americans resulted in black artists having to struggle with being pigeonholed as a "Negro writer" or a race writer, as well as being simply a writer. For Baraka, the appellation "Negro writer" implied a second-rate talent at the mercy of the white middle-class critical establishment. Baraka rejected such reductive terms, insisting that *Dutchman* in particular be allowed to speak for itself as art, rather than as "Negro art," as a play, and not as a "civil rights" play.[23]

Baraka's refusal to take advantage of the civil rights mood stands in sharp contrast to Baldwin's desperate attempts to publicize his contemporaneous play, *Blues for Mister Charlie*. Although Baldwin claimed that part of *Mister Charlie*'s box office failure was due to the fact that many people simply considered it a "civil rights" play, he did not shy away from explicitly appealing to consciences pricked by the civil rights movement in order to forestall the play's closure. *Mister Charlie*, which opened mere weeks after *Dutchman*, also presents characters trapped in roles determined by societal structures that are beyond their control. Inspired in part by Baldwin's fury at the murder of Medgar Evers and loosely based on the murder of Emmett Till, *Mister Charlie* tells the story of a black activist, Richard Henry, who returns south to his segregated hometown, Plaguetown, after failing to become a successful actor and subsequently becoming a drug addict in New York City. Henry is a deliberately belligerent character, whose continued agitation for black civil rights and refusal to observe the race/caste system in Plaguetown, as embodied in his flirtation with a married white woman, provokes a member of the white community to murder him. Fidelity to the southern code of honor prevents a witness (who considers himself sympathetic to local blacks) contradicting the false evidence given by the murderer's wife. Inevitably, the murderer is acquitted by an all-white jury.[24]

The predictable nature of the play is signaled in the reference to Camus in the name of Henry's hometown. The basic question that Baldwin poses involves not Henry's attack on segregation and his provocation of the local community, but whether anybody has the right to kill him for his militancy. As if to compensate for the simplistic plot, setting, and premise, the play is extremely long and has a deliberately confusing structure. It contains similar shifts in time as Baldwin's *Go Tell It on the Mountain*, offering the denouement at the outset followed by a series of flashbacks, a structure that makes considerable demands of the audience. Apparently, the length was a deliberate ploy to remind Baldwin's white audience of the time it took white Americans to recognize that a racial problem existed. A few hours in the theater did not bear comparison with the centuries that African Americans had spent waiting for Mister Charlie. Both felt like purgatory.[25]

Politics was never far from Baldwin's thoughts during the play's gestation. Elia Kazan and the white-run Lincoln Center were slated to produce the play's opening run. Baldwin, concerned at the play's relation to the civil rights movement and the troubling racial connotations of it being produced by whites, transferred production to the more visibly integrated Actors' Studio theater group and the more sympathetic direction of Burgess Meredith. So, although Baldwin complained that *Mister Charlie* was not a "civil rights" play, he decided to move the production to a company whose staff more closely reflected the racial identity of the movement, suggesting that civil rights issues were central to the play's production. Beyond this, Baldwin wanted his close friend, the Congress of Racial Equality (CORE) activist Jerome Smith, to be kept on the payroll as a consultant, and it is clear that Kazan was less keen on Smith's role. More troubling was Baldwin's refusal to relinquish control of the direction. The success of his early novels had given him a certain freedom from editorial interference, a level of control that he hoped to exert over the play and that could not be possible in theater. The racial implications of Baldwin's interpretation of the power imbalance between author and studio are clear. A white-run studio was preparing to exploit black art to promote its own liberal credentials, a state of affairs that Baldwin abhorred. In removing his play from white hands, he was not only reasserting his control over the play but also reaffirming black American's right to their own culture. That the Actors' Studio was less wealthy than the Lincoln Center and would therefore be more keen to produce the play according to the author's whims was mere detail to Baldwin, as were the facts that Burgess Meredith was more accommodating to the author's directions and that Smith remained on the payroll. Baldwin also insisted that ticket prices be as low as possible in order to attract New York's black community. In conducting such an operation, Baldwin firmly positioned the play within the racial politics of 1964.[26]

Initial reports in the black press were kind. *Ebony* hailed the play, explicitly linking it with the civil rights movement. *Jet* agreed, feeling that Baldwin's zeal for the civil rights struggle transcended the play's limitations and its didacticism. Less kind reviews in the white press hindered the play's appeal to white theatergoers. Almost inevitably, *Mister Charlie* did not generate the revenues needed to prolong its run. Even Baldwin noticed that the low prices were not attracting enough paying customers to cover the production costs. He failed to discern that the reticence of black New Yorkers to attend Broadway shows was not wholly a financial issue but one related to the racial politics of the overwhelmingly white Broadway and to local geography. The thought of traveling through the white areas of Manhattan was not attractive to many African Americans. Although few black subway riders would have been forced to relive Clay's encounter, some would have been subjected to a muted form of Lula's abuse through accusatory glances and general white discomfort with their presence. Baldwin instead reasoned that ordinary people, much like the reviewers, erroneously considered *Mister Charlie* to be a play about civil rights, failing to comprehend that it was rather about how race corrupts personal relationships and the American mind. For him, the lack of box office was less the fault of the play than the demands of Broadway.[27] Baldwin reacted by enlisting a group of friends—including Harry Belafonte, Sidney Poitier, Lorraine Hansberry, Marlon Brando, and Roy Wilkins—to harangue Broadway and the black community. Baldwin couched his protest at the play's failure in political terms, which suggests that he had conceded that it was now a "civil rights" play. In the event, even the liberal appeal failed. A large donation from the Rockefeller family ensured that the play limped on until August.[28]

Baldwin implicitly accepted that racial identities were crucial to the success of his art. He could not resist using his own fame to interfere in the play, and his constant presence on set reflected his belief that *Mister Charlie* was such an important statement about race in America that it could not be left alone to find an audience or to stand apart from its author's fame (or indeed his race). It is only fitting that a play so dependent on politics for its creation and production was also dependent on politics for its performance.

The comparison between *Dutchman* and *Mister Charlie* reveals the struggle between separatism and integrationism within the movement during this period. Baraka cared not for acceptance in high art circles; Baldwin's play was an almost self-conscious attempt to create high art and great theater. *Mister Charlie* was consumed by Baldwin's insistence that he could speak to both blacks and whites; Baraka gave no hint that he was concerned about the white response to his work. As a less public figure, Baraka could allow *Dutchman* to speak for itself. *Dutchman* also succeeded outside the spotlight of Broadway, where costs and ticket prices were lower. Its distance from the Broadway establishment gave *Dutchman* an appeal beyond the patrons of most Broadway shows. Moreover, its off-Broadway status reinforced the play's antiestablishment aura. Baldwin wanted *Mister Charlie* to move beyond a middle-class constituency, as demonstrated by his principled stand on the price of tickets for the play. Yet *Mister Charlie* needed white patrons. Its inability to attract such an audience was in part a reflection of the attitude toward black art, and therefore black people, in the white community. Whites had no interest in being hectored by another angry young black writer. The white rejection of *Mister Charlie* echoed the white rejection of black militancy. Just as black civil rights organizations lost white support as their attacks on the Democratic Party and white liberals in general increased, Baldwin's play, which suggested that white liberals were prepared to betray blacks if the demands of the white race at large required it, touched raw liberal nerves and found itself shorn of a natural support base. In this sense, the rejection of *Mister Charlie* by a white audience reflects white indifference toward integration. Baldwin also found himself trapped by the politics of the civil rights movement: in publicizing his play and using the support of liberal icons, he could not move beyond liberal entreaties, whereas Baraka was simply unconcerned with integration and its implications. Baraka's art stood alone; Baldwin's relied on a crutch formed by the liberal conscience and black politics. That *Dutchman* was far more compact in setting, plot, and execution than the sprawling and fractured narrative of *Mister Charlie* also suggests much about the appeal of Baraka's work: it was more comprehensible, even though its meaning remained ambiguous, whereas Baldwin's negotiation between the worlds of black and white America served only to confuse. Thus the political, economic, and cultural milieu in which *Mister Charlie* operated contributed in many ways to the play's failure, as did class politics. Its failure was compounded by the fact that it was not good art.

Through his art, Baraka claimed that American society was corrupt, oppressive, and doomed to failure. He suggested that the only viable alternative was black nationalism, and that within black nationalism, blacks should focus on the unity that their culture could produce. He thus rejected the implicit message of Baldwin's art: that black and white Americans were locked in a mutually degrading embrace that could only be transformed through open and honest communication. Baraka also maintained that art and the artist had a central role in the African American liberation struggle. Despite being painfully aware that whites would not walk down the street and differentiate between a "cultured nigger" and a "plain nigger," he urged blacks to affirm and organize around their separate culture.[29] Baraka maintained that the culture of the rice plantations and the cotton fields was central to the African American experience. Statements such as this, though, highlight the inherent contradictions within Baraka's thought. While he maintained that there were various strata within black culture—"cultured" and presumably "uncultured" African Americans—he was also insisting that there was one unified black culture around which all African Americans could unite. Unlike Clay, rather than shying away from his identification with his racial identity, Baraka, like Vessels, fully embraced the notion that color and culture were one and the same.

Robert F. Williams and Radio Propaganda

Like Baraka, Robert F. Williams was galvanized by his experience in Cuba and returned to the island upon his exile from the United States, using it the base for an assault on America's ears during the early 1960s. Williams first attracted national attention to Monroe, North Carolina, through the sensational Kissing Case in 1958. Two African American boys, "Fuzzy" Simpson and Hanover Thompson, aged eight and ten, had been arrested and sentenced to a decade or more in reform school after playing a game in which

Thompson and an eight year old girl kissed each other. Linking the case to the fight for African American freedom, Williams coordinated a massive publicity campaign, placing enormous pressure on Governor Luther H. Hodges to overturn the conviction. The boys were released after only three months. Williams, however, soon found himself isolated within the NAACP as a result of his frank espousal of the right to bear arms in support of the freedom struggle.[30] He became acutely aware of the effects of propaganda through his clashes with the NAACP hierarchy in the late 1950s. In July 1959, he initiated the publication of the *Crusader*, a weekly pamphlet that was designed to counteract the distortions of the NAACP and the white power structure. The pamphlet often featured articles and columns on black history, confirming Williams's awareness of the Orwellian notion that those who control the past control the present, and of the value of African American heritage and culture to the present struggle. Further isolated by his support for the Cuban Revolution, Williams developed an aura of a maverick "crazy nigger" who behaved as though he had nothing to lose, which was cemented when he was forced into exile in order to save his own life.[31]

Since childhood, Williams had been aware of how history could be used to inspire and motivate people. He held particularly fond memories of history lessons at school; his favorite stories were those of black men deciding to fight in no-win situations rather than meekly accepting their fate. These lessons taught Williams that the only honorable response to desperate situations was defiance. In the *Crusader*, Williams was not averse to comparing himself with other historical figures who advocated violence in order to redress injustice, such as George Washington and Thomas Jefferson. Overlooking their complicity in slavery, Williams took inspiration from their refusal to accept British tyranny meekly. While praising the American Revolution, Williams raged against the Civil War centennial, denouncing it as a "[c]entennial of shame."[32]

As a child, Williams had heard Cuban radio broadcasts and knew that people would be listening if programs were broadcast in English. In July 1962, he cheerfully announced that he would soon be doing so. *Radio Free Dixie* would offer regular reports on the civil rights struggle. Williams wanted to position the most progressive jazz and soul, which mainstream radio ignored, at specific points in the broadcast in order to complement the subject matter of the spoken element of the show. Williams sought to manipulate his listeners' emotions through music, using it to accentuate the feelings that his commentary generated. This provocative music would demand the listeners' attention, deliberately anger people, and provoke them to action.[33]

Aside from explicitly political music, Williams also wanted to experiment with the power of African-influenced polyrhythmic drumming that added urgency and complexity to the work of drummers such as Max Roach and Art Blakey. This music would be ideal for grabbing the listeners' attention. For Williams, music also produced an emotional reaction, one that he hoped to exploit, "in the same vein as the preacher but it would have more of a political theme than religious—in other words, it was to adapt this religious concept to propaganda." While he thought that the black church was often too conservative and gradualist, Williams was aware of the massive cultural role that it played and consciously structured his broadcasts like church services. Preacher Williams was able to benefit from a reciprocal relationship with his listeners, notably Amiri Baraka, relying on them to donate new records. Williams, then, developed a variation on the call-and-response method of black sermons, both in the relationship between his oratory and the music and in the interplay between his listeners and himself.[34]

The broadcast signal of *Radio Free Dixie* was so powerful that the program could be heard throughout the South. Thanks to an underground railroad of private individuals and broadcasters, recordings of the program spread through many areas of the North. By March 1963, the program was being aired three times per week, allowing for even more recording and dissemination.[35] Over the stentorian drumming of *Radio Free Dixie*'s introduction track, Mabel Williams would announce, "From Havana, Cuba, free territory of the Americas, *Radio Free Dixie* invites you to listen to the free voice of the South."[36] The link between African American music and the freedom movement was made clear from the very beginning of each broadcast. Musical hostess Jo Salas introduced modern songs before moving to Mabel Williams's folklore section. Mabel Williams often read from Langston Hughes's prose and poetry; "When a Man Sees Red" was suggestively selected for one show: the double meaning of red was an indication both of the show's mood and its politics.[37] Robert Williams's commentary on the freedom struggle would be introduced by "John Brown's Body," linking Williams with the interracial abolitionist crusade and, more pointedly, with one of the few whites whom he admired. Occasionally, Robert Williams was introduced by a rendition of "Dixie," intended as a sarcastic swipe at the South. Williams's apocalyptic commentary typically castigated the hypocrisy and self-righteousness of the U.S. government, hammering home the gulf between American ideals and American reality. Occasionally, Williams would offer a critique of nonviolence, pointing out that it often offered only "empty promises instead of positive results [for] the impoverished black ghettos." Nevertheless, Williams was consistent in declaring that white supremacy was doomed: either "King's love and understanding" would overthrow it or it would be destroyed by "the enraged masses' force and violence." After a reading of the week's news by Carlos Moore, the program drew to a close.[38] Williams rarely failed to invoke the ramifications of the Cold War in his monologues, frequently suggesting that U.S. activities in Central America could lead to a third world war.[39] Even the title of the show was intended to call to mind Cold War cultural politics. Broadcasting in sixteen languages to a huge European audience, Radio Free Europe included jazz music in its programming in order to demonstrate the vibrancy of American culture and to open European Communist minds to the political propaganda in the broadcasts. Similarly, *Radio Free Dixie* broadcast underground jazz, opening listeners' minds to the vibrant culture of black Americans and to Williams's uncompromising spoken editorials.

While Williams held an internationalist perspective on the worldwide struggle against oppression, he understood that this was a racially polarized struggle. Even though he publicly rejected black nationalism in the early 1960s, in practice he tended toward sympathy with certain black nationalist precepts. Williams's editorials emphasized the need for black unity in the face of white supremacy and were particularly scathing of white liberals who urged African American patience. There were very few calls for class unity in *Radio Free Dixie*, an omission that troubled a number of high-ranking Cuban Communists.[40]

Throughout this time, Williams retained his tendency to sneer at official organizations, notably the Cuban government. He became frustrated with the Cuban attitude to propaganda, possibly as a result of criticism from the party hierarchy that he was peddling imperialist nonsense in the form of jazz music. Williams was a passionate believer in the African roots of jazz, and wrote as such in response to this criticism, arguing that music that originated from slaves, and which was being exploited by whites, could never be described as imperialist. Williams considered himself to be returning the music to its original intention as music of the oppressed. Thus he acknowledged that art could be subverted, yet also have its message reconfirmed, by the changing context in which it was heard, a situation that he took full advantage of through his program. He opened minds to the African American freedom struggle and also to new forms of music, uniting the two to create a hugely powerful and relevant piece of propaganda that emphasized blackness and the powerful role of cultural forms in the political struggle.[41]

In 1965, following the demise of *Radio Free Dixie* amid increasing pressure from the Cuban Communist Party, Williams left for China, taking the *Crusader* with him. Although named president-in-exile of two militant groups, the Revolutionary Action Movement (RAM) and the Republic of New Africa (RNA), Williams had no direct involvement with the struggle. Much as he supported the concept of Black Power, he was reluctant to become involved in internecine warfare and rejected the Black Panther Party's call to denounce cultural nationalism. His return to the United States in 1969, courtesy of a private flight from Trans World Airlines, confirmed his incorrigible contrariness: soon after, he chose to resign from both RAM and the RNA and from front-line involvement in the national struggle.[42]

Baraka's and Williams's cultural productions help to broaden our conception of the resurgence of black nationalism in the mid-1960s. They also enrich our understanding of the militant mood among some blacks, notably the relationship between this militancy and black identity and culture. Williams concluded that African American cultural expressions should become weapons in the struggle. He found the support in Cuba through which he could realize his ideas. He had been aware of the power of music and history since a young age, and the civil rights movement presented him with a means through which he could test out his theories. As the civil rights war raged in the South, Williams used jazz and the songs of the movement to reinforce his conviction that black and white Americans were in a struggle to the death, adding nuance to Malcolm X's allegation that revolutionaries did not do any singing because they were too busy swinging.[43] For Williams, revolutionaries could also swing—to jazz. Baraka was similarly convinced of the efficacy of art as a medium for spreading a political message. His writing expands on Williams's broadcasts by explicitly linking jazz with the freedom movement while castigating the civil rights movement's lack of radicalism.

Baraka's theatrical work is similarly unconvinced of the progress that the civil rights movement had made for African Americans. Clay's sartorial conservatism reflects that of the major movement organizations (excepting SNCC) when *Dutchman* was written; contemporary audiences would have recognized him, or at least figures like him, from television broadcasts of civil rights marches. His acknowledgment that his suit effectively protected both him and his fellow white passengers from his violent side reflects the duality that many white contemporaries saw between King's dream and Malcolm X's nightmare: beneath these marches lay the threat of black violence. Clay's adherence to nonviolence, however, is his major weakness and leads to his death. Walker Vessels represents a further step in Baraka's move toward black nationalism. Having rejected his civilized background, Vessels suggests to his wife that he is reclaiming his daughters for their race. The race war means that they are no longer living as blacks in a white world but are at the dawning of a new era of black dominance. The question of whether Vessels has killed them (presumably since they demonstrate his profound links with integration) is left deliberately unanswered, although Vessels's final transformation suggests that his double consciousness has not yet been resolved.

While not as apocalyptic, *Blues for Mister Charlie* is similarly circumspect about the relationships between whites and blacks. Like Baraka, Baldwin believed that fidelity to racial identity was at the core of the problem of the color line, although he was more concerned with the nature of white identity than with black, and with pushing his sincere belief that a color-blind civic code was the only positive solution available. *Mister Charlie* demonstrates the shortcomings of developing a close relationship between the arts and the movement. The author attempted to cover up the failure of his play as art by pointing to its relevance to the prevailing political mood and its reimagining of recent events in the civil rights movement. Yet alongside the murders of Emmett Till and Medgar Evers, the bombing of Birmingham's Sixteenth Street Baptist Church, and the horrifying violence in St. Augustine, Florida, that occurred during the play's initial run, *Mister Charlie* seemed dull and unmoving.[44] Where audiences flocked to *Dutchman* to find themselves challenged as well as shocked, those who attended *Mister Charlie* were simply baffled by its structure or bored by its length. The contrasting box office returns for *Dutchman* and *Mister Charlie* also suggests that urban audiences were moving away from what might be termed a traditional view of the civil rights struggle, one that concentrated on the actions of whites. *Dutchman* might have revolved around the control exerted by its white protagonist over its black character, but it certainly had more to say about the nature of black identity in modern American society and about the tense relations between blacks and whites. Similarly, *The Slave* was less concerned with the liberalism of Easley and Grace than with Vessels's increasing militancy and his internal battle over his own identity.

As suggested by Clay's demise at the hands of a woman and Easley's abuse of his ex-wife, Baraka's work included a troubling misogynist streak. His was a largely macho world, where women were supposed to defer to men. While Williams's gender politics were less distasteful, he was of the opinion that the man's role was to defend "himself, his family, his home and his dignity," and this dignity was in part achievable through the protection of his wife and children. Admittedly, Williams was at pains to involve his wife fully in their struggle, to the extent that he trained her to shoot a pistol, but his ideas regarding gender equality were always filtered through his firm adherence to a form of masculine physical superiority. Malcolm X's masculine view of the world was more discernible in his speeches, not least through his frequent references to the damage that the white man has caused the black man and how the black man was to attain his manhood. Baraka took this masculine view of the world to an extreme, adopting a hypermasculine pose that largely denied women agency in the black struggle. While his divorce might be interpreted more as a black nationalist than a misogynist action, his treatment of his female characters in his plays confirms his male chauvinism, a position that became ever more extreme as the decade wore on.[45]

Williams developed his conception of the use of cultural expressions through his critique of the civil rights movement. Baraka's interpretation, on the other hand, also developed out of the broad leftist movement in the postwar years. His first encounter with political activism came through the sponsorship of the FPCC, which had links with both the Old and the New Left. Baraka remained aloof from the mainstream civil rights movement, choosing to ally himself with Williams's struggle in Monroe and the worldwide struggle against racial oppression largely because of his experience of the Cuban Revolution. Yet as his racial identity—and his own sensitivity toward it—asserted itself, Baraka believed that he had to separate himself from these links in order to maintain his image as a black militant.[46] Although neither he nor Williams became involved to a significant extent with the major civil rights organizations, both concluded that a movement based on racial unity should acknowledge the value of black art as an organizing tool and understand the relationship between color and culture. Baraka emerged from a northern middle-class background and Williams from a southern working-class background. Both learned at an early age that the white power structure was no friend of blacks. Independently, they concluded that culture could be a political weapon and an organizing tool in the freedom struggle.

They were not alone. In 1964, Malcolm X told his friends, "We must launch a cultural revolution to unbrainwash an entire people. . . . This cul-

tural revolution will be the journey to our rediscovery of ourselves." To this
end, the OAAU proposed to establish a cultural center in Harlem to conduct
workshops in history, writing, theater, art, and music. A liberation school
was established in summer 1964 to offer Harlemites education in politics,
consumer skills, and African and African American history. Although it did
not become a reality—the OAAU's organizational instability and Malcolm
X's assassination saw to that—the cultural center was clearly part of Malcolm X's plan to ensure the complete freedom of African Americans, beginning with the liberation of the African American psyche. He placed black
history and culture at the center of a human rights struggle and was well
aware of how an individual's worldview, and that of the African American
population in general, was shaped not merely by politics but also by cultural
influences. The black struggle, then, was not to be fought only on the political battlefield but was an all-encompassing fight for psychological, spiritual,
cultural, and political freedom.[47]

4

The 1964 Mississippi Summer Project

The Student Nonviolent Coordinating Committee's (SNCC) Mississippi Summer Project was the central event of the civil rights movement in 1964, perhaps of the entire movement.[1] Inspired in part by Highlander's concept of education, the Summer Project engaged in cultural organizing to broaden the political message of the freedom movement and to include heretofore alienated members of the black community in the movement. Indeed, the Summer Project was SNCC's most effective and ambitious attempt to unite culture and politics. It crystallized the value of a cultural approach to movement work, integrating music, theater, art, poetry, and history into the development of political awareness among the black Mississippian population. Children and adults were encouraged to explore their own culture and heritage and, through this engagement, were given the opportunity to develop the psychological armor that was necessary to sustain their long-term political struggle. SNCC's experience of organizing prior to 1964 led the group to conclude that one of its failures was its inability to get deep into the community. Simply stimulating local people to action was not deemed enough to justify SNCC's existence. Many in SNCC concluded that education and culture were crucial to the establishment of deeper links between the organization and local people. The Summer Project was the apotheosis of this impulse and of Highlander's influence on the organization. Following Freedom Summer, SNCC became ever more radical and grew ever more aware of the value of black culture to the emerging Black Power generation. Thus the Summer Project represents the great turning point in SNCC's history and arguably of the entire civil rights movement.

While SNCC was immersing itself in the wider ramifications of the freedom struggle, the Congress of Racial Equality (CORE) undertook similar organizing efforts with a more ambivalent approach to cultural organizing.

Although CORE's point man in Mississippi, Dave Dennis, adopted SNCC's approach to freedom schools in Mississippi's Fifth Congressional District, the organization as a whole preferred to focus on the political effects of freedom education and attempted to use the freedom schools as a recruitment device. Early in 1964, Dennis told CORE's National Action Council that the primary purpose of CORE-run freedom schools was to train "action orientated Mississippi high school students . . . *on political issues.*" In contrast to SNCC's view, education might produce a free thinker, but might not produce a CORE activist or member. For CORE as an organization, educational programs were in essence propaganda vehicles designed to boost membership rolls and lead people straight toward voter registration. CORE's lack of central control, however, allowed activists to develop projects that did not necessarily reflect the attitude of the central office toward cultural protest or cultural development. During 1964, Dennis was assistant program director of the Council of Federated Organizations (COFO), the umbrella organization established to coordinate civil rights activism in Mississippi, a position that entailed working closely with SNCC and influenced him to move beyond CORE's ideas for the Mississippi project. Dennis's reasoning is anomalous within CORE. Of all the proposals for community action in the South put before CORE committees between 1960 and 1964, only his emphasized the benefits of a cultural focus to political organizing. It is no coincidence that he worked so closely with SNCC during this period.[2] Meanwhile, the Citizenship Education Program (CEP) continued to educate and register adults using the Highlander technique. It made small inroads into Mississippi during 1964, although the organization made a negligible contribution to COFO.[3]

SNCC and the Summer Project

On 30 December 1963, SNCC's executive committee approved Bob Moses's proposal for a summer voter registration project involving hundreds of white volunteers. Initially intended to highlight the brutality inherent in Mississippi's culture and to register large numbers of disfranchised black voters, the plans expanded to include more long-term and holistic methods of addressing civil rights, including educational and social programs. As SNCC's freedom school coordinator Liz Fusco asserted, this represented an acceptance that what could be done in Mississippi "could be deeper, more fundamental, more far-reaching, more revolutionary than voter registration alone. . . . [It was] a decision to enter into every phase of the lives of the people of Mississippi . . . a decision to set the people free for politics in the only way that people really can become free, and that is totally."[4]

The early planning stages of the 1964 Mississippi Summer Project confirm that SNCC was expanding its focus beyond political action. The Tougaloo Literacy Project, a pilot project to develop literacy materials related to the cultural environment, was central to the Mississippi plans. Church- or school-based community centers were to be a focal point and safe haven for the community and SNCC. When pressure from local whites became dangerous, SNCC prepared to use local houses and, in some cases, build new centers. The community centers were also a place for training, where local people could learn new skills, and a cultural space where films were shown, drama and reading groups met, and a library was available. These facilities were expressly designed to meet community needs that were not being served by state and local authorities. The few cinemas that existed in black neighborhoods were fleapits that presented poor quality Hollywood films. Libraries were either woefully underfunded or nonexistent, and there were no child-care centers, health clinics, or employment and training centers. The SNCC community centers would address these shortcomings and try to introduce a deeper conception of how to tackle the problems that faced black southerners.[5]

Community centers and freedom schools were central to SNCC's program. Both institutions emphasized the worth of culture to the individual's political and intellectual growth. In the freedom schools, students would be encouraged to think freely and develop their own ideas about a free society. They were to be places where students could feel free to question and debate any issues that concerned them. Movement historiography has generally been reluctant to examine the schools in depth.[6] The roots of this historiographical oversight derive in part from the attitude of movement participants themselves. The prestige assignment for volunteers and staff was voter registration, whereas teaching was accorded relatively little respect and was often delegated to female volunteers. Teachers were also expected to drop their commitments if the voter registration campaign needed extra bodies. This might suggest that the freedom schools were something of an afterthought, but there is little doubt that they were central to the operation of the Summer Project and were one of the summer's major achievements. Furthermore, the identity of many of the teachers confirms that the role of the teacher was not only racialized but gendered, and that the civil rights movement was an important crucible in the development of the women's movement.

The schools were an integral part of COFO's 1964 activities, providing new leadership and attacking what SNCC considered to be the stifling and repressive Mississippi educational system. This system was designed to ensure that Mississippi's African American population remained largely uneducated. The 1954 *Brown v. Board of Education* decision had little impact in Mississippi where, at the state level, four times as much money was spent on white as on black schools. By the 1960s, the average white Mississippian received eleven years of education, but black Mississippians averaged a paltry six years. To SNCC, it was clear that education was a central pillar of the Mississippian caste system, one that had to be reconstructed. SNCC had always envisaged itself as an interim organization. Its modus operandi was to develop independent local structures and leaders to such an extent that SNCC was no longer needed in the community: SNCC effectively hoped to organize itself out of existence. This was certainly the goal of the 1964 Summer Project. It hoped that the schools would become the foundation for a statewide youth movement that would produce a new generation of community leaders and for the Mississippi Freedom Democratic Party (MFDP), a parallel structure to the regular white-only state Democratic Party, to become the primary political vehicle for black and poor Mississippians.[7]

SNCC defined the numeracy and literacy skills of adults and children and the lack of cultural knowledge among the black population as the problem areas that needed addressing. Freedom schools were designed to offer remedial instruction in basic educational skills and to expose the students to cultural influences not normally available in the Mississippi education system. The core curriculum consisted of supplementary education in English language, mathematics, history, political and social studies, literature and film studies, and other basic educational subjects, plus cultural programs such as art, music, dance, drama, creative writing, and the appreciation of these cultural forms. Reflecting the theory behind Highlander's citizenship schools, SNCC intended the curriculum to derive from the students' background and planned to base classroom activities around the students' experiences, thus ensuring that school activities remained fully grounded in Mississippian culture. As SNCC's Jane Stembridge, a white southerner who was involved in setting out the freedom school curriculum, suggested to new freedom school teachers, classes should discuss concepts in applied terms: instead of launching into a discussion of the concept of economic pressure, the students should discuss the closure of black stores in Jackson. Stembridge argued that the students would relate to these concepts as realities, thus helping them understand the conceptual framework behind the discussion. The aim of the curriculum, in traditional educational (and gender) terms, was "to challenge the student's curiosity about the world, [and] introduce him to his particularly 'Negro' cultural background." Cultural activities were central to the curriculum: black history was taught in the morning, and less formal subjects such as art and music were generally studied in the afternoon. The latter aspect of the curriculum was designed both to provide for relaxation from the students' more intense studies and to give them the opportunity to express themselves more freely and in new ways. The timetable was also dictated by the weather: more relaxed work was better suited to the demands of working in the blazing afternoon sun.[8]

SNCC's community centers provided a similar function to the schools, offering educational and recreational structures for local communities, although only thirteen were established during the summer. Again, educational programs were central to their operation. Instruction in job training, literacy, pre- and postnatal care, nutritional advice, and home improvement was available, as were various extracurricular programs for grade school and high school children. Similarly, the community centers provided a space for cultural activities in order to broaden the cultural horizons of local people. SNCC intended to show films that the black community would not have seen and to provide music appreciation classes and workshops alongside arts and crafts workshops and literature, drama, and current affairs discussions, as well as performances from outside entertainers. Naturally, visitors would be able to take advantage of the citizenship education that was available at the centers, which would include instruction in African American and American history and assistance in using federal antipoverty programs. Conceived as a permanent institution and as a focal point for the entire community, the community centers developed out of SNCC's concept of parallel structures: institutions that challenged the state's failure to provide for the basic needs of its black citizenry. As the freedom school prospectus established, "If we are concerned with breaking the power structure, then we have to be concerned with building up our own institutions to replace the old, unjust, decadent ones which make up the existing power structure. Education in Mississippi is an institution which can be validly replaced."[9]

At the beginning of the Summer Project, there were forty-one functioning freedom schools in twenty communities spread throughout Mississippi. By 26 July, 2,135 students had enrolled, double the expected number.[10] The freedom school curriculum centered on the courses on citizenship and American government, with New Left historian-activists Howard Zinn and Staughton Lynd insisting that black history and literature be accorded equal prominence. One SNCC document called black history white America's blind spot and claimed that in most American public schools, history was a "bleached product." It was sterile in its failure to engage students and colorless in its refusal to acknowledge the contribution of blacks to world civilization. Significantly, of African American historical figures, only Booker T. Washington was well known to the Mississippi students. The state education structure clearly approved of his acceptance of segregation and his emphasis on vocational education. For SNCC, the absence of other African American historical figures was not only a disservice to the state's black students, but it was also shaping their entire lives. Lynd and Zinn, like many New Left historians, advocated the concept of a usable past and encouraged SNCC to stress the continued relevance of African American history to the black Mississippian population. Even at the preliminary stage, the curriculum was designed to link the 1960s movement with the African American oppositional tradition, emphasizing a multigenerational history of struggle. Through an awareness of these movements, SNCC hoped that a new generation of leadership would emerge. Just as historians like Zinn—who was then working on a history of SNCC, suggestively subtitled *The New Abolitionists*—strove through their writing to establish that the protest tradition was inherently American, SNCC intended to demonstrate the importance of the African American contribution to the United States. History would justify and elaborate on SNCC's insistence that black Mississippians agitate to play a full role in state politics.[11]

A special concern was to explore African American contributions to American culture, again underlining SNCC's insistence that culture was one of the keys to liberation. SNCC's curriculum used the work of Baldwin, Ellison, and Wright to establish the genius of African American letters and provide an African American canonical literature. It solicited charities, organizations, and individuals to provide books that emphasized the black contribution to American life. W. E. B. DuBois's *The Souls of Black Folk*, John Hope Franklin's *From Slavery to Freedom*, Carter G. Woodson's *Negro Makers of History*, and Langston Hughes's *A Pictorial History of the Negro People in the United States* formed the core of the history curriculum, with *Ebony*'s September 1963 issue, a commemoration of the Emancipation Proclamation, a supplementary text. These readings both affirmed the durability of the African American oppositional tradition and insisted that African Americans should define their own history. While the books were not intended to present a black nationalist interpretation of history, that the authors were African American is a subtle indication that SNCC was aware of the psychological value of self-definition and that African American history need not be written by whites. Elsewhere in the curriculum, biographies of Harry Belafonte and Frederick Douglass examined notable black figures. Pen portraits of figures such as Gwendolyn Brooks, Douglass, and Crispus Attucks stressed the multifaceted contributions of African Americans to American life. These profiles again emphasized the oppositional tendencies of the African American people. SNCC highlighted not only how these African Americans contributed to American life but also how they challenged discrimination. The portraits helped to establish a centuries-long tradition of opposition within the African American community, one that SNCC intended to reenergize. Through learning about African American history, the matrix of African American protest became clear to the students. The links between Harriet Tubman and Fannie Lou Hamer, Frederick Douglass and James Forman, and gospel music and the freedom songs started to take shape in the students' minds. This was, however, no segregated program. Works by white writers such as Guy Carawan's collection of freedom songs and W. J. Cash's *The Mind of the South* were studied along with Martin Luther King Jr.'s books to emphasize the importance of biracial understanding to the modern South.[12]

Despite his exile in Cuba, Robert F. Williams's ideas were also spreading though SNCC. Williams's *Negroes with Guns* featured in the freedom school curriculum, offering a pugnacious counterpoint to King's texts. In June, when SNCC activists Sam Block and Willie Peacock were arrested in Columbus, Mississippi, on a traffic charge, they were in possession of thousands of copies of the *Crusader*. Their cargo, and the existence of *Negroes with Guns* in the curriculum, suggests that the Summer Project was exposing Mississippi's blacks to a militant African American politics that acknowledged the practical necessity for armed self-defense. Williams's rugged politics provided a useful contrast to King's faith in nonviolent direct action and suggested that self-defense was a political act. His account of black resistance in Monroe, North Carolina, related more directly to the experience of many blacks in Mississippi who carried guns for their own protection than to King's appeals to their Gandhian and Christian faiths. It was also interesting reading for the SNCC devotees of nonviolence who might not have experienced the brutality of small town or rural life in the South and the necessary adjustments that black Mississippians made to nonviolence. As such, Williams's work provided a political framework around which activists could incorporate ideas about self-defense within the movement. While SNCC insisted that its activists practiced nonviolence, the organization's sensitivity toward the decisions made at a local level resulted in a tacit acceptance of many Mississippians' decision to carry weapons. The distribution of Williams's work corresponds with the Summer Project's goals of opening the political and cultural consciousness of black Mississippians to many tributaries of African American thought.[13] Williams's message was being heard loud and clear in Mississippi, and not only through SNCC. His Cuban-based radio show, *Radio Free Dixie*, broadcast weekly during summer 1964 on a signal so strong that it reached much of the South, continued to mix political comment and music, including the freedom songs. Also on his playlist that summer was Nina Simone's caustic swipe at the slow response to the civil rights movement, "Mississippi Goddam," which featured within its jaunty melody the Williamsesque couplet, "This whole country is full of lies/You all gonna die and die like flies."[14]

In selecting its study material, SNCC wanted to address two issues: the lack of African American visibility in American life and the racially polarized depiction of black and American history. SNCC noted that "black" history was often isolated from American history. Thus a separate and unequal view of history was relayed to young generations. The task of the freedom schools, therefore, was not only to explore black history in itself but also to desegregate the history of nations by focusing on multiracial and international history. African history, for example, would not focus exclusively on the impact of white settlers and colonialism, but would encompass tribal society and African culture as well. The negative experience of slavery would not be separated from the concept that slavery led to the development of a unique African American culture, and the contribution of whites would not be written out of the history of the civil rights movement. COFO's Lois Chaffee solicited a number of handbooks on Africa for use in the schools to help enrich the students' discussions. At Holly Springs, a discussion of Haitian history included the involvement of France in abolishing slavery during the French Revolution and the subsequent Haitian defeat of the English, Napoleon's reinstatement of slavery, and the final creation of an independent Haiti before a comparison with the African American struggle for freedom. These discussions reveal that, while a desire to redress the historiographical balance and a hint of black nationalism led SNCC to focus on black history, its commitment to integrationism ensured that this history was not ghettoized.[15]

Significantly, in the CORE freedom schools, SNCC's curriculum was adapted to fit CORE's ideas about the project. Classes were held in social sciences, languages, and music. A course, simply titled "Freedom," was designed to help students understand what the freedom movement was and how it related to them and their community. The CORE freedom school and community center in Meridian stressed the political aspects of CORE's involvement in the community. CORE's conviction that political strength would end discrimination led to the organization considering the freedom schools and community centers as political training centers. Staff member Eric Morton suggested that the simple fact that the Summer Project involved itself in the community would give local people the incentive and courage to resist oppression. For him, this long-term involvement differentiated CORE from the other civil rights organizations. As for the community centers, CORE staff did not expect cultural activities to be popular: the Meridian project director was rather surprised to discover that the students actually enjoyed listening to the Beatles, Bach, and Berlioz.[16]

SNCC's influence on the subjects and materials was evident when CORE engaged with the wider concerns of freedom schools. Its curriculum followed the same format as the SNCC curriculum and generally used the same books. The CORE curriculum differed from SNCC's, predictably, on the historical significance of the twentieth-century freedom struggle, with CORE's involvement emphasized much above that of SNCC. Still, the knowledge and learning that came out of the history classes were corollary benefits. CORE's Western Regional Action Council asserted that the classes were to be used as a means through which the community would become involved in CORE work and, crucially, not as an end in themselves. Less concerned with the wider implications of citizenship education, CORE largely saw this educational program as an opportunity to boost its own support among blacks in Mississippi.[17]

Further demonstrating its distance from CORE's freedom school praxis, SNCC devised an arts and crafts program for freedom school students. In addition to the expected focus on the development of manual and design skills, the curriculum also explored the application of such skills to everyday life. Thus woodworking skills were directed toward the construction of household objects such as tables, benches, and bookcases, with the intention of encouraging the students to use their income more effectively by making what they would normally buy. This aspect of the curriculum hints at the lasting influence of Booker T. Washington on black activism. Few SNCC activists would have admitted the value of Washington's advocacy of agricultural and vocational training as the key to the solution of the southern race problem. Nevertheless, the focus on manual labor and the production of low-cost utilitarian objects that could be used to increase the self-sufficiency of the black working class suggests that Washington's legacy endured and that a conservative streak remained in the Summer Project ethos.[18]

Departing slightly from this Washingtonian plan, the graphics workshops of the arts and crafts program were geared toward developing awareness of "communications of community importance" alongside the intrinsic value of the printed or reproduced matter. Students were instructed in the operation of mimeograph machines in order that they could mass-produce leaflets for the community. Similarly, the visual art component focused on the social and cultural role of art. Students would discuss the role of African American art in American history and compare it with African art, providing for an implicit critique of American society and accentuating the relationship between art and the society around it. The freedom schools would also be a forum for community art, where local people could display their work and discuss how to address it to their political and social experiences. As a result of observing the students in the creative classes, Liz Fusco came to the realization that expressing oneself through cultural forms was central to the freedom movement. Thus social and cultural action could be united in striving for a common goal, in the process benefiting and strengthening each other. One of the primary concerns of the curriculum was the relation of the artist to his or her surroundings. The curriculum suggested that teachers raise questions such as whether social guilt could cripple artistic creativity, the relationship between art and propaganda, the legitimacy of art as social protest, and whether there is a connection between suffering and creativity. These questions raise the issue of the role of culture in society and make it clear that SNCC viewed African American culture, in its many forms, as a central battleground for the hearts and minds of black Americans.[19]

Influenced by the citizenship schools, and again displaying elements of Booker T. Washington's ideals, SNCC used pedagogic techniques that stressed the everyday application of academic disciplines. Thus economics could be presented as the effects on the individual of a loan and the individual's responsibilities rather than as a set of potentially intangible concepts. Staughton Lynd was keen that SNCC give its curriculum a Socratic air, to provoke and stimulate its young students, many of whom had previously been discouraged from questioning much about the world around them. Through such methods and with a more creative attitude toward teaching, SNCC hoped that black Mississippians would rediscover a thirst for learning and an appreciation of their own talents, spurring them on to further individual and group development. For SNCC, education was, or at the very least should be, a creative experience for student and teacher, where both could learn about themselves and each other. Ultimately, the goal was to develop a new way of thinking and to provoke Mississippi's black population to question everything.[20] This process developed from relatively simple questions such as "what is the freedom movement?" and "why do the freedom schools exist?" to examining issues such as the role of majoritarian culture, its relationship to minority groups, and the development of oppositional culture in response to its deficiencies. The freedom schools encouraged students to broaden their horizons and look beyond their immediate surroundings to the wider world beyond Mississippi's limiting environment. They also compelled the teaching volunteers to do the same, urging them to question what brought them to Mississippi, whether middle-class whites could truly understand what it meant to be black, and why many African Americans no longer trusted white liberals. The volunteers' commitment to nonviolence also had to be reaffirmed at regular intervals—not least when white violence reemerged—and they were encouraged to rethink their definition of freedom. These questions, according to SNCC, were at the core of American democratic society.[21]

Fundamentally, the teachers had to challenge themselves. Their biggest hurdle was to resist the temptation to talk at the students and instead learn how to teach creatively through listening and questioning. For example, rather than letting students focus on their desire to leave Mississippi, teachers were encouraged to provoke debates on the status and condition of northern blacks. As Fusco notes, the students "did not change their minds just because the truth about the North began to shatter their dream of it as a paradise. Their need to escape stemmed from the fact that they really did not know what it was about Mississippi that they hated." The cultivation of this questioning attitude was, according to Summer Project volunteer Sally Belfrage, one of the summer's major accomplishments.[22]

To engender a greater sense of group loyalty, freedom school students were encouraged to express themselves through whatever means were at their disposal and in whichever way they felt most comfortable. In one of the Jackson freedom schools, a history teacher used a session to discuss that morning's local newspaper editorial. He encouraged the students to consider how they would write a letter to the editor in response, and the best two were sent to the newspaper. For Howard Zinn, "this was not education for grades . . . but for an immediate use." Students were encouraged to reject their forebears' acceptance of, and even complicity with, the racial status quo. Teachers encouraged them to contrast such common misconceptions with the message, both symbolic and political, of the civil rights movement and their own involvement in the freedom schools. Encouraging students to reverse the roles and exploring how this related to the American democratic ideal of every person being equal challenged the lessons that many students learned at home, such as never openly questioning the authority of whites. Through such exercises, freedom school students developed a greater ability to think critically and act according to their conscience. This change was crucial to SNCC's insistence that the culture of the South be transformed. Students in Hattiesburg were inspired by their freedom schools to draft their own Declaration of Independence, which began, "In this course of human events, it has become necessary for the Negro people to break away from the customs which have made it very difficult for the Negro to get his God-given rights." That the new version featured vernacular English suggests that the Summer Project was extending its plans to include a critique of the varied hegemonic practices of the American state. Although a political document, its mere production suggests much about the creation of an oppositional culture within the freedom schools and how the students were beginning to translate this culture into their own lives. Students were encouraged to see the world outside their community and take from mainstream American culture what they thought was useful while challenging what they considered unacceptable.[23]

In October 1964, Myles Horton wrote to Liz Fusco in support of a plan to establish poetry corners in libraries throughout the South. Having witnessed the keenness of students to read and write poetry during the Summer Project, Fusco told Horton that she was anxious to expand the experience to other communities. Fusco's enthusiasm for the subject filtered through the freedom schools. In Harmony, freedom school students were encouraged to read their poetry out loud in order to stimulate discussion. Ida Ruth Griffin read her poem in which she referred to herself (and by implication all Mississippi blacks) as a slave. This led to howling protests from the class and developed into an intense discussion over the validity of her statement. Members of the Holly Springs freedom school were encouraged to publish their own newspaper in which students wrote poetry and articles about their hopes and fears. Some students articulated their feelings about John F. Kennedy's assassination.[24]

The promise of freedom loomed large in the freedom school poetry, alongside the Christianity that formed the backbone of southern black society and a social realism that was encouraged by the freedom school teachers. Most of the freedom school poetry reflected the Summer Project's Highlander-derived philosophy of introducing complex or abstract subjects through examples from everyday life. Potential poets were encouraged to write about what they knew, in order that universal truths might be revealed through individual experience. Beulah Mae Ayers used her personal experience as a metaphor, writing about teachers being afraid to teach and of one teacher who rejected this obsequiousness and inspired hundreds of young women to learn. Ayers then linked this experience to the wider issue of black women hiding from their reality, scared to show their face, and warned them, "When God gets ready for you/There'll be no hiding place."[25]

Langston Hughes's poetry was a point of reference for a number of students. His endearing lyricism and accessible form encouraged many freedom school students to enter the world of poetry. Northward travel was a frequent theme, paralleling the concerns of some freedom school students. Firmly located within the organic African American folk tradition, Hughes's work could translate easily from the Harlem Renaissance to 1960s Mississippi, and certainly influenced the more impressionistic poetry of the Summer Project.[26]

It would be overstating the case to argue that all the poetry from the freedom schools was heavily influenced by Langston Hughes. Yet it is not surprising that his work was a key reference point for the poets of 1964. The themes within his work and his deceptively straightforward poetry were of universal appeal. The links between his poetry and that of the students, with a central theme being the relationship between the mundane and the transcendental, suggest that the shared memory of slavery and its aftermath loomed large in the minds of African Americans. Hughes's poetry—and its influence on the freedom school students—reinforced the Summer Project's insistence that African Americans had a usable past.

Highlander assisted in the development of the freedom school curriculum, hosting a COFO conference in March 1964 at which the curriculum was discussed. Its influence also extended to the Mississippi Caravan of Music, which toured the state during the summer. The Caravan involved over twenty-five singers and musicians performing and leading workshops in movement meeting centers. Len Chandler; Peter, Paul, and Mary; the Staples Singers; Pete Seeger; Guy Carawan; SNCC's Freedom Singers; and others helped to spread folk culture through the state. The Caravan also worked to establish the close relationship between black culture and protest, as exemplified in the slave songs and the freedom songs, with its participants often attending black history classes during which they sang spirituals and slave songs. It also introduced black Mississippians to the work of artists such as Lead Belly and Big Bill Broonzy as part of the Summer Project's goal to emphasize the contributions of African Americans to American cultural history. Seeger talked of music's power to transcend racial and cultural divides, and sang songs from a variety of national traditions. He also taught schoolchildren songs in African languages, thus linking them once more to their heritage. The Caravan provided a vital new cultural arena for black Mississippians. The music workshops and hootenannies introduced local people to new and old forms of music from both the white and the African American folk traditions, further ensuring the perpetuation of these traditions.[27]

The Free Southern Theater

Theater played an important role in the freedom schools, helping to develop group bonds and individual confidence. Role-play was often used to illustrate many issues, encourage empathetic skills, and nurture creativity. The students at Holly Springs wrote and performed a play based on the life of Medgar Evers; McComb students performed a play about the local movement; and Clarksdale students presented a production of *Blues for Mister Charlie*. The arrival of the Free Southern Theater (FST) in thirteen COFO centers between 1 and 13 August heralded the most explicit union between theater and the Summer Project. Of the cultural events and programs that summer, the FST tour was easily the most significant and successful.[28]

The FST brought theater and drama workshops to the black community in an attempt to broaden the struggle into the cultural sphere and fill a cultural void in the black community. Journalist Gilbert Moses and SNCC activists John O'Neal and Doris Derby were instrumental in establishing the FST and in its alignment with the civil rights struggle. Moses studied at Oberlin College before joining the staff of the *Mississippi Free Press* in Jackson. O'Neal left his psychology and philosophy studies at Southern Illinois University to join SNCC's Southwest Georgia Project in 1962. Influenced by Charles Sherrod's missionary zeal, he took a similar enthusiasm and single-mindedness to Mississippi, where he helped to plan the 1964 Summer Project. Derby, an artist, dancer, and elementary school teacher from New York City, traveled to the South to become part of the Albany movement in 1962. Derby and O'Neal joined SNCC's Tougaloo Literacy Project, where they first met Moses and began to develop the idea of the FST. All three became convinced that a cultural approach to SNCC's organizing would be a valuable addition to the movement. The FST's work would be the catalyst for further community development. The community would become involved in cultural activities alongside politically oriented actions, and thus the work of the civil rights movement would expand into the cultural sphere.[29]

The FST was initially to be composed of students and both professional and amateur actors at Tougaloo College. As a result of their movement experiences, the founders of the nascent company thought it important to use works by black playwrights. They were, however, aware that the development of black theater had been sorely limited by the closed society and so prepared to produce their own work, particularly through improvisation, in order to develop a style that best reflected the singular experience of southern blacks. Such a technique placed the FST within the African American improvisational tradition. Despite these aims, the FST's relationship with this tradition was never fully consummated. After failing to develop workable productions of plays by Lorraine Hansberry, Langston Hughes, and Ossie Davis, the FST also failed to devise a suitable improvisational piece. Consequently, for its first tour, it chose to present *In White America*, the white historian and sociologist Martin Duberman's first published play. The play developed out of Duberman's interest in the civil rights movement, New Left politics, and history. The play was undoubtedly influenced by the concept of a usable past: the preface revealed that the author "wanted to combine the evocative power of the spoken word with the confirming power of historical fact . . . [in order that] past reality might enter into present consciousness."[30]

The play uses primary sources, including Jefferson's *Notes on Virginia*, antebellum period letters between a slave mistress and her former slave, excerpts from speeches in Congress, and the Works Progress Administration slave narratives, as a historical backdrop, with dialogue constructed around the original documents. Opening with a brief scene set in January 1964, the play examines the black experience in the United States through "400 years of barbaric treatment," beginning with the slave trade. Act 1 moves from the Middle Passage through the framing of the Constitution and the antebellum black experience, including Nat Turner's revolt and John Brown's failed insurrection and subsequent trial, before concluding with the Civil War. Act 2 begins with white missionary activity in the South before moving the narrative through Reconstruction, the Washington–Du Bois debate, the Depression, and World War II, which is examined through Walter White's reports for the National Association for the Advancement of Colored People

(NAACP) on black combat troops. The play concludes with a dramatization of the 1954 *Brown* decision and the 1957 Little Rock crisis. Duberman chose not to extend the narrative to link up with his opening scene because he thought that the subsequent events were sufficiently familiar to his audience and that Little Rock was difficult to better dramatically. Recent events in Mississippi, however, provided a provocative and emotive conclusion, so Gil Moses added two scenes centered on the murder of COFO workers James Chaney, Andrew Goodman, and Mickey Schwerner. Moses also interspersed the play with freedom songs, linking African American history and culture in an even more explicit manner. Each FST performance was accompanied by a workshop in the local freedom school on the same day, in which the company introduced students to theater participation. The FST's tour was explicitly conceived as an addition to the Summer Project curriculum, establishing that *In White America* was the most appropriate play for the theater group to present.[31]

In White America's plot accurately represents the aims of the Summer Project, which O'Neal helped to define. The FST at this point was firmly committed to integration, so presenting a play that explored the interrelated nature of African American and white American history was an excellent opportunity to demonstrate this commitment. The selection of *In White America* also confirms that the FST was influenced by Lynd's conception of a usable past. Duberman's play perfectly complemented the Summer Project's history curriculum. As Moses notes, the play was chosen because it suggested that the civil rights movement was analogous to the American Revolution, just as New Left historical writing (such as Duberman's on the abolitionists) suggested that the New Left had deep roots in American dissent. *In White America* reveals the FST's keenness to ensure that its work contained an accessible yet pertinent political message. It integrated with the Summer Project aims of exposing universal truths through personal experience and emphasizing the concept of a usable past, and appealed to the FST's target audience. The FST was to perform for church congregations, schoolchildren, civil rights workers, and the community at large throughout Mississippi. Clearly, the play had to be comprehensible to a potentially ill-educated audience. The play's accessible dialogue and documentary feel rendered it palatable to a wide audience and thus made it a natural selection. To criticize the FST over the choice of a white play aimed at a sympathetic yet generally uninformed audience would be to ignore the historical reality of white Mississippi's refusal to educate its black populace. *In White America* told the story that the FST wanted its audience to hear and become involved with. Although the FST was later to reject works by white playwrights out of hand, in summer 1964 it was unconcerned with the symbolism of presenting a play that, through its author's racial identity, might have suggested that the white interpretation of black history remained dominant.[32]

Movement historiography has underestimated the significance of the FST's Summer Project tour.[33] Yet the tour was one of the most significant and successful events of the summer. Staughton Lynd cites the FST tour as one of the three most important of the planned events for that summer (the others being the freedom school conference and the schools themselves). For him, the FST's work was to drama what the freedom schools were to education: revolutionary in its conception of student or audience participation. Sally Belfrage and Florence Howe lavished praise on the performances. Audiences responded energetically and ecstatically to the FST, not least because *In White America* portrayed historical incidents that they had discussed in freedom school classes. Through this, they began to understand the matrix that united history, politics, art, and activism. Kirsty Powell, a freedom school coordinator in Ruleville, applauded the FST's performance as "a great success. . . . [T]he [200–strong] audience almost became a part of the play. . . . [T]here was an intimacy and informality about the performance that underlined for me the impression that the play was woven out of the very stuff of these people's lives." Most audiences understood that they were learning while being entertained, although an anonymous black Mississippian argued that "the theater is a wonderful idea. It takes more than learning to make the whole man." This might suggest that some considered the play to be mere entertainment, but, more significant, it indicates that audiences were primarily engaging with the theater as a cultural activity, that the FST was stealthily educating while entertaining, and that it was broadening the scope of the Summer Project. This testimony suggests that audiences were aware of the vital importance of cultural activities to personal and political development, and that they were fully cognizant that the civil rights movement existed not only to give them voting rights but also to enable full participation in American society.[34]

Performances began with John O'Neal impressing on the audience that "you are the actors," thus making explicit the relationship between the play and African American life, emphasizing the FST's belief that the seeds of change took root in the black community and that ordinary people were history makers. During the Greenwood performance, one member of the audience took O'Neal's opening statement literally and briefly joined the actors on stage. Although it desired to break down the traditional barriers that existed between performers and audience, the FST was rarely able to translate its interaction with the community into the performance sphere, as demonstrated by Gil Moses's attempt to maneuver the Greenwood improviser back into the audience. Its choice of material played no small part in this: since *In White America* explored actual events primarily from a factual (rather than dramatic) perspective, improvisation was a difficult proposition. This tension between accuracy and improvisation remained with the FST throughout its life. Elsewhere, forty-two armed police and a deputized posse descended on the performance at Indianola, in Sunflower County, suggesting that the popularity and notoriety of the play had spread to the white community. Somewhat inevitably, the county clerk declared that the play served to confirm that Communists had infiltrated the Summer Project. The arrival of the whites led to fervent renditions of freedom songs from the black audience, including a pointed "Which Side Are You On?"

Most audiences responded favorably to the FST's appearance in their locality. Greenwood locals, in addition to the improviser, were enraptured by the FST's work, and some became even more vociferous in their support for the movement after experiencing *In White America*. One native Mississippian bore witness to the power of the FST's production: "I sat there on the edge of the seat, with one hand holding me to it, to keep from jumping up and screaming through the veil of heaven, 'Yes! Tell it!' With the other hand, I was wiping tears from my eyes that were laden with love, sorrow, joy, pity—and hate. . . . They were telling my story on that stage. Oh, they were telling it . . . and telling it like it *really* is."[35]

The FST had a profound impact on the 1964 Summer Project and on the thousands of Mississippians who witnessed its performances. Its work illuminated the history curriculum and gave added impetus to the students' studies. *In White America* succeeded in provoking its audience to think deeply about theater and the movement. While some Mississippians focused on what it said about white people, others found it to be a superlative examination of what it meant to be black. For some, it told a story, while for others it presented a documentary. It challenged the preconceptions of its audiences, and it convinced many to rededicate themselves to the civil rights movement. The FST tour resulted in the cultural enrichment of the Mississippians who witnessed it. It remains as a powerful memory of summer 1964 and illustrates that protest could come in many forms and move the individual in many ways.

Despite this success, the COFO Summer Project did not result in vast numbers of newly registered voters. The MFDP's attempt to unseat the regu lar Mississippi Democrats at the national convention in Atlantic City later that summer ended in failure. Yet SNCC's decision to enter into every facet of black life in Mississippi was crucial to the development both of the organization and of civil rights protest. In accepting that the culture of the South needed changing, SNCC went further than other civil rights organizations dared. Through its educational and cultural activities, SNCC hoped to create a new self-awareness and a new generation of leaders in Mississippi. It made African American history part of the civil rights movement's weaponry to establish that the 1960s struggle was part of a long-term historical process. While its political campaign was questioning America, its cultural campaign was reinforcing American ideals and emphasizing the American roots of African American protest. Freedom school education encompassed more than simply education for qualifications; it was more a holistic plan to enter into every aspect of black Mississippian life and a concerted effort to legitimize African American culture as a counterhegemonic force. This neo–Du Boisian faith in the utility of education to racial uplift was fused with a Washingtonian belief in the application of skills to everyday life. The role that African American cultural forms played in the 1964 Summer Project reveals how the long-term traditions of accommodation and resistance were perhaps more entwined than even SNCC appreciated.

Although the short-term political aims of the Summer Project collapsed amid the chicanery of American party politics, the long-term and more abstract proposals in the project opened up the possibilities for thousands of Mississippians. Despite idealism not triumphing in the Democratic Party's national convention in Atlantic City, SNCC could legitimately claim that its successes were in the tradition to which the organization aspired. Its work instilled a new sense of community and history in black Mississippians. From this, SNCC hoped to develop the community's confidence in its own abilities to organize and to agitate.

Many volunteers and staff burned themselves out over the course of the summer, and SNCC simply did not have the finances to repeat the experiment. Despite this, a number of volunteers wanted to ensure that the freedom schools continued to offer a different experience of education for young Mississippians, although the new school year was to affect attendance. In the months after the Summer Project ended, Mississippians frequently used the facilities that SNCC left behind. Political classes attracted numerous individuals and voter registration classes met regularly in Holly Springs, Itta Bena, and Philadelphia. Moreover, all the major movement centers reported ongoing activities after the official conclusion of the Project. Following the

Hattiesburg Declaration of Independence, students from around Mississippi organized a conference to develop a youth platform for the MFDP, which proposed housing and health programs and school boycotts. This political consciousness remained through the fall, as students continued to protest the murders of Schwerner, Chaney, and Goodman in Philadelphia and students in Issaquena and Sharkey counties boycotted their schools over the issue of free political expression. The FST took inspiration from its audiences to prolong the experiment in developing protest through theater, deciding to settle in New Orleans in order to cement its relationship with the local black community. The betrayal of the MFDP might only have confirmed the mendacity of mainstream American politics, but education in the Summer Project suggested that black culture could be an effective alternative weapon for the civil rights movement.[36]

The freedom schools continued to inform SNCC practice well beyond the conclusion of the 1964 Summer Project. SNCC Arkansas set up a cluster of freedom schools in 1965 using the 1964 syllabus.[37] In August 1965, SNCC announced that it had published a black history primer for schools designed to address the failure of American history textbooks to acknowledge the contribution of African Americans to the United States. The fifty-one-page book began life as a freedom school coloring book, but developed following SNCC's realization that a suitable survey text was needed for people with limited reading skills. In Albany, Georgia, SNCC proposed to extend the freedom school concept to nursery schools, hoping to offer a nurturing environment for preschool children. Creating a positive self-image was the central goal of the nursery in order to propel the children toward language development, concept formation, and perceptual discrimination. The organization continued to stress the importance of bringing resources into local communities and experimenting with new programs to broaden the parameters of the movement, citing the success of the FST as a prime example of its own innovation. In addition to such programs, SNCC debated the legacy of the freedom schools, desperate to fine-tune their implementation and ensure that the questioning attitude that the schools inculcated be transformed into action.[38]

In August 1965, not long after she had established a freedom school in southwest Georgia, Judy Richardson established a residential freedom school. Involving a hundred black students—fifty urban northerners and fifty rural southerners—the school ran for two sessions, one in a northern urban setting and one in the rural South. Richardson hoped that the experience would strengthen cultural bonds between the two groups and offer a practical response to the many questions that Summer Project students had about life in the North. SNCC hoped that the exchange would help African American students comprehend the essential similarities between life in the North and the South, in order that they better understand the extent to which American racism, discrimination, and economic inequality were national phenomena. For Richardson, the development of this common ground could aid the destruction of the urban-rural and sectional divides within the national African American community. The students would take part in a wide variety of activities designed to facilitate discussion and forge working relationships among them. Richardson and her colleagues Sherron Jackson and Nancy Cooper hoped that as many of the southern students as possible would be housed in the ghetto during the tour's northern leg in order that they might experience all aspects of their counterparts' lives. Generally, the experiment was a success, although Richardson noted occasional outbreaks of civil war. In emphasizing that class oppression united the black community, Richardson hoped that the students would start developing a black working-class movement that would overcome the struggles that the southern civil rights organizations were encountering in their attempt to move from southern communities to the urban North.[39]

This was the only time that SNCC experimented with a residential freedom school, which in a number of respects represents SNCC's transitional phase. It reveals how SNCC became increasingly interested in developing a black working-class consciousness that might be able to sustain a protest movement after the demise of legal segregation. It also hints at SNCC's struggles to expand its program, particularly the discovery that its resources could not cover both rural southern and urban northern activism. Some SNCC activists such as Richardson struggled to comprehend the lack of unity between northern and southern blacks, becoming drawn into the violence of northern ghettos and away from SNCC's initial programmatic focus. The trouble between the student groups also suggested to SNCC how difficult it would be to translate the lessons of the southern movement to the North.

The Summer Project convinced many SNCC activists that African American culture was a viable organizing tool and a vital component of the freedom struggle. The freedom school curriculum placed African American history at the center of the freedom struggle and SNCC urged the freedom school students to consider themselves historical actors. Students of all ages were encouraged to learn about their own history and culture and understand the depth of the contributions of African Americans to the United

States. Thousands had their minds opened to theater, poetry, and new forms of music. But the legacy of the Summer Project went further. The collapse of the MFDP challenge and the pressure that SNCC staff members experienced over the summer thrust the organization into a period of self-analysis, which transformed its philosophy and from which it arguably did not recover. The psychological trauma of the summer of 1964 resonated for some time, particularly in the organization's central cadre. Physically and in some respects politically exhausted, ten senior SNCC staff members gratefully accepted Harry Belafonte's offer to visit the African continent. Designed as a restorative, it arguably served only to raise more problems. The trip helped to expand the visitors' conception of the civil rights struggle beyond the United States but led the delegation to conclude that SNCC had to turn to Africa for further inspiration. It deepened SNCC's appreciation of the worldwide struggle against oppression and pushed the organization toward a closer embrace with the psychology of being black in the United States.[40]

5

Integrationist Cultural Organizing in the Black Power Era, 1965–1969

Black Power became a clarion call for young black activists in the wake of Kwame Ture's utterance of the slogan during the Meredith March in Mississippi on 17 June 1966. While no fully coherent Black Power philosophy emerged in the 1960s, one of its key appeals was the call for African Americans to embrace their cultural heritage, to stop being ashamed of being black, and to celebrate their own blackness. Even moderate magazines such as *Ebony* jumped on the bandwagon, publishing articles that celebrated African-influenced fashions and hairstyles. This cultural appeal, and its attendant psychological benefits, remains among the most enduring legacies of the Black Power era.[1]

Amid the rise of Black Power, the Southern Christian Leadership Conference (SCLC) explored the psychological ramifications of the civil rights movement in greater depth. Although it began to come to terms with the importance of black cultural advancement to the movement, its commitment to cultural organizing was relatively limited. The SCLC's understanding of the relationship between African American politics and cultural forms was defined by its commitment to the Christian church and by its respectable middle-class image. Even so, during the late 1960s the organization began to acknowledge the importance that many young urban blacks placed on celebrating African American identity, heritage, and culture. Martin Luther King Jr. took the psychological impact of Black Power very seriously. His wife, Coretta Scott King, attempted to widen her involvement with the movement through a series of "Freedom Concerts," which were similar in form to the Student Nonviolent Coordinating Committee (SNCC) Freedom Singers' concerts but differed widely in terms of content. Coretta Scott King was arguably more interested in displaying her own talents than on encouraging a greater understanding of the relationship between the singing culture and the political aims of the movement. This exemplified the difference between the organizing styles of the SCLC and SNCC. The SCLC's embrace of cultural organizing was tempered by the organization's belief that secular black cultural expressions were ultimately relevant as fund-raising tools and indeed by the organization's leadership-centered strategy. The SCLC's engagement with cultural organizing was largely rhetorical, as evinced by the organization's 1967 annual conference, at which the SCLC attempted to hitch itself to the soul culture bandwagon and where Andrew Young took the opportunity to reemphasize the debt that African American culture owed to the church. His statement defined the SCLC's relationship with African American culture and its strained relationship with Black Power.[2]

Highlander continued to inspire and sustain the commitment of a number of civil rights activists even though it shifted its focus from the quest for integration to the problems facing the Appalachian poor. At Resurrection City, the SCLC's quixotic attempt to rejuvenate the integrated movement, Highlander was given the opportunity to link communal song with political organizing once again. Cultural events became important methods through which the increasingly demoralized residents could come together and build a sense of community, one of the few positives to emerge from the SCLC's last major campaign. Guy Carawan continued to organize and sing at music festivals. His work compelled a Southern Student Organizing Committee (SSOC) activist, Anne Romaine, to expand her folk revival work in the South. She worked briefly with Bernice Reagon, who had left SNCC's Freedom Singers to pursue other activities. Their organization, the Southern Folk Cultural Revival Project (SFCRP), represents one of the last attempts at biracial organizing during the 1960s civil rights movement and offers further insight into the effects of Black Power on southern organizing.

The National Association for the Advancement of Colored People (NAACP) managed to survive the Black Power insurgency, even though it also experienced a period of decline. Amid the rise of Black Power sentiment within its own ranks, the NAACP hierarchy attempted to triangulate its position, offering stern criticism of Black Power's fiery rhetoric while privately maneuvering to take advantage of Black Power's ambiguous relationship with American capitalism. The NAACP's ambivalence toward Black Power and its outright rejection of Black Power's cultural campaign, exemplified in the NAACP's insistence that "Negro" remain the accepted nomenclature, was wholly consistent with the organization's class identity. Even though it entered the post–civil rights era with a reduced membership, its decline did not compare with that of the other major organizations of the period. Ultimately, its mass membership—not to mention the conservatism of most members—enabled it to resist the Black Power tide.

The SCLC and Black Culture

In spring 1965, Coretta Scott King tried to break out of her role as a wife and mother by undertaking a brief singing tour in support of the SCLC. She had previously performed in a benefit concert for the Montgomery Improvement Association in 1956, singing spirituals and reciting her interpretation of the bus boycott. The 1965 concerts followed a similar pattern. King sang movement standards alongside Christian hymns, interspersed with a self-penned narrative of the movement from Montgomery to the present. For King, these concerts combined art and the movement in a "practical, relevant, meaningful way," and utilized her unique gifts as an orator, singer, and activist to the full. The concerts were an undoubted success, netting the SCLC approximately $20,000.[3]

The concerts reveal much about the SCLC's attitude toward organizing through cultural forms, and reflect the long-established struggle to emphasize the high-cultural credentials of black folk culture. Like the Freedom Singers, King brought the indigenous folk culture of the black South to the concert halls of the North. Yet her concerts did not focus so much on demonstrating the intrinsic beauty and value of the songs but on establishing her own credentials as a singer. King wore lavish concert gowns rather than work clothes, accentuating the distance between the concert and its politics, and hinting that the concerts were more about her own ambitions and dreams than that of the grassroots movement. While the acquisition of such an impressive wardrobe was no doubt an ambition of some African Americans, many were concerned with more pressing needs, such as adequate political representation and economic stability. Where the Freedom Singers stressed that the movement needed the audience's participation, King took full control of the repertoire and did not encourage audience participation in the songs. By maintaining a clear distance between herself and her audience, she suggested that the movement existed away from the concert hall and far from the audience's doors. Debate was thus stifled, and the audience's role was reduced to that of benefactors rather than participants.[4]

King's target audiences were the well-to-do, who could lavish relatively large amounts of money on such concerts. The struggle was presented in respectable, even aspirational terms (King was, after all, a classically trained singer), and the concerts were carefully designed to avoid contentious and non-SCLC events such as the 1964 Summer Project. This narrative structure discouraged the audience from considering the ordinary African American people of the South as political actors in the civil rights movement. Instead, King's audience was led toward a leadership-centered interpretation of the movement that focused only on the major marches and campaigns rather than its underlying structures. Indeed, her control of the repertoire is reminiscent of the control that her husband and his lieutenants hoped to exert over civil rights demonstrations. In contrast to the Freedom Singers, King reinforced the notion that working-class blacks were simply waiting for leadership. Rather than pointing to the deep roots of the freedom struggle, she presented Montgomery as "A New Hope" for black Americans. Rather than exploiting the distance between the concert hall and the public arenas of the civil rights campaigns, she reinforced this divide, suggesting that the wealthy need not make a personal commitment to the movement beyond donating money. King did not see the concerts as a tool for recruiting movement activists. Nor did the concerts aim for verisimilitude. Instead, they were to publicize the SCLC, and perhaps even to reinforce the cult of personality around her husband.[5]

By 1967, Martin Luther King Jr. had come to the conclusion that a social and political movement needed a psychological appendage, and he saw much of use in Black Power's insistence on racial pride and of the glory of African American culture and heritage.[6] His acknowledgment during a late 1964 interview of the increasingly important symbolism of Africa to the American freedom struggle suggests that King was exploring the intellectual limits of his early philosophy of nonviolence and was coming to terms with the gradual shift of emphasis in the movement from the social to the psychological. He accepted that there were clear, direct, even inevitable parallels between the African independence movement and the rise of Afrocentricity in the American movement. King did not explicitly suggest that a psychological or cultural return to Africa was essential, but the lessons of the anticolonial struggle and the growth of black consciousness on the continent were clear to him. Stronger ties between the two movements would strengthen the resolve of black people on both continents. The SCLC even tried to develop these bonds, inviting the Nigerian ambassador to the United Nations, S. O. Adebo, to address its 1965 convention. Yet Adebo's address ruffled a few nonviolent feathers in its call for a worldwide black revolution. Significantly, no more Africans—diplomats or revolutionaries—were invited to address the SCLC convention during the 1960s.[7]

King acknowledged the impact of double consciousness and the frustrating search for heritage and culture, concluding that African Americans simply had to embrace their hybrid identity to avoid losing themselves in a spiral of despair and rage. He considered such dual heritage an advantage to the African American. Despite this positive outlook, King was increasingly worried about the pernicious effects of the militant mood, and addressed these feelings at a staff retreat in November 1967. He mused whether the antiwhite rage that was allied to this feeling could be channeled more effectively. As he put it, "to develop a sense of black consciousness and peoplehood does not require that we scorn the white race as a whole. It is not the race *per se* that we fight, but the policies and idiolody [*sic*] formulated by leaders of the race to perpetuate oppression." "We must also be the custodians of creative black power," King argued. "We need to be proud of being black and not ashamed of it."[8]

Even when the SCLC began to respond to this new mood in the African American community, like Coretta Scott King's Freedom Concerts, it remained slightly aloof from the grittiness of African American culture. Its 1967 conference was the most explicitly cultural event in the organization's life, at which Sidney Poitier addressed the delegates. Four years earlier, he became the first black to win a Best Actor Oscar. The Oscar offered him a gold-plated opportunity to bring the civil rights movement firmly into the public consciousness. He declined, choosing instead to declare his indebtedness to numerous unnamed friends, telling *Jet* that his award constituted only "a mandate to intensify my moves toward increasing my potential as an artist." His SCLC speech was slightly less self-centered and focused more on his contribution to the freedom struggle. Feeling that the current political situation was too depressing for consideration, Poitier dedicated himself to promising the delegates that he would henceforth "try to make a new world full of love."[9]

That same night the SCLC commemorated Aretha Franklin's vocal contribution to the advancement of the freedom struggle. The theme of the SCLC's first "Negro Culture and Heritage Evening," "black is beautiful, it's beautiful to be black," reflected King's message in his annual report. Bernice Reagon was invited to perform alongside Emory and the Dynamics, an SCLC rock group of freedom singers. *Ebony's* senior editor, Lerone Bennett Jr., gave the keynote address, in which he argued that the movement had become both a social and a psychological struggle, and concluded that identity—African and African-American—was central to the revolution. Nevertheless, the struggle between secular and Christian culture in the SCLC was always to be a lopsided battle. Andrew Young, also speaking at the event, reiterated the value of religion to the organization: "You know in this church, nobody needs to tell you about black culture, because this church is black culture." "Never in this world," concluded Young, quoting Curtis Mayfield, "can there be too much love."[10]

The invocation of Curtis Mayfield is significant. He had achieved national renown as the principal singer-songwriter with his band, The Impressions. His lyrics were characterized by gentle social commentary, notably his 1964 hit, "Keep on Pushing," which was often sung at Chicago civil rights rallies, and "People Get Ready," an allegorical take on the movement's goals in which a train acts as a metaphor for the freedom struggle. His sound grew out of his upbringing in the church and his membership in a number of gospel vocal groups in his early teens. As such, he was a perfect example of the SCLC's interpretation of African American culture. His metaphorical lyrics made few explicit claims for the movement, but their message was clear to those who wanted to seek it. His church roots and belief in interracial liberalism did not alienate older elements of the SCLC's constituency, while his critique of racism, insistence on black pride, and musical genius ensured that he was popular with a youthful fan base, one that the SCLC desired.[11]

Young's statement encapsulates the attitude of the SCLC toward black culture. While the SCLC acknowledged that the mood of black Americans was increasingly linked to cultural expression and the desire to legitimize an independent African American culture, it could not conceive of this culture without Christianity, which was the only culture able to protect the individual and the collective from the physical and spiritual ravages of segregation and white oppression. Where many Black Power advocates were arguing that embracing secular black cultural forms and practices was the answer to the psychological oppression imposed by white Americans, the SCLC maintained that a firm commitment to Christianity was just as important. As Young pointed out, the SCLC believed that there was no need to embrace a secular black culture, for the church provided all the culture that black Americans could want: their music, their literature, and their theater. Even as the SCLC was affirming that black was beautiful, it was stressing that Christianity was fundamental to the acceptance of this beauty. King, too, was convinced that the black church provided the only culture that African Americans needed. He was quite happy to be pictured alongside Aretha Franklin, but his appreciation of her as a cultural icon was shaped by his knowledge of her family background and her roots in gospel. Ultimately, for King and the SCLC, black culture represented little without the black church.

This attitude is visible in the SCLC's plans to spread the Citizenship Education Program (CEP) northward. In March 1967, it made a proposal to the Ford Foundation for the funding of a project designed to train neighborhood leaders in five major cities and establish a network for church leadership in twenty-five cities. Aware of SNCC's focus on developing indigenous leaders and of the growing militancy in the ghettos, the SCLC proposed that the church be emphasized as a safeguard against the growth of this political and racial radicalism. The SCLC intended to coordinate church leadership to contain the rising militancy and ensure the continued viability of the church in the inner cities. The proposal emphasized the cultural element of the CEP, arguing that it had "capitalized on this need for racial identity by emphasizing Negro history and current events of immediate relevance to the participants." The SCLC was aware that religion was losing ground in the inner cities, as it had painfully witnessed in its Chicago campaign, and hoped that an emphasis on religion was necessary. In July 1967, the SCLC announced that an education program had started in Chicago, which, it hoped, would become the model for similar programs throughout the nation's inner cities. Classes would run through the summer and, along the same lines as the CEP and SNCC's Summer Project, would concentrate on remedial instruction in communication skills, writing, arithmetic, and consumer education.[12]

Almost paradoxically, just as the SCLC was beginning to appreciate the value of blackness to the movement, the organization was planning a mass multiracial campaign that would reenergize the movement and return its focus to the federal government. Reflecting a subtle change of the organization's attitude to cultural organizing, the Poor People's Campaign (PPC) drew much sustenance from the Highlander ethos that embraced the use of song as a political weapon. Rev. Frederick Douglas Kirkpatrick, the director of the campaign's cultural program, set out to address the issues of pride, heritage, and common roots. Kirkpatrick, an ordained minister, had previously been involved with the Congress of Racial Equality (CORE) in Jackson, Louisiana, and the Deacons for Defense, a local organization that rejected nonviolence. King convinced him of the futility of this stance, drawing him into the SCLC and toward a realization that poetry and song could play a role in the freedom struggle. Kirkpatrick wrote and performed songs for the SCLC alongside white folk singer Jimmy Collier, believing that song was a perfect vehicle with which to promote interracial understanding. Kirkpatrick thought that an encounter with heritage and roots proved the essentially American nature of the African American experience.[13] For this reason, there was a folk culture tent in Resurrection City, and a culture department was planned for the SCLC. The PPC distributed a songbook, which featured movement standards alongside some of Kirkpatrick's compositions. *True Unity*, a PPC newsletter that often included poetry by the city's dwellers, was distributed around the shantytown. King also promised that the SCLC would institute freedom schools in Resurrection City that would emphasize the black contribution to philosophy and culture.[14]

Kirkpatrick's work served to prolong Highlander's contact with the movement. One of his assistants was Anne Romasco, who had worked at Highlander developing the use of art, dance, and literature as means to create interracial understanding. Musicians and artists associated with Highlander, including the Georgia Sea Island Singers, were invited to Resurrection City. An evening of folk music and poetry was organized in May, where American Indians performed traditional songs and spoke of their solidarity with the white poor, Bernice Reagon talked of and sang freedom songs and spirituals, and Pete Seeger led a trademark hootenanny. Highlander ran a tent at Resurrection City, where Myles Horton and others led discussion groups and Guy Carawan continued his music workshops. Carawan's work again emphasized the cross-cultural bonds of music. Mexican Americans, Puerto Ricans, American Indians, and whites were encouraged to merge their singing traditions with those of the black freedom struggle. As Mike Clark noted, for Highlander, Resurrection City was not a political campaign, but a "huge educational experiment."[15]

Highlander's scheduled sessions frequently developed into lengthy discussions, arguments, and celebrations of cultural diversity. For Carawan, one of the most important facets of Highlander's work in Resurrection City was the simple fact that it ensured that white faces who were not exploiting or oppressing peoples of color were constantly present. These meetings formed a beacon of hope amid the desperation of the campaign and a bulwark against the racial essentialism that bubbled under the surface of the city's life. Such was the success of the Highlander sessions—or the desperation of the city's organizers—that the PPC invited Highlander's delegation to merge with its own cultural program. Thus, even as the SCLC struggled to prolong the campaign, cultural workshops were positioned even closer to the center of Resurrection City. Faced with the immense problems of coordinating the shantytown, still reeling from King's assassination, and suffering from damning press coverage, the SCLC focused on day-to-day organizing of protests and, later, on negotiating a face-saving retreat from the protest.[16]

Following the demise of Resurrection City, the SCLC attempted to instigate a "Many Races Culture" program to combine the musical and cultural heritage of American minorities and build on the few successes of Resurrection City. The increasingly apocalyptic timbre of the SCLC's campaigning can be discerned in its statement of purpose, which warned that "this may well be one of our last chances to eradicate racism . . . [this] may be a last ditch effort to heal the sickness of racism which threatens to destroy our country." Notably, the SCLC intended to use cultural organizing to unite the many races. The program, however, could not contend with the problems that beset the SCLC in 1968. While the SCLC was beginning to appreciate that a cultural appeal could reinvigorate the movement, its organizational problems ensured that it could not capitalize on this realization.[17]

The SCLC's ambivalence about cultural organizing prevented the organization from fully committing itself to such work. Although certain activities suggest that the organization continued to test the water in this area, the fact that it proposed so few programs illustrates that the organization preferred not to concede that secular culture was as important as religious culture. The "black is beautiful" evening at the 1967 annual conference was largely a propaganda exercise to win young hearts and minds. In the face of the increasing militancy of Black Power, the SCLC felt compelled to address issues such as race pride. Its continuing programs, however, served to confirm that, for the SCLC, the church was paramount. Even though Highlander insisted that positives could be drawn from the experience of Resurrection City, the initiative proved to be a disaster for the SCLC. Highlander's presence could not prevent the shantytown's decline into petty criminality and despondency. The turmoil that resulted from King's assassination and the failure of the PPC confirm that, from early 1968, the SCLC was responding to events rather than creating and developing them. Always a low priority, cultural organizing was further marginalized as the organization stumbled toward its uncertain future.

Highlander's Continuing Influence

Highlander was more assured of its future in 1968, having recently decided to return to a focus on Appalachian organizing while maintaining a limited commitment to the development of the civil rights movement. Guy Carawan remained convinced of the value of folk song to the movement. Late in 1965, he organized a folk music workshop at Highlander to reacquaint southern black youth with their music and spur further meetings throughout the South. Some of the Georgia Sea Island Singers were present, as were Esau Jenkins; a number of SNCC activists, including Charles Sherrod, Willie Peacock, and Sam Block; and CORE's Jerome Smith. Bernice Reagon, the singer and SNCC activist Julius Lester, and Carawan were chosen to coordinate an effort to preserve indigenous African American culture. A statement of intent declared that black culture was an integral part of the freedom struggle and asserted that, through music, black and white southerners could begin a process of honest and mutually beneficial dialogue.[18] The statement reflected Highlander's insistence that in spite of slavery and segregation, black and white southerners shared a common heritage and that the bifurcation of southern culture had a central role in upholding segregation. To address this issue was to strike at the heart of segregation: its cultural foundations. Reagon proposed to further her work with black college students in Atlanta. Lester began touring the South as a roving fieldworker, reporting on cultural activities that resulted from the conference. Willie Peacock, who had concluded that developing pride through culture and heritage was fundamental to the struggle, and Sam Block established their own festival, courtesy of funds from the "We Shall Overcome" royalty trust. Peacock was certain that racial identity was a central issue in the struggle for equality. His series of festivals that toured the South in 1966 were designed as a means through which this identity could be confirmed, celebrated, and developed, spurring the black community to further action and strengthening its bonds with Africa. He envisaged emphasizing African culture in an attempt to highlight the common bonds that united the global black population.[19]

During a tour of the South, Julius Lester met the piano- and guitar-playing SSOC activist Anne Romaine. She was keen to involve the SSOC in community cultural revival programs, including a tour of the South by a collection of folk singers and performers. Brought up in rural North Carolina, Romaine was profoundly influenced by the culture of the southern church, and by Presbyterian tent meetings in particular.[20] Her initial idea, influenced by several SNCC activists including Robert Parris (formerly Bob Moses), was to import northern folk singers to combat miseducation in the South. Her enthusiasm for cultural revival spread to Bernice Reagon, who had retired from the SNCC Freedom Singers to concentrate on working with Guy Carawan. In return, Reagon convinced Romaine of the value of using community-based performers from the South. For Reagon, northern folk singers offered a distorted view of the South because they could not fully understand the subtleties of southern culture.[21]

The first Southern Folk Festival tour organized by Romaine and Reagon offered twenty-two afternoon workshops and evening performances in March and April 1966, mostly for white college audiences in towns including Richmond, Durham, Atlanta, Birmingham, Tougaloo, and New Orleans. A rolling bill of twenty performers, including Georgian balladeer Hedy West (daughter of Highlander's cofounder Don West); Eleanor Walden; Mable Hillery of the Georgia Sea Island Singers; the Reverend Pearly Brown (a blind street singer from Americus, Georgia); and Romaine herself took to the stage. Romaine's and Reagon's concept for the performances and the accompanying workshops was in the Highlander spirit, encouraging audience-performer interaction. Each performance was structured around a historical narrative that drew on the expertise of the performers to flesh out the story. The use of white and black musicians was a deliberate attempt to illustrate that southern cultures emerged from a common tradition of resistance against oppression. The entire troupe sat on stage together, taking turns singing songs to illustrate a particular singing style, a historical period, or even a philosophical point. Although Romaine and Reagon were no class warriors, the inference that a common bond united the lower classes of all races was a result of this tactic. For Romaine in particular, the folk culture of the South had been split along racial lines during slavery. Since white songs tended to shy away from racism and slavery's legacy, a burden was placed on black culture to explore both, resulting in black folk culture focusing overwhelmingly on the negative experience of the South. Romaine's thesis derived from a misreading of antebellum and postbellum black culture that focused too exclusively on the work songs and the pleas for emancipation of the spirituals. Her insistence that certain fundamentals united the two, however, was intrinsic to her folk festival work. For her and Reagon, black and white southerners, especially students, had become ashamed of their culture, an emotion heightened by the experience of the civil rights movement and the consequent media portrayal of the white South as a decadent, racist, and corrupt society. Their festival would instead celebrate the South as a culturally diverse and distinct area of the United States whose proud tradition of resistance ran from the slave revolts into the present. So successful was the Southern Folk Festival that SSOC historian Gregg Michel maintains that it was the most noteworthy project that the organization implemented in its entire history.[22]

Romaine arranged a workshop at Highlander in early September 1966 at which she discussed further ideas for cultural organizing with Carawan, Lester, and other folk singers and activists. Even at the planning stage, Romaine was being buffeted by the racial turbulence of southern organizing. Lester was in favor of moving the program into the white community, while Eleanor Walden preferred to maintain an interracial focus. Highlander staff, reflecting the center's increasing focus on Appalachia, were meanwhile encouraging Romaine to emphasize the intercultural links between black people and white Appalachian people. Romaine hoped that the workshop could establish common ground and discuss the value of using southern culture and folk revival as organizing tools.[23]

In spring 1967, Romaine organized a second Southern Folk Festival tour without the assistance of the poverty-stricken and increasingly unintegrated SSOC. Some of the performers from the 1966 tour, including Hillery, West, Brown, Carawan, and Reagon, were augmented by local performers at each concert to emphasize the links between different folk cultures and to remind audiences of the heterogeneity of southern culture. The 1966 tour had featured cameos from Pete Seeger, Len Chandler, banjo-playing folklorist Charles Joyner, and DeFord Bailey, a black harmonica player who had performed at the Grand Ole Opry for some thirty years. Most gave repeat performances in 1967, and even the Seeger-pursuing John Birch Society joined in the fun, distributing handbills that, much to Romaine's annoyance, billed its quarry above the other performers. The success of this tour led Romaine and Reagon to incorporate the festival as an organization to facilitate a wider range of programming and fund-raising. The SFCRP reiterated that by emphasizing the historically biracial nature of southern culture, the two races could be brought together. The grassroots tradition of biracial cooperation, Romaine and Reagon believed, offered a template that could be used to rebuild southern society. By perpetuating the best of this biracial southern culture, the SFCRP could lead the South toward a future without racial inequality.[24]

Bernice Reagon might have been involved with the SFCRP from its inception, but she was never a driving force. Her organizing commitments in Atlanta led her to decide that the 1967 tour would be her last. Her proposal to work with young African Americans in an urban center might suggest that she was drawing closer to a black nationalist position. This was not the case. In June 1968, Reagon reunited with Romaine to lead a short-lived Atlanta schools program that promoted the teaching of black history through song. After promising to continue her work with the young people of Atlanta, she organized an Afro-American cultural program to be made up of a history festival, a music festival, and a cultural library. Influenced by Highlander and her experiences with SNCC, Reagon thought that programs should be established that would address the failures of the local educational system in alerting people to their history and to the substantive changes that black protest had wrought in the South. The Penny Festival (so called because of its entry fee) was presented in conjunction with Negro History Week 1967. It was the direct offspring of Highlander's insistence that local folk culture be used as an organizing tool and SNCC's focus on education as a means with which to combat oppression and promote understanding.[25] The popularity of the Penny Festival confirmed Reagon's suspicions regarding the promotion of history and culture as a means to create racial understanding—in her words, "that Negro history is not only important to us but to everyone." The festival was so successful that an excited Reagon planned for it to become an annual event. Yet within two years, Reagon had left Atlanta, serving notice on the festival's demise. Without her leadership and contact network, the Penny Festival was effectively doomed. Its short-term success suggests that the black community responded well to cultural organizing, but the fact that nobody built on Reagon's momentum indicates the fragility of such initiatives and their reliance on the vision of their leaders.[26]

Reagon's withdrawal from SFCRP activities—at a time when many civil rights organizations were jettisoning their white members—effectively left Romaine without a biracial organization from which she could be expelled. So, in fall 1967 she organized a tour featuring only white performers, a decision that responded to SNCC's call for whites to organize in white communities and reflected recent changes in the SSOC. Many SSOC activists were attuned to the importance of country music to the South, not least because of their increasing interest in southern working-class culture and because the SSOC was based in Nashville, home of the Grand Ole Opry. The tour was a struggle due in part to the SFCRP's failure to raise support from major grant-giving foundations. Matters were worsened by Romaine's curious decision to take the tour to a black college audience in Morristown, Tennessee. The audience was not pleased. To her credit, Romaine invited black performers on the 1970 tour, but as a consequence of the decline of the movement, the civil rights message of the SFCRP was receiving less emphasis. With the waning of the movement and a consequent drop in audiences, Romaine was forced to retreat into white communities and gradually strip the SFCRP of its political message to concentrate on southern history and local concerns. By the early 1970s, the SFCRP was effectively committed to the preservation of white culture, performing at folk festivals and revival meetings, a reorientation that ensured that it continued to operate into the 1980s.[27]

For Romaine, the SFCRP was a natural extension of her civil rights work and the zenith of her life's work. She had become aware of the powerful role of music in shaping personal political and social perceptions and directed her work at challenging mistaken prejudices. By attempting to prolong the interracial dream, she tried to fight a rearguard action against the growth of black nationalism and racial essentialism in the South. In attempting to promote and preserve the traditional music and culture of the South, the SFCRP hoped to overcome the divisive society of the modern South. The SFCRP represented another example of the power and utility of the Highlander approach to organizing, and of SNCC's search for innovation in the struggle. In Romaine's view, its great failure in the 1960s was its inability to address the tendency of white performers to emphasize the positive aspects of the poor white South and the common oppression of the working class, thus leaving the black folk tradition to deal with racism and the negative side of the South. This was a failure compounded by the decision of many black performers to concentrate on the black community in the wake of Black Power.[28] In fact, the failure of the SFCRP was its timing. By 1966, black audiences were growing less interested in white culture and were exploring their own heritage at the expense of their common bonds with white Americans. The SFCRP was not able to adjust to this new racial sensibility and found itself swimming against the tide of history. Its failure suggests that class-based organizing was also unsustainable in the later years of the 1960s, and its ultimate depoliticization reflects much on the attitude of many previously "friendly" whites who became alienated from a movement that was urging them to look into their own psyche.

The NAACP and Black Power

During the early 1960s, the NAACP had not been unduly concerned at the resurgence of black nationalism, largely focusing its energies on the legislative assault on segregation.[29] While smaller organizations tied themselves in knots over Black Power, the NAACP's sheer size enabled the organization's leadership cadre to keep the new radical movement at arm's length.

In the field, the NAACP's programs tended to focus on voter registration drives, the push for greater employment opportunities, and protests against segregation and racial violence. Broader activities designed to reduce the educational and cultural gap between white and black Americans tended to be minor programs, developed through the initiative of local leaders.[30] The former aims were the overwhelming focus of a series of Summer Projects in the late 1960s, which suggests that the NAACP was less interested in the wider ramifications of SNCC's 1964 experiment than in the degree to which SNCC managed to mobilize the local community. An eight-week project was planned to run between July and August 1965 in South Carolina, Mississippi, and Alabama, staffed by over 1,200 NAACP volunteers. While literacy training for adults and tutorial classes for children and teenagers were available, the NAACP's primary concern was with voter registration. The NAACP accepted only volunteers who were "mature enough to understand and accept discipline." Significantly, the Mississippi operation relied only upon the local NAACP, ignoring structures such as the Mississippi Freedom Democratic Party (MFDP), which might have broadened the campaign but which also might have challenged the authority of NAACP organizers and might have widened the scope of the project. The Mississippi project brought the NAACP closer to the church, with a "Citizenship Sunday" being established in local churches at which services would be augmented with NAACP proselytizing. This focus certainly worked, adding over 50,000 people to the voter rolls. While representing only half of the NAACP's target figure, it dwarfed the number registered in SNCC's 1964 Summer Project and trebled the number that SNCC enticed merely to attempt to register. Undoubtedly though, the legacy of politicized communities that SNCC and the MFDP left behind smoothed the NAACP's path. Even though the 1965 Voting Rights Act certainly helped, it is notable that 26,975 registrants were passed before the bill became law.[31]

At a leadership level, the NAACP insisted that Black Power was synonymous with black nationalism. Its treatment of Black Power suggests that the NAACP was troubled by the new rise of black militancy and that it was struggling to redefine itself in the wake of the legislative breakthroughs of 1964 and 1965. The NAACP was desperate to stress that, at heart, both Black Power advocates and NAACP members sang from the same song sheet. Had these nationalists attended their local NAACP's Negro History Week events, they would have understood that there was little need to look to Africa for inspiration and might even have concluded that Kwanzaa, Maulana Ron Karenga's Afrocentric celebration of black heritage and history, was missing the point slightly. The NAACP's public stance on Black Power was also related to its fear of losing control of the movement's public agenda: Gloster Current, the NAACP's director of branches, might have denounced Kwame Ture as a "termite" in public, but on the same day, the organization's Assistant Secretary, John Morsell, admitted in private that the NAACP and Ture had many areas for agreement.[32]

The NAACP attempted to plot a steady course through stormy waters, exemplified by its refusal to change its policy on nomenclature. In 1929, the NAACP had pressured the major American newspapers to capitalize "Negro" as a matter of policy; within five months, the *New York Times* and twenty-seven other newspapers had adopted the capitalization. By the 1960s, the NAACP's policy had solidified into an unquestioning belief that "Negro" was the only correct name for Americans of African descent. The *Crisis* editor, James Ivy, dismissed a 1960 call to replace "Negro" with "Afroamerican," claiming rather ingenuously that "words have no power to alter matter and circumstance."[33] Ivy seemed unaware—or unconcerned—that language was an important element in the quest for black American redefinition. Kwame Ture often argued that power could be reduced to the question of who speaks loudest and most eloquently, and that many working-class black leaders such as Fannie Lou Hamer found themselves marginalized by the white power structure because they did not speak in a traditionally intellectual or educated manner. For Ture, even at its most simplistic level, Black Power was a powerful slogan, since the very combination of the two words implied first of all a rejection of white cultural hegemony and second a challenge to white political hegemony.[34] Although sentiment in the NAACP grew toward the idea of self-redefinition, an attempt by a group of so-called Young Turks to substitute "Black" for "Colored" in the organization's name was rebuffed. This, and the general clamor for black redefinition in the late 1960s, led Morsell to remind everyone that "Negro" was the only "clear, specific and exclusive denotation" for people of black African origin or descent, whereas the voguish "African-American" or "Afro-American" had the potential to include Ian Smith, the white prime minister of Rhodesia, should he claim American citizenship. "Black" was simply too broad.[35]

The 1968 convention was the closest that the NAACP came to an official adoption of Black Power. Conference delegates submitted a series of Black Power–influenced resolutions, all of which were deleted from the NAACP's official program of resolutions at the behest of the NAACP board.[36] Yet at a practical level, the NAACP insisted that its program could be reconciled with aspects of Black Power: an internal memo talked about transposing Black Power into green power by pumping loans and investment into the inner cities. Stephen Spottswood, chairman of the NAACP board of directors, claimed that Black Power was fundamentally the same as the NAACP's traditional approach: both focused on urban problems; both advocated the expansion in size and numbers of black-owned businesses and more jobs for African Americans; and both stressed the importance of knowing one's past and supported black artists, as demonstrated in the purchase of Charles Alson's *Black Man and Woman* for the NAACP's offices in New York City. And black political power, of course, was one of the NAACP's rallying cries, but it would seem that class was of little concern to Spottswood.[37]

Even as NAACP executive secretary Roy Wilkins was comparing Black Power advocates with Klan members and Nazis, the NAACP was attempting to wrestle the Black Power debate on its own terms. Wilkins's indignation stemmed from his adherence to pluralism and his belief that Black Power was attacking the ideal of racial harmony. In his less agitated moments, Wilkins took a more moderate position, offering New York congressman Adam Clayton Powell Jr. a few pointers as to common ground between Black Power philosophy and the NAACP and even admitting that, like most Black Power supporters, the NAACP was totally in favor of building black pride, economic power, and political strength. The organization's only differences with Black Power concerned separatism and Black Power's lack of a concrete program. Characteristically, Wilkins found other things to do when Powell invited him to discuss Black Power at a 1966 conference, but Wilkins's insistence that there was common ground to be found indicates that the NAACP was taking Black Power seriously (in private, Wilkins admitted that his reason for turning down the invitation had more to do with adverse publicity than with the terms of debate).[38]

The NAACP also insisted that the new attitude toward black education was consistent with its own policy. John Hope Franklin noted in the *Crisis* that one of the most significant breakthroughs of recent years was the revision of the portrayal of black Americans in educational material for history and social studies, which would surely aid the psychological development of young blacks.[39] Amid calls for community control of public schools in the inner cities, the NAACP reminded its members that such a policy had long been an NAACP concern. The organization solidified its stance on the depiction of African Americans in school textbooks, averring that racism was at its worst in such books and calling for mandatory education in African American history for elementary and secondary school pupils and college students. The 1969 annual convention program hammered home the message that the NAACP was fully committed to fighting racism in education, and included a report on the recent campus unrest involving African American students that was less critical of the students than of their oppressors. Education expert Doxey Wilkerson addressed the delegates on the need for higher standards in inner city schools. Spottswood offered his approval of black studies programs, but his support was qualified on the grounds that white students needed these courses more urgently than black students, for they were most ignorant of the facts of black history and life, a message endorsed by Wilkins in his address to the youth delegates.[40]

By 1969, the NAACP's position on black artists had shifted enough for it to sponsor a touring exhibition featuring the work of twelve African American artists. Despite vetoing the appropriation of NAACP funds for the tour, Roy Wilkins acknowledged that the action was a valid part of the NAACP's plan to integrate African Americans into American society, since highly capable artists were often being denied access to commercial galleries for reasons linked to race. The exposure offered by the tour would benefit both the artists and the wider culture. When the *New York Times* offered a critical review of the exhibition, Wilkins was moved enough to complain in public, noting that the artists just "*happen[ed]* to be black" and that to exhibit such artists as a collective was no different from holding exhibitions featuring only Mexican artists or just Italian frescoes. These comments certainly suggest that Wilkins was slowly coming to appreciate the value of holding a black nationalist stance when it was convenient, although the NAACP's relationship with the exhibition is more reflective of the general interest in black culture of the time than an acceptance of black nationalist tenets.[41]

Despite its weakened position, the NAACP was the only civil rights organization to weather the Black Power storm. This relative stability was entirely consistent with the class identity of the organization. Its struggles in certain inner cities are related to this identity. In Harlem, the NAACP's lack of dramatic action, its moderation, and its association with middle-class, comfortable lifestyles alienated many working-class blacks, as did the publicity that the organization courted for its society events. West Coast organizers became increasingly concerned about the NAACP's failure to embed itself in post-Watts Los Angeles. By 1968, fewer than 500 NAACP members remained in the city. The San Francisco branch similarly struggled to stem a membership hemorrhage.[42] Quite understandably, the organization was disinclined to address these image problems because they reflected the mood of Black Power, which the NAACP hierarchy believed to be a passing fad. Nevertheless, the organization survived, suggesting that (from an organizational perspective) it was correct to resist Black Power numbers. Its survival further suggests that the cultural turn was a chimera, and perhaps a desperate attempt to wring a positive outcome from the devastating effects of the civil rights movement's failures.

The descent of the SFCRP into irrelevancy confirms the vast problems that the cultural turn and Black Power brought to integrationist organizers. In splitting the SFCRP from the SSOC, Romaine and Reagon deprived the latter of its only successful interracial project. Nevertheless, the SFCRP remains significant, not least because it confirms the struggle to promote biracial understanding in the Black Power era, particularly when firebrands such as Kwame Ture were calling for African Americans to reclaim black history and culture from the pernicious effects of white dominance.[43] It represents a noble attempt to emphasize the biracial tradition of southern protest, establishes the continuing influence of Highlander's organizing style, and suggests that folk culture remained an important organizing tool. Ultimately, however, the SFCRP was paralyzed by the political whirlwind that surrounded it. The civil rights movement's focus on the North hindered the work of the SFCRP, leading it to be virtually ignored by the media and almost unable to call on the support of other groups with similar integrationist aims. That the SFCRP failed is not proof that cultural organizing was not viable; instead, it indicates that Romaine's idealism was out of step with the racially polarized spirit of the time.

Indeed, Highlander's involvement in Resurrection City suggests that cultural organizing retained value in the late 1960s, as demonstrated by the fact that many participants regarded the Highlander programs as one of the few successes of the PPC. Despite this, the SCLC remained ambivalent about cultural organizing, not least because its leadership remained fully convinced that their movement was to be firmly wedded to Christianity. Yet by 1967, the SCLC was aware that its constituency was growing older and that it was not attracting a new generation of African Americans who were more responsive to messages of black pride and racial solidarity. Hence it tried to woo black youths through its acknowledgment that black was beautiful and by its attempt to exploit the rising popularity of soul music. Martin Luther King Jr. was also coming to the conclusion that the movement was becoming increasingly black in outlook and constituency. Indeed, during the planning of the PPC, King talked of the value of African American culture to the freedom struggle. Echoing the message of Negro History Week and the 1964 Summer Project, King acknowledged the need to celebrate African American cultural achievements.[44]

The inclusiveness of integration was seen by many Black Power activists as a weak answer to the race problem that did nothing to address the issue of identity within the black community. Where Anne Romaine insisted that biracial culture could unify the South, the SFCRP's experience suggests that such an appeal was doomed to failure. When the SCLC finally came to terms with the power of culture, it relied on a simple "black is beautiful" message.

This did little to endear the SCLC to Black Power activists, not least because it was not matched by the creation of a new generation of SCLC leaders. Those in the "old guard" were strongly identified with the gradualism and integrationism of the early 1960s movement, and their insistence that revolution was not necessary did little to convince younger activists that they were changing. Although numerous movement activists and sympathizers retained the hope that integration was possible, the SFCRP and the SCLC's experience during this period suggests that the cultural politics of the Black Power period rendered such a goal largely illusory. Ultimately, almost all the avenues for the integrationist movement had been exhausted. The cultural thrust was too alienating for whites and moderates, and the multiracial army of the poor did not appeal to militant blacks.

6

Black Cultural Nationalism, 1965–1969

Although Black Power did not completely overrun moderate elements within the movement, its radicalism influenced the major civil rights organizations and informed the rise of a new generation of activists and agitators. Cultural nationalism was arguably dominant within Black Power philosophy. Most Black Power activists implicitly or explicitly acknowledged that the black diaspora was in part defined by culture. Indeed, the promotion of black cultural forms as political weapons was a salient feature of the Black Power period. Even the notorious dispute between the Black Panther Party (BPP) and US was defined in part by rival theories concerning the role of black culture in the struggle.

After the successes of 1964, Amiri Baraka's work, including his jazz criticism, increasingly deferred to his nationalist interpretation of black history. He also attempted to bring black theater to the black community, his first major attempt to become involved in community activism. His so-called revolutionary plays tend toward a simplistic, even Manichaean, interpretation of the black struggle influenced in part by his interest in the Nation of Islam and black nationalist politics.[1] Yet *Slave Ship*, the finest of these plays, transcends these influences to offer a forceful exegesis of black history. Perhaps as important, the play powerfully confirms Baraka's insistence that free jazz was the true music of black liberation.

Slave Ship's union of black suffering, resistance, and struggle proved attractive to the Free Southern Theater (FST), which had been searching for a play that truly reflected the politics of its members since its inception. In a number of respects, the FST's experience of the Black Power years is emblematic of the integrationist response to the challenge of Black Power. The 1964 Summer Project had convinced the group that the black community needed theater as a forum for both cultural and political expression. Following its formal break from movement activities and the commensurate loss of publicity, the FST found its audiences dwindling and concluded that community activism was the only viable means through which it would survive. Some FST members turned to black nationalism and led the FST toward a new conception of the role of African American culture in the freedom struggle. This development also had an impact on the FST's audience and the group's relationship to its predominantly white funding sources. Successful in establishing an organizational base in New Orleans, the FST failed to make an impact on the national stage and isolated itself from the Black Arts Movement. While this isolation starved the FST of national publicity, it enabled the group to maintain its own identity and allowed it to ride out the Black Power storm. Although the FST's philosophy was defined in part by Malcolm X's conception of black nationalism, its reading of Malcolm X was filtered through its experience of the South. *Slave Ship* was the culmination of its quest to unite art and politics in a meaningful and inspiring way.

The West Coast rivalry between the BPP and Maulana Ron Karenga's US organization was the most notorious feud of the Black Power era. This dispute has become caricatured as gun-toting Marxist revolutionary nationalists facing off against gun-toting African cultural nationalists. In fact, the BPP was closer in spirit to the cultural nationalists than even its own members appreciated. The difference between US and the BPP largely surrounded the political use that could be made of black culture and the relative merits of an exceptional African American culture versus an all-encompassing African culture. Both organizations emerged from the cultural nationalist Afro-American Association. Moreover, thanks to its artist-in-residence, Emory Douglas, the BPP engaged wholeheartedly in a form of artistic propaganda that was not far removed from the radio broadcasts of Robert F. Williams or the theater of Baraka and that was underpinned by a strikingly similar artistic philosophy to that of Karenga. The BPP's appreciation of African American culture both prior to and following the eruption of the feud in 1969 was an important facet of its critique of American society and reveals that the philosophies of the two groups—and the impulses behind these philosophies—were by no means mutually exclusive.

Amiri Baraka, Black Culture, and Black Liberation

The assassination of Malcolm X convinced Baraka that black unity was fundamental to the survival of the black nation. Malcolm X's understanding of the importance of black consciousness to the liberation struggle was, furthermore, confirmation that black culture should be wedded to the political struggle. "The Black artist," Baraka argued, "is desperately needed to change the images his people identify with, by asserting Black feeling, Black mind, Black judgment." From this culture, a politics that offered a new social order could emerge. For Baraka, the black artist was a Fanonist activist, devoted to the destruction of white America by any means necessary. Frustrated at his own lack of involvement in the movement and piqued by white criticism of his politics, within days of Malcolm X's death he relocated to Harlem, cutting his ties with the interracial bohemia of Greenwich Village.[2]

Late in 1964, Baraka wrote that revolutionary theater should "force change; it should be change." The Black Arts Repertory Theater/School (BARTS) represented Baraka's first organizational attempt to force this change. The concept for BARTS was relatively simple: by uniting radical politics with avant-garde art, the organization was to become the vanguard of the impending black revolution. In his position as director of the operation, Baraka called on African Americans to reject white cultural and intellectual norms and unite around their blackness. During its twelve-month life, BARTS employed nearly 200 people and inspired many artists who later became involved in the Black Arts Movement. Alongside amateur and professional theatrical productions, BARTS organized outdoor art exhibitions, jazz concerts, poetry readings, and classes in playwriting, music, art, and black history that educated some 400 students. Among teachers from both the public and private sectors, Harold Cruse taught black history to classes that occasionally included Federal Bureau of Investigation (FBI) agents. Musicians such as Archie Shepp performed in playgrounds and parks. Sun Ra both performed and taught cultural philosophy at BARTS. One BARTS benefit concert featuring Shepp, Albert Ayler, John Coltrane, and Bobby Hutcherson was recorded and released commercially on the Impulse jazz label. Baraka even headed a march through Harlem that featured Sun Ra's Arkestra as part of the program to bring art into the public arena.[3]

Despite its high profile, BARTS suffered from financial problems. Initially funded by the profits from the productions of Baraka's plays and a large Harlem Youth Opportunities Unlimited (HARYOU) grant, BARTS was never able to generate enough autonomous funds to maintain its programs. The benefit concert and album could not cover BARTS's operating expenses. Baraka sincerely believed that he was subverting HARYOU through his insistence that the black community could develop a revolutionary ideology through its own art and culture. Yet BARTS's need for federal funds suggests that Baraka's nationalism was somewhat compromised and reveals the extent to which black cultural nationalism was unable to develop true autonomy from white America. Baraka's initial optimism for BARTS also did not last. Increasing factionalism and the demagogy of certain members propelled Baraka out of Harlem, leaving BARTS to flounder in his wake.[4]

In August 1966, inspired by his return to Newark, New Jersey, Baraka organized the Afro-American Festival of the Arts, hoping to stimulate local black pride and self-awareness. Kwame Ture, Harold Cruse, Ossie Davis, and other speakers shared stage space with poets such as Larry Neal and jazz performers including Coltrane and Sun Ra. Art exhibitions, drama, and dance performances also featured in the program. The festival again illustrates Baraka's keenness to unite art and politics and so reenergized him that he soon established the Newark Spirit House, which became one of the most significant institutions of the Black Arts Movement. Baraka wanted the Spirit House to "present whatever the community wants," performing plays (occasionally with musical accompaniment from Sun Ra's Arkestra), offering lectures, and putting on children's activities.[5] During a brief sojourn as a visiting professor at San Francisco State University, Baraka also became involved in the Black Arts West organization, helping to develop a repertory group that performed in Bay Area schools and community halls. Part of the Spirit House program included education in black consciousness, which involved "cultural-political-socio-economic classes" and instruction in black history, philosophy, and heritage through drama, poetry, art, and dance. Street theater involved the community, and newsletters were widely distributed.[6]

The Spirit House instituted educational programs, focusing on black pride and spreading African values, in an attempt to separate Newark blacks from the pernicious effects of double consciousness. Black history, literature, and languages formed the core curriculum, with reading, writing, and arithmetic instruction taking a secondary role. This eschewed traditional (white) educational principles in favor of inculcating racial consciousness before encouraging political and cultural activism. The Spirit House educational programs represent a black nationalist overhaul of SNCC's 1964 Summer Project curriculum. Where the Summer Project stressed the need to integrate into mainstream American democratic practice, the Spirit House elevated issues related to black consciousness. In this, the Spirit House suggested that mainstream education was failing young black Americans not by neglecting to offer them enough formal education but by denying them their racial consciousness. Control of the education process and rejection of white educational goals were fundamental to the cultural revolution that the

Spirit House workers believed was under way. Yet the Spirit House education program did not refuse to acknowledge the importance of the political
process to the black community. It might have emphasized African American spirituality, but it also encouraged voter registration. In one crucial respect, however, it reinforced normative discriminatory practice. Its gender
politics reflects those of both the 1964 Summer Project and wider trends in
American society: teaching roles were considered to be beneath men. More
troublingly, Spirit House women were expected to be subservient to their
male colleagues, a factor that severely circumscribed the Spirit House's commitment to a revolution in values.[7]

Following the example of BARTS, the Spirit House enticed the community with cultural programming before propelling it toward political
action. Its success encouraged Baraka to plan another arts convention in
1967. During the planning for this event, he met Maulana Ron Karenga and
became seduced by the cultist aura that surrounded the US leader, not least
because Karenga believed that black culture was central to the revolution.
Under Karenga's influence, Baraka concluded that blacks were instinctive
beings who had been tricked by whites into reasoning, thus making them
"the most schizophrenic people on this planet." Baraka declared that "the
socio-political must be wedded to the cultural." Politics went hand in hand
with culture.[8]

By the late 1960s, Baraka was becoming increasingly concerned about the
elitist turn of certain free jazz musicians and started to argue that jazz was
losing sight of itself as it moved farther from the blues. In the early 1960s,
Baraka thought that the free jazz players were conveying some sort of elemental truth about the black condition through their rejection of Western
form and structure. The 1968 publication of *Black Music*, a collection of
reviews, opinion pieces, and essays on jazz dating back to 1961, hinted that
Baraka's criticism was increasingly subservient to his political views. Its final
essay, "The Changing Same (R&B and New Black Music)," declared that
saxophonist Pharoah Sanders incanting "OMMMMMMMMMMMMMM-
MMMMMMMMMMMMMMMMMM" was a more radical political state-
ment than direct action protests against segregation. More controversially,
Baraka stated that "the more intelligent the white, the more realization he
has to steal from niggers."[9]

In 1967, Baraka argued that the jazz musicians of the 1960s were able to
articulate a black sensibility through their music better than singers and
musicians were through the less expansive artistic palette of soul. Yet he
believed that soul music's social consciousness would develop and inten-

sify over the coming years as a consequence of the liberation struggle. By the end of the decade, he was arguing that soul was more relevant to and in tune with the black masses. Tired of the increasingly challenging compositions of free jazz players, Baraka began arguing that the music had to come from the spirit of the people as a whole, rather than the select few. It had to be functional rather than contain "meaningless abstractions." James Brown's simplistic "Say It Loud—I'm Black and I'm Proud" was therefore a perfect example of soul music at its finest. Based around a simple guitar riff and a syncopated drumbeat, the song is chiefly notable for a chorus in which Brown orders his listeners and backing vocalists to "Say it loud!" The famous retort became a favorite among black radicals and instantly lost Brown much of his white audience. That Brown's position on Black Power was dominated by his faith in black capitalism was of less interest to Baraka than the racial politics the song espoused; that the backing vocalists were a motley crew of white and Asian American children was far less important than the song's popularity with a young, urban, working-class black audience.[10]

Baraka desired to abandon any vestiges of his middle-class background (including his prior association with Beat Generation writers) in favor of developing a working-class black identity. His increasing identification with the black working class rendered his earlier position on music untenable. Perhaps foreshadowing his adoption of Marxism, Baraka's ideas concerning cultural production were becoming more class oriented. As free jazz grew more experimental, it increasingly became the preserve of middle-class audiences. The musicians' fondness for experimentation led the music farther away from a mainstream black audience.[11] In *Blues People* and "Jazz and the White Critic," Baraka identified the exact moment when black music ceased to be inspirational and pioneering: it was the point at which white middle-class jazz hobbyists started to appreciate it. With the increased visibility of this previously underground phenomenon and its steadily increasing appeal to white middle-class listeners, Baraka felt compelled to seek out music that was inspiring the same sort of people who first responded positively to bebop: young, urban, working-class blacks who liked to dance. They were listening to soul, and so Baraka concluded that soul was the true voice of black America. The jazzmen, Baraka perceived, were alienating themselves from the masses by demanding that their audiences follow them.

By 1969, Baraka was praising Curtis Mayfield's "We're a Winner" as a more revolutionary statement than most jazz music. Soon after, he was dismissing saxophonists Ornette Coleman and Albert Ayler as "bullshit" for their self-consciousness and failure to follow a black nationalist line. Mayfield's audience—younger, hipper, blacker, potentially more radical, and certainly larger than Coleman's or Ayler's—represented the constituency that Baraka hoped to win over to black nationalism, and so he simply realigned his musical sensibilities to reconnect with the masses. In praising Mayfield, Baraka ignored the fact that Coleman's and Ayler's politics were more in tune with his than the avowedly integrationist Mayfield. Even a cursory glance at Mayfield's lyrics reveals his abiding faith in integrationism: "People Get Ready" references the March on Washington, and 1970's "Mighty Mighty (Spade and Whitey)" declares that Mayfield was black and proud but reminds listeners that "there really ain't no difference/if you're cut you're gonna bleed." That the cultural nationalist organization, US was concurrently attempting to attract a number of jazz players to its cause adds to the irony of Baraka's decision.[12]

Baraka's plays in this period also point to his increasing fascination with cultural nationalism. After abandoning allegory, Baraka argued that truly black theater dealt with the lives of black people and committed its audience to involvement in the freedom struggle. "Black Theatre," he stated, "has to be making a dynamic statement and be of itself an act of liberation." He pared his work down to its base elements, stripping his plays of extraneous detail and making characterization subordinate to the political message behind the work. Short poems and single-act plays were a more populist art form than longer formats and were not laden with so much high cultural baggage that supposedly "ordinary" folk avoided them. Furthermore, Baraka had witnessed how successful an amalgam of popular and high culture could be at the July 26 Celebration in Cuba. In rendering theater more accessible to the black population, Baraka was able to break down cultural barriers and to legitimize an African American theatrical tradition. Through these forms, Baraka did not necessarily want to popularize "high" culture but to erase the boundaries that traditionally associated theater with a European (or Arnoldian) cultural model and that suggested that no similar traditions existed for non-Europeans.[13]

Experimental Death Unit #1 (1964), the first of the revolutionary plays, features two Beckettesque white male characters, one of whom is addicted to drugs and the other to sex, and an aging female prostitute who seduces them. An argument develops between the two men, leading one to kill the other. At the play's conclusion, a black revolutionary army discovers the scene and shoots the remaining characters. *A Black Mass* (1965) is Baraka's interpretation of the Nation of Islam's Yacub myth, set to a cacophonic Sun

Ra soundtrack. In the Nation's mythology, a powerful scientist named Yacub brought about a holocaust after creating a white race to conquer the world. Baraka's Jacoub, an iconoclastic and sinister black magician, creates a soulless and evil white man named The Beast who kills Jacoub's fellow magicians. The Beast transforms all he touches into his own image, reducing the other black characters to mindless, gibbering fools. At the play's conclusion, The Beast enters the audience to continue his depravity. *Jello*, a 1965 satire, converts Jack Benny's assistant Eddie "Rochester" Anderson into a revolutionary who robs Benny and his friends before absconding. Baraka's publishers, fearing libel actions from Benny's representatives, refused to publish the play.[14]

Great Goodness of Life: A Coon Show concerns the framing of a black postal worker for harboring a murderer. The worker, Court Royal, is forced to defend himself in front of a kangaroo court led by a disembodied white judge. Royal's attorney, who is under the control of the court, advises Royal to plead guilty. At one point, the murder victim is identified as the Prince, in a clear reference to Malcolm X. After being convinced of his own guilt, Royal is given an opportunity to redeem himself. To do so, he is ordered to kill the murderer, who is his own son, and who might be interpreted as a metaphor for the African American spirit. After killing his son, Royal declares that his soul is "as white as snow" and returns to his middle-class life. In *Madheart*, the only white character is Devil Lady, whom Black Man kills in order to free himself. Now free, Black Man is empowered to reassert his natural dominance over black women, who, in awe of his masculinity, submit to him.[15]

Although Baraka never joined the Nation of Islam, the influence of the racial essentialism that pervaded Black Muslim thought is apparent throughout his black revolutionary plays. Baraka's white characters are either mendacious and savage or guileless and foolish. The degeneracy of these characters and the simplicity with which they are drawn are major uniting features. The black characters who consort with these whites become infected by this degeneracy. Only those who kill whites, namely the army in *Death Unit* and Black Man in *Madheart*, survive and flourish. Both Court Royal and his attorney have become alienated from their race (a point hammered home during the trial when Royal fails to identify a succession of images of black leaders, including Malcolm X, Patrice Lumumba, and Medgar Evers). Having let themselves be exploited by the white power structure, Royal and the attorney, blind to the realities of American race relations, betray their own race in order to preserve their careers. The explicit reference to the civil rights movement in *Great Goodness* suggests a degree of ambivalence about integrationists. Although Baraka acknowledges Evers and other murdered activists, only Malcolm X assumes physical form. Other aspects of Baraka's didactic politics emerge in the black revolutionary plays. His anti-intellectual streak reveals itself in Jacoub's misguided immersion in scientific knowledge, Court Royal's erroneous trust in his lawyer, and the lawyer's compromised position as a middle-class black man. The Manichaean relationship between the races in the plays indicates that Baraka's move toward racial essentialism, which was explored in his 1964 plays, was largely complete.

Baraka believed that black culture was vital to black liberation, and in all his plays the virtuous black characters are in tune with their natural rhythms and other black people. Moreover, this black culture and life were not only to reflect each other, they were to be one and the same. Thus Jacoub's assumption that creation is an end in itself produces only evil. One key issue at the heart of these plays is the status of black Americans as victims. Rejection of this status was a central element of Black Power, as was the rejection of white cultural hegemony. Moreover, this rejection of victim status relates directly to Baraka's insistence that the black male reject the supposed matrifocal tendencies of the black community. Baraka considered such a focus to be a result of white America's dominance over the black male. Slavery, segregation, and white racism had not only subjugated the African American community, it had stripped the black male of his previously exalted position in black society. Baraka looked back to premodern African gender relations, expressing his disappointment and disgust that black men had effectively ceded their position at the head of the black community to their women. Baraka extended Malcolm X's insistence that men protect while women nurture to an aggressively masculine black nationalism. Only by reasserting male dominance within the African American community could the black male return to his position at the head of his own community.[16]

Slave Ship, an impressionistic, episodic play about the Middle Passage, initially received little attention but has since become appreciated as one of Baraka's greatest accomplishments in theater. It towers above his other black revolutionary plays.[17] Where his other 1960s plays refer (occasionally obliquely) to the civil rights movement, *Slave Ship* comments directly on its shortcomings, and where they offer snapshots of the black freedom struggle, it encompasses the entirety of African American history. Its relationship to

Baraka's other plays is akin to the relationship between *Blues People* and his early 1960s jazz criticism: the culmination of his thought on the subject and the most complete expression of his artistry.

Eschewing a formal plot, Baraka constructed the play as a tableau of black suffering, resistance, and liberation. The play opens in darkness, and gradually the sounds and smells of a slave ship headed for the Americas emerge. The largely wordless action focuses on the lower decks, with drums pounding out a rhythm punctuated by women's and children's screams, whips lashing against flesh, and chains being dragged along the floor. Amid the cacophony one woman strangles herself and her child to death with her chains, and men start fighting among themselves. The transition between scenes 1 and 2 juxtaposes heroic African warriors dancing to the rhythm of the drums with an obsequious, "raggedy ass" slave obeying his master. The passage of time has transformed the warriors into slaves and the white sailors into plantation owners. A slave offers a shuffling dance for the whites as banjos gradually replace the drums. The scene shifts to the same slave discussing a planned revolt with Nat Turner. In return for a pork chop, the slave informs his owner of the plot, enabling the whites to gather together an army strong enough to defeat the uprising. The audience only hears the battle. After its conclusion, some slaves, whose voices were heard in the first scene, plead to African gods for salvation. Gradually the sound of the spiritual "Oh Lord, Deliver Me" emerges from the background, and the slaves start appealing to Jesus, signaling the start of a second transition scene. Here, a preacher in a modern business suit echoes the chants of "Jesus." He is revealed as the race traitor from the second scene. He speaks in "pseudo-intelligent patter," and his body is contorted by his attempt to appear dignified. His speech is a grotesque parody: "We will be nonviolenk . . . to the last . . . because we understand the dignity of Pruty McBonk and the Greasy Ghost. . . . I have a trauma that the gold sewers won't integrate. Present fink. I have an enema . . . a trauma, on the coaster with your wife bird shit."[18] In the background, a woman screams for the return of her child, embarrassing the preacher. The preacher's discomfort is compounded when the burned and bloody corpse of a child is placed at his feet. Continuing to "Tom," and talking of integration, the preacher attempts to push the body aside with his foot.[19] His speech is interrupted by the squeal of a saxophone, which starts playing free jazz, accompanied by a band that includes the African drums from the first scene. A black voice shouts, "Beasts! Beasts! Beasts! . . . Give me the spear and iron. Let me kill." Other voices chant "ommmmm," as the lights dim. The music prompts the bodies of those killed on the slave ship and in the Turner revolt to rise up. The cast begins to sing to music played by the jazz sextet:

Rise, Rise, Rise
Cut these ties, Black Man Rise . . .
When we gonna rise up brother
When we gonna rise above the sun
When we gonna take our own place, brother
Like the world had just begun?[20]

Mixing modern and traditional African dances, the cast advances toward the preacher, who reveals his true colors: "Please, boss, these niggers goin' crazy; please, box, throw yo' lightnin' at 'em, white Jesus boss, white light god, they goin crazy! Help!" A disembodied voice chuckles and denounces him as a fool before the masses surround and kill him. The cast then turns toward the source of the voice, which suddenly loses its tone of authority: "You cain't kill white Jesus God. . . . You love the way I look. You want to look like me. You love me. You want me. Please. . . . I'll give you anything you want." The lights dim as the sound of struggle returns, which is broken only by the death scream of the voice. At this point, the cast turns toward the audience and, as the jazz music returns, begins to dance the "Booga-looyoruba," a hybrid traditional African and modern youth dance. Black audience members are invited to join the dance. Once the audience is comfortable with the dancing, the preacher's severed head is thrown onto the dance floor to conclude the play.[21]

The play's critique of integrationism and King in particular reflects the frustration with the civil rights movement in numerous urban black communities. The King figure's gibberish suggests that the real King only spoke to white people. Those who attended the play—presumably, in Baraka's mind, African Americans who rejected integration, the people to whom Baraka addressed his work—could not understand King's rhetoric. The preacher's "Jesus" incantation suggests that the real King could offer only Christianity; in contrast to Walker Vessels, he has no plan of action. That this religion mutes the African revolutionary spirit in the play constitutes a further denunciation of the close relationship between the movement and Christianity. The symbolism of the dead child—designed to prompt thoughts of the 1963 bombing of the Birmingham, Alabama, Sixteenth Street Baptist Church—is the final nail in King's coffin. The King figure's fate during the final dance in the play almost strikes an ironic chord. Baraka's intention was to provoke his audience further and to remind them that they had to kill false idols if they were to become truly revolutionary. The severed head returns to the dance floor to prompt the audience to focus their energy on challenging their leaders, reminding them that the fervor of the dance could be translated into political action. The play, however, first attracted attention after King's assassination. In this context, the act of throwing the preacher's head onto the dance floor jolts the audience further, as if to remind them that they should not let the dance distract them from the political reality they face as blacks living in white America. It leads the audience to question the act of dancing when King is dead: should they be celebrating his death or using it as a spur to further political action?

In *Slave Ship*, Baraka wrestles the ritual element of the civil rights movement from the integrationists. In an echo of his grand BARTS parades, Baraka replaces the set-piece marches of the integrationists with black nationalist dances and pageantry steeped in an exclusive African American history rather than in racial hybridity. In *Slave Ship*, free jazz rather than freedom songs provides the soundtrack for black liberation. Extending the thesis of much of his jazz writing, *Slave Ship* suggests that music is fundamental to African American life. The racialized aspect of his later work adds a separatist tone to *Slave Ship*'s use of jazz. In "The Changing Same," Baraka argued that the slave ship "destroyed a great many formal art traditions of the Black man." The polyrhythmic drumming throughout *Slave Ship* is Baraka's indication that the whites failed to destroy the most important tradition of all. Baraka's disavowing of any white influence on the new wave of jazz suggested that this was a black music for a black movement. Through music, he suggests, the spirit of Africa has been preserved among the African American people, in spite of the attempt to replace this musical tradition with white cultural practices, as suggested by the banjo picking and the Christian hymns in the plantation scene. The return of jazz at the conclusion represents the final rejection of these white influences for a music steeped in the African American experience. The lyrics of the song urge the cutting of ties with white America, while the instrumentation suggests a reconnection with black African traditions. This music provides a direct link between individual and group freedom in the African past and a future freedom in the United States.[22]

Even the play's script possesses numerous similarities to free jazz, in line with Baraka's insistence that the music played a key role in black liberation. Echoing Baraka's interpretation of the essence of jazz, *Slave Ship* privileges the emotional feeling of the play over fidelity to the text. The spare script is similar in style to the scoring indications of numerous jazz composers. John

Coltrane, for example, regularly offered guidelines rather than scores to his band members, trusting in their ability to respond to the feel of the music. Coltrane was not alone in allowing soloists room to interpret the music according to their own ears; improvisation is central to jazz.[23] Key moments in the text are used to propel the play toward the conclusion of each scene, in a similar fashion to the use of certain riffs and melodies to signal particular changes by free jazz musicians. One might even suggest that the frequent shrieking by the women on the ship and through the rest of the play was designed to recall the screaming and wailing tones of saxophonists like Coltrane, Ayler, and Shepp.

The centrality of music to African American culture and history is reinforced by the "Boogalooyoruba." This dance acts as a metaphor for the culture of black America, one that reflected an African ancestry combined with the African American present. Baraka's insistence that only black members of the audience be invited to dance is further confirmation of his dismissal of the white contribution to the freedom movement and another assertion of the singularity of the African American experience. Of course, this racialized action comes close to suggesting that all black people possess natural rhythm, but it is clear that, in Baraka's mind, the act of excluding whites contains the more significant message.

Slave Ship has a visceral energy that is absent from Baraka's other late 1960s plays. It taps into the shared historical memory of slavery and the civil rights movement, and includes a cathartic ending designed to facilitate the release of the audience's pent-up energy. It thoroughly deconstructs the actor-audience boundary, encouraging the physical liberation of the audience's rage at white America that has been built up by the play's performance. Crucially, it rejects the victim status of African Americans that had informed many of Baraka's previous plays. Whereas Clay's victimhood concluded *Dutchman*, and the ambiguous conclusion of *The Slave* suggested that Walker Vessels remained enslaved, *Slave Ship*'s slain characters achieve a life after death. By rising from their graves to take part in the revolutionary pageant, they receive affirmation of their role in the freedom struggle, and Baraka restates the central position of black history in the African American psyche. The disembodied voice of white power, which controls Court Royal in *Great Goodness of Life*, ultimately loses its omnipotence, unable to suppress the revolutionary fervor of black Americans finally reconciled with their history. The play is undoubtedly nationalist in its insistence that common bonds of culture and experience unite the black diaspora, in its condemnation of Uncle Toms, and in its unflattering portrayal of whites, from their capturing of free black Africans through enslavement and into hegemonic control. Yet unlike *The Slave*, it is not consumed by its disgust with white Americans. Instead, it suggests that black Americans could turn in on themselves and learn to celebrate their proud heritage of resistance. This black nationalist historical consciousness would enable a psychological freedom that would eventually lead toward complete freedom from white Americans. Indeed, the play's conclusion offers a more complex interpretation of freedom than does Baraka's previous work. The attack on the white voice could simply be interpreted as the final slaying of white America, but it more accurately represents a psychological assassination of the white element in the black mind. The revolution was not necessarily in the streets but could be played out in the mind, where its effects might be more liberating. That this complete freedom is primarily one of the mind and not of the body—and that it has not yet been achieved—is accentuated by two crucial aspects of the play. The emancipation of the slaves is ignored in the play's historical narrative. To have included it would have accepted that black Americans had to rely on whites for their own freedom. This suggestion is deepened by the play's setting, which never leaves the slave ship. The audience is reminded of their continued enslavement and that the only viable response is to free the mind. The body will surely follow.

The Free Southern Theater and Black Nationalism

During 1969, the FST toured an intense production of *Slave Ship*, scored by Gil Moses and Archie Shepp. Using the entire theater as a stage and taking advantage of the considerable room for interpretation in the script, the FST encouraged individual and group improvisation. The fervent reactions of southern audiences to *Slave Ship* suggest that the FST, helped by Baraka's liberating final scene, had to an extent overcome its distrust of its audiences.[24]

Since its inception, the FST had searched for a play that truly embraced black history and the experience of black southerners while also reflecting the improvisational tradition. After ending its formal relationship with SNCC, it settled in New Orleans to continue this quest. Experiments with whiteface performance failed to engage audiences in Beckett's *Waiting for Godot*. The reversal of racial norms confused many southern audiences and led to a period of self-doubt within the group.[25] An ambitious fall 1965 tour hoped to reach a succession of integrated audiences in six southern states. The repertoire was designed to suggest that "sometimes bloody struggle [was needed] to organize grievances for effective political change and action," and included *In White America*, Bertolt Brecht's *The Rifles of Senora Carrar*, and Sean O'Casey's *The Shadow of a Gunman*. It is clear from the selection of these plays that the FST was developing an ambivalent attitude toward nonviolence, which was a direct result of the company's experience of Mississippi in 1964. *In White America* had been a great success; a repeat performance made perfect sense, since it was effectively the FST's signature piece. *Senora Carrar* explores the eponymous heroine's dilemma, whose husband has been killed fighting Francoists during the 1934 Asturian uprising that anticipated the Spanish Civil War. Determined to prevent her sons from suffering a similar fate, she confronts her brother, who wants to use her rifles to continue the fight against fascism. Events compel Carrar to realize that even inaction involves taking a stand. O'Casey's tragicomedy is similarly concerned with the actions of individuals caught up in historical forces beyond their control. Set during 1920, the play features a poet and various other characters in a Dublin slum trying to live as though Ireland were not occupied by the British. "They all talk about bravery and freedom," noted the FST, "but only one of them . . . does anything about it."[26]

The plays indicate that the FST was already reconceptualizing the civil rights movement and its own relationship with its southern black audience. While O'Casey's play could conceivably have been performed for audiences in 1964, it is unlikely that the FST actors at that time would have considered *Senora Carrar* suitable. Initially, the FST was firmly convinced of the value of nonviolence to the southern black community, but its Mississippi experience led it to question the assumptions of nonviolence. The choice of *Senora Carrar* indicates that the FST, like SNCC, had come to appreciate the role of guns in the social network of the South, and that the FST was moving toward an acceptance that the threat of retaliatory violence from blacks helped to maintain the peace. Indeed, the FST benefited from this itself—the heavily armored Deacons for Defense protected them during their visit to Louisiana in 1965. Furthermore, the existence of Brecht's play in the repertoire helps to contextualize why FST later accepted Malcolm X's philosophy of self-defense.[27]

The FST's 1965 tour foreshadows the conclusions that many black nationalists arrived at later in the decade. That the tour collapsed due to a lack of funds after the FST visited only five locations, most of which were in poor black neighborhoods, furthermore anticipates the struggle of many Black Power organizations to develop autonomous funding networks within the black community. Due to the choice of locations and the FST's association with the movement, white audience numbers were conspicuously low. The FST's refusal to charge admission fees, a vestige of its commitment to destroying class boundaries, compounded the financial mess. The tour's failure led to a period of intense debate within the FST as to the organization's future. The company realized that it could not contend with the South's social structure: its integrated company could not perform in the white community, and performances in the black community (to which it consciously addressed its work) could not attract whites, who were major sources of financial assistance. For FST actress, Denise Nicholas, who had been with the company since 1964, this failure derived just as much from the FST's growing belief that its improvisational work was more exciting in both theatrical and political terms: the relatively static performances of scripted material, most of which was written by whites, did not appeal to the FST's black audiences or, indeed, to the company.[28]

The tour helped to precipitate the FST's final divorce from integrationism and accelerated its move toward black nationalism. In November, Gil Moses proposed that the group demonstrate its blackness by producing an adaptation of *Dutchman*. Stung by the FST's reliance on white donors, he suggested that the company redirect its fund-raising efforts to the black middle class. Tom Dent, whose association with black nationalist politics went back to his membership of the Umbra Poets Workshop, also urged the FST to develop a repertoire of plays by black playwrights. Somewhat unsurprisingly, *The Autobiography of Malcolm X* became required reading for every FST member. Soon after, discussion moved from whether the FST should expel its whites to the implementation of their expulsion, although the process took eighteen months to complete.[29]

Malcolm X's work resonated with the FST's continuing search for "blackness" in theater. Just as Baraka found that Malcolm X's words gave expression to the feelings inside his own head, the FST identified with and found solace and justification in Malcolm X's autobiography. Malcolm X spurred the FST to embrace a secular black working-class culture. His words encouraged the FST to become more skeptical of integration and even more focused on looking to non-European theatrical traditions for inspiration. This identification manifested itself both in the FST's racial identity and in a new faith in improvisation: like Baraka, the FST became convinced that truth revealed itself in the unrehearsed moment of action. Nicholas's and Dent's suspicions were confirmed by the rapturous receptions of Louisianan audiences to the improvisational pieces based on the history of the local movement during late 1965 and early 1966. While this reaction might have been due to the immediacy of the material and its direct relevance to the local experience of civil rights organizing, Dent concluded that audiences related more easily to improvisational performances. This, he said, was "a significant breakthrough toward cultural development of untouched, yet amazingly sophisticated and responsive audiences."[30]

The FST was always desirous of a symbiotic relationship with its audience. It desperately wanted its audience to relate to the theater, and often tried to replicate the lived experience of southern blacks onstage. This lived experience incorporated an ambivalence toward integration that increasingly became a motif of the FST's work. While Malcolm X's autobiography crystalized the suspicion that integration was doomed, the choice of plays for the 1965 tour suggests that the disillusionment began before the autobiography was published. One of the underlying messages of *Senora Carrar* was that inaction in the face of a changing situation was tantamount to treason. From a civil rights standpoint, it might be suggested that Carrar's adherence to nonviolence was congruent with Martin Luther King Jr.'s position. More troubling was the suggestion that, in her refusal to accept the necessity of sending her guns to the front, Carrar was effectively aiding fascism. One of the debates in Mississippi during 1964, where the FST received its most profound political education, concerned the issue of the commitment to nonviolence. In this context, the play suggested that working alongside those who advocated complete adherence to nonviolence—many of whom happened to be integrationists—was tantamount to supporting the segregationists, a position that was not far removed from Robert F. Williams's stance. The only chance of surviving was to accept the views of the more extreme elements of the resistance (such as Carrar's husband and brother), who accepted the necessity of violence and who, in the black community at least, rejected alliances with whites. Rather than defining the FST's drift toward black nationalism, Malcolm X's autobiography served to clarify the FST's thought at a time when some members suspected that the integrationist message of *In White America* had become outmoded. The FST concluded that to pursue an integrated audience was an impracticable task; rather, the organization's energies should be focused on developing black consciousness among its audiences and within its own ranks. The early 1966 experience in Louisiana suggested that southern black audiences responded to theater that directly reflected their own lived experience; metaphors and allegories were not as successful as "telling it like it *really* is." Coupled with its resurgent commitment to improvisation, it meant that the FST continued to move toward theater as an expression of an elemental black consciousness.[31]

The rise of black nationalism within the FST led to further internal tensions. Still reliant on white largesse, the company grew increasingly alienated from the black middle class. Despite the FST's all-black personnel, its inability to find a substantial audience, coupled with its increasingly fiery rhetoric, failed to attract black middle-class support. The resultant shortfall in the FST's funding left it in debt to white foundations, a paradoxical relationship that reflects the broader relationship between many black nationalists and money from whites. Although black nationalist rhetoric repelled many whites, the inability of black nationalist organizations to attract money from the black community, and particularly from the middle class, forced them to accept white support when it was offered. In 1966, foundation support had been half that of the FST's own fund-raising income, but the following years saw a steady decline in the FST's precarious financial state. By 1967, foundation grants dominated the FST's income. In 1968, the Rockefeller and Ford foundations alone contributed more than half of the FST's income. Both donated even larger amounts in 1969.[32] Although Dent had few qualms about lambasting the Rockefeller Foundation for its patronizing middle-class attitude and its use of the FST to keep the natives quiescent, he needed its money to prolong his quest to inculcate an oppositional consciousness in the black population.[33]

Following the collapse of the 1967 summer tour, the FST abandoned touring to concentrate on developing black nationalist theater in New Orleans. Its community theater project, led by John O'Neal, expanded to weekly acting, writing, dance, and technical workshops.[34] O'Neal envisaged the creation of a new documentary theater project that built layers of script and improvisation on preexisting facts and ideas, a method that owed a considerable debt to *In White America*. This would create a new repertory and become a forum for the FST's ideological development, making the FST a more democratic organization. O'Neal, further influenced by Malcolm X, asserted that all true African Americans descended from the field hands during slavery and that therefore the real African American experience was also a class experience. For him, the new theater that the FST was developing had to reflect this common, working-class oppositional heritage, which again referred tangentially to the betrayal of the modern black middle class. The workshop had two objectives: making political points and reflecting real life. As Tom Dent argued, "the blood of the experience our people know, in all its joy and hurt, must *flow* on the stage."[35]

The black nationalist impulse caused a shift of emphasis in the FST's view of art. Initially, the organization intended to spread culture to the masses in order to help black people actualize their dignity. Black Power pushed the FST toward the realization that African American culture was already the richest and most complex culture within the United States. The FST's task, then, was to affirm the value of this culture and help the masses to develop and adapt it to their own uses, thus reinforcing their own cultural autonomy. Although the FST was initially committed to integration, the group's primary focus was always the black community. Its attempts to promote integration, by integrating itself and by trying to attract an integrated audience, only revealed to the FST that this was an illusory goal. Its encounter with Malcolm X served to confirm this feeling. The FST feared that its work would become reduced to minstrelsy, and so set out to create its own repertory that rejected the influence of whites. For Dent, presenting white plays was effectively saying to the black community, "'What you have ain't shit. If you want to be "cultured" you got to dig *Godot*.'" "Well I say goodbye *Godot*," he continued, "we'll stick with Otis [Redding]. . . . And the hell with what the white critics say or expect." In accepting that the artist needed to break out of the double consciousness straitjacket, the FST firmly positioned itself within the Black Arts Movement's philosophical spectrum. Yet despite its pioneering role, the FST did not play a significant role in the Black Arts Movement itself. The FST's geographical distance from the northern urban centers ensured that interaction with such groups as the New LaFayette Theater and Baraka's Spirit House was minimal.[36]

Although the FST began to withdraw from the front line of the freedom movement, its actions between 1965 and 1969, particularly its focus on local activism and its increasing commitment to reflecting the lived experience of African Americans, served as a template for the many black nationalist theater groups that emerged during this period. Its members went on to influence a number of Black Arts Movement groups and individuals: Roscoe Orman joined the New LaFayette Theater in Harlem, Denise Nicholas joined the Greenwich Village–based Negro Ensemble Company, and Gil Moses collaborated with Melvin Van Peebles before directing the blaxploitation film *Willie Dynamite* (starring Orman) and working on the television adaptation of Alex Haley's *Roots*.[37] The FST's success was, however, tempered by its failure to develop an audience outside New Orleans. This was partially a consequence of the end of its formal relationship with SNCC. It was also influenced by the FST's failure to acknowledge the worth of Christianity to the black South, one of the crucial differences that separated the FST from the southern movement. Although it often performed in church halls, the FST remained steadfastly atheist and skeptical of the church's role in the development of black consciousness. A union with the church might have provided an alternative source of support when the FST ventured beyond New Orleans. Ultimately, the FST's reluctance to engage actively with black Christianity suggests that it did not quite come to terms with the complexities of the relationship between African American culture and politics in the South. Yet to argue that the FST should have paraded Christianity would be to ignore many other facts. Its core members were northern and not overtly religious. The early influence of existentialism initially kept the FST away from the church; its reading of Malcolm X's *Autobiography* removed it further. The FST began operating in the Desire housing project in New Orleans and became concerned with the economic realities of being black in the South. That New Orleans also reflected many Creole and other religious influences complicates the relationship between religion and activism in the area and in the FST, helping to explain why the group remained relatively small. Despite its lack of success on tour, this local focus enabled the FST to weather the Black Power storm, ensuring that the organization continued to function well into the 1970s.

Yet the FST failed to win the support of middle-class blacks in New Orleans. Such people might appear to be the natural constituency for a black theater group, but the FST's rejection of integration did not chime well with middle-class blacks; nor did its general aura of nonconformity. As Gil Moses and Tom Dent commented, the FST brazenly disregarded social convention in terms of dress, behavior, and interracial interaction. The very things that made the FST unique—its links with the movement, its irreverence, its perpetual search for new and exciting content and form, its rejection of theatrical tradition—perhaps made it unappealing to mainstream theatergoers. Had the FST been a more "traditional" theater company, it might have attracted greater audiences, but this would have been anathema to the FST actors. Nor did its choice of location help: the racial climate in New Orleans was very different from that of many other southern localities. As Moses and Dent later commented, the FST did not instantly develop a rapport with the local black community, not least because the FST's first home was in an area of New Orleans heavily populated by people who identified as Creole. While Creole identification did not necessarily preclude sympathy for Black Power, the overwhelmingly racial subtext of Black Power did not exactly reach out to all sections of the nonwhite community, particularly in New Orleans.[38]

Nevertheless, the triumphant performances of *Slave Ship* were a fitting end to the FST's work in the 1960s and constituted the culmination of the

FST's search for a black play that truly reflected the experiences of southern blacks and that embraced the improvisational tradition (a point that was underscored by Archie Shepp's score). They also represented the achievement of Tom Dent's desire for the blood of the African American experience to flow on the stage. *Slave Ship* finally allowed the company to be comfortable with both the message and the medium and with its own ability to reinterpret and reimagine scripted material.[39] Yet the significance of this production goes far deeper. As it rejects King's influence, *Slave Ship* explicitly places the civil rights movement within the longer tradition of African American resistance, one that rejected white involvement. That Baraka felt compelled to indict King as an Uncle Tom indicates that the playwright was worried about the repercussions of the integrationist movement for the development of African American consciousness: never before had a representation of King appeared in physical form in Baraka's plays. *Slave Ship*, then, links the radical cultural nationalism of Baraka with the integrationist movement that the FST had earlier embraced. The FST developed out of the nonviolent movement and became influenced by SNCC's commitment to local people and Highlander's antidogmatic pedagogy before embracing black nationalism. Baraka's trajectory went from a Beat-inspired disinterest in politics through Cuban-inspired activism and into militant black cultural nationalism. Both Baraka and the FST arrived at their positions via Malcolm X, and the play symbolizes the final convergence of their political beliefs. The play's use of music indicates the importance that Baraka and the FST placed on cultural forms as political weapons. Most significant, *Slave Ship* presents African American culture as a process through which black Americans could be reawakened to their heritage and tradition of struggle against opposition: it is a message very similar to that encoded within SNCC's 1964 Summer Project. The blood of the African American experience truly flowed on stage during these performances.

While its production of *Slave Ship* did not signify the FST's acceptance of Baraka's cultural nationalism, it does represent the convergence of two strands within late 1960s black nationalist thought. The FST reveals that the new black theater of the late 1960s owed a profound debt to the southern organizing of the civil rights movement. As Richard Schechner concluded, the FST "was never—and perhaps should never be—an 'independent' theater. It is tied to the Freedom Movement and to the fate of black people in America."[40] By contrast, Baraka developed his critique of the civil rights movement in relative isolation from movement activities. Baraka gave no indication that BARTS was influenced by the civil rights movement's organizing structures, and his political critique was more influenced by his interaction with black politics in New York City. Yet, like the FST, BARTS was to bring cultural programs to the masses. Both hoped to challenge the community's self-perception and push it toward political action through theater. Both certainly proved that black theater could be brought to the black community and confirmed that African Americans were not necessarily alienated from it; rather, that economics and location played lead roles in this relationship. That Baraka and the FST deliberately addressed their work to the freedom struggle in the United States suggests that the cultural aspect of Black Power emerged out of the civil rights movement just as much as it emerged as a critique of the very same movement.

The Black Panther Party and US

An almost monolithic interpretation of the feud between the BPP and US has emerged in the thirty years since its bloody nadir on 17 January 1969, when two Black Panthers were murdered on the University of California–Los Angeles (UCLA) campus in broad daylight, an event that apparently served to complete the BPP's alienation from West Coast cultural nationalist organizations. The feud established a historiographical orthodoxy that asserts that the BPP rejected cultural nationalism in favor of revolutionary political activism, which some allege resulted in the BPP's ultimate alienation from the black community, one that places the BPP within a restrictive political framework. This reduces the complex relationship between the BPP and US to a caricature of gun-toting political revolutionaries facing off against dashiki-clad African cultural nationalists and devotes little attention to the cultural element of the BPP's philosophy and praxis.[41]

A full examination of the relationship between the BPP, US, and African American politics and culture reveals that the two organizations were by no means mutually exclusive. The BPP was closer to African American cultural nationalism than it cared to acknowledge. Its appreciation of the relationship between culture and politics was an important facet of its critique of American society, and the party placed considerable importance on the role that African American cultural expressions could play as a weapon in the liberation struggle. It had a minister for culture, who defined much of the BPP's cultural action during the late 1960s and early 1970s and who held an artistic philosophy similar to that of Karenga. It formed its own singing group, which was intended to unite political sloganeering with soul music in a fashion similar to US's dance troupe. The founders of the two organizations had also previously been members of the same Californian cultural nationalist organization. These common bonds should not be underestimated.

By the mid-1960s, an explicitly cultural interpretation of black nationalism was growing on the West Coast. A black student union at the University of California–Berkeley, founded by Howard University graduate Donald Warden, was attracting interest in the local black community. Initially a reading group, it gradually moved beyond the campus boundaries, and after evolving into the Afro-American Association (AAA), developed a large membership in the Bay Area black community. AAA members founded a quarterly journal entitled *Soulbook* and organized cultural education programs for children in the Bay Area. Various members, motivated by the organization's focus on black nationalism and their own frustration with the hesitation of national black leaders, agitated for the group to become involved in action-oriented politics. Rather than reading to each other, they began speaking on the streets in the Fillmore area of San Francisco and in the Oakland black community. This led to the AAA instituting community programs designed to promote racial pride and cultural awareness. Young Bay Area students such as Huey P. Newton increasingly found inspiration in Warden's cultural nationalism and the words of Malcolm X and Robert F. Williams. Although SNCC, CORE, and the NAACP were active in the Bay Area, the growth of the AAA suggests much about the failure of traditional activism outside the South. None of the leading civil rights organizations were truly able to come to terms with the demand in the Bay Area black community for a direct link between black cultural awareness and political organizing.[42]

Maulana Ron Karenga was appointed chairman of the Los Angeles AAA chapter in 1963. The first black student president of Los Angeles Community College, Karenga had been profoundly influenced by Marcus Garvey, Kwame Nkrumah, Sekou Toure, and elements of socialist thought. Initially impressed with the AAA's focus on study sessions, tutorials, and instruction in language and history, Karenga began speaking on Los Angeles street corners predicting a revolt. By 1964, his geographical and increasingly significant intellectual distance from Warden led to his isolation and separation from the AAA to form his own organization, US.[43]

After becoming increasingly skeptical of the direction of the AAA, Huey P. Newton set about honing his own ideas about inner-city organizing in

Oakland, founding the Black Panther Party for Self-Defense in September 1966 with Bobby Seale, another AAA dissident. Newton's differences with Warden stemmed from the AAA's refusal to come to terms with the plight of black Americans and Warden's approval of capitalism. Newton did not reject Warden's cultural stance. He appreciated that the African American struggle had to challenge white cultural hegemony, and he recognized the benefits of the AAA's cultural awareness programs and had successfully agitated Oakland's Merritt College to offer instruction in black history. For Newton, the failures of existing black organizations were largely a consequence of their misunderstanding of class politics in the African American community, notably their refusal to engage the lumpen proletariat. Thus Warden's nationalism was just as ineffective as religious black nationalism and middle-class liberalism because none paid attention to the gamblers, ex-convicts, and other lumpen elements of the black community. Similarly, Newton and Seale initially reacted against cultural nationalism in order to attract the "brothers on the block," as they often termed lower-class blacks, in accordance with Frantz Fanon's formulation of revolutionary Marxism. Cultural nationalists, they believed, directed their appeal too heavily at the middle-class blacks, who were obsessed with African accoutrements to the detriment of revolutionary activity. Yet the BPP retained a proximity to cultural nationalists that it rarely dared to make explicit.[44]

The early BPP's philosophy was indebted to two people whom Newton cited as the most important black men of the twentieth century. Marcus Garvey's black nationalism informed the BPP's insistence that race overrode class and that control of the black community be placed in black hands, and its demand that education reveal the true history of black and white America. Early copies of the *Black Panther Black Community News Service*, the party's newsletter, contained pictures of Malcolm X, urging readers to remember the example of the other central influence on the early BPP.[45] The right to self-defense was one of Malcolm X's mantras and completed the full title of the BPP. Newton readily invoked Malcolm X's "field nigger–house Negro" analogy, stressing its relevance for contemporary black organizations, and the BPP insisted that its members read Malcolm X's autobiography.[46] In February 1967, the BPP offered protection to Malcolm X's widow, Betty Shabazz, upon her arrival at San Francisco airport to attend a rally commemorating her late husband. Newton and Seale had no faith in the ability of other local black nationalists to protect Shabazz from assassination and decided to provide security themselves. Their very public parade of loaded weapons at the airport was not only a display of brinkmanship with the local police but also a symbolic capture of Malcolm X's legacy, confirming the BPP as the most dangerous and militant black organization in California.[47]

From Robert F. Williams, the BPP took inspiration that fleshed out Fanon's concepts of retaliatory violence. Newton devoured Williams's *Negroes with Guns* and must have been impressed with Williams's description of the oddly impotent fury of the Monroe, North Carolina, white community when it came into contact with armed blacks. Echoes of Williams's very public display of black power can be distinguished in Newton's actions when faced with a crowd of belligerent observers and local police in numerous events around the Bay Area, most notoriously his October 1967 shoot-out with police officers John Frey and Herbert Heanes. Newton's and Williams's subversion of the "crazy nigger" image attacked a core element of the American psyche in their adoption of the Cold War arms race ideology. Both affected a pose that promised their foes mutually assured destruction, backed up with visible displays of lethal weapons. Just like Richard Nixon's "madman theory," Newton and the BPP hoped to convince whites that they were prepared to do anything to achieve their goals.[48]

Malcolm X's thought became less important to the BPP's philosophy as the party moved away from black nationalism. He was more useful as an example of black fortitude, militancy, and martyrdom than a political philosopher, as demonstrated by the few references to him in BPP speeches and writings after 1968. Documents from the post-1968 BPP were more likely to feature approving references to Che Guevara, Mao Tse-Tung, and Frantz Fanon. Black Panther booklists eschewed *Malcolm X Speaks*, a collection that emphasized Malcolm X's socialist leanings, instead citing *The Autobiography*, which emphasized his devotion to Islam and belief in black nationalism and offered fewer hints as to his political development.[49] Although his equivocal stance on violence remained central to BPP philosophy, his personal association with black nationalism underestimated the value of class solidarity. As Fanon argued, "nationalism is not a political doctrine, nor a programme," it was merely a step toward political and social consciousness. Nor was Malcolm X's mystical conception of Africa as a cultural and spiritual homeland appropriate to the stark realism of BPP doctrine. While the BPP did not reject outright his belief that black culture could assist the revolution, his amorphous and incomplete philosophy gave way to the more specific and overtly revolutionary work of Mao and Fanon.

Fanon's *The Wretched of the Earth* became central to BPP philosophy, and his ideas came to dominate the BPP's conception of the African American struggle.[50]

Most historical accounts interpret the relationship between the BPP and Fanon through Fanon's insistence that violence can eradicate colonialism. This overlooks his sincere belief in the value of cultural expressions to the freedom struggle. For Fanon, revolutionaries would have to cite and/or create a revolutionary culture specific to their immediate situation. Newton and Seale noted that Karenga and the cultural nationalists had not advanced beyond a homogenized African culture. Herein lies the BPP's rejection of Malcolm X's interpretation of African culture: the reliance on an idealized and vague African past was inadequate for a revolutionary campaign that demanded a culture that was directly relevant to the present situation. African American cultural nationalists were thus at an intermediate stage in their development. Newton and Seale adopted Fanon's dictum that cultural nationalism was a dangerous diversion from revolutionary activities but did not publicly acknowledge Fanon's insistence that African American culture could play a central role in the revolution. The actions of the BPP, however, indicate that the party retained a keen interest in the value of culture and that its antagonism toward cultural nationalism derived from other sources. Far from stripping and robbing culture of its liberating content, as Karenga claims, the BPP was very much aware of the role that culture could play in the revolution. The BPP's acceptance of the value of art to organizing can be discerned in the pages of its official newspaper. Primarily a vehicle for the propagation of the thoughts of the BPP's leadership, community news, and socialist revolutionary thought, the newspaper became central to the BPP's operation and allegedly reached a peak weekly circulation of over 100,000.[51]

Revolutionary art was fundamental to BPP philosophy and was featured prominently in the newspaper. Its chief architect was the BPP's minister for culture, Emory Douglas, a trained artist who had designed theater sets and props for Amiri Baraka at San Francisco State and who was heavily influenced by the socially conscious work of Charles White and Elizabeth Catlett.[52] Douglas was courted by Newton and Seale, who wanted an artist to design posters and newsletters to publicize the nascent BPP. Although he was interested in Baraka's cultural nationalism, Douglas joined (largely because he was entranced by Newton's and Seale's image) and was invited to spearhead the party's Ministry for Culture. He soon developed a hybrid Fanonist-Maoist conception of his work, agreeing that artists had to involve themselves completely in the struggle. Mao demanded "the unity of politics and art, the unity of content and form," but rejected both art with the wrong political perspective and the leftist "poster and slogan" style, which lacked artistic power.[53] Douglas concurred, asserting that revolutionary art could enlighten both the party and the masses. This was "an art that flows from the people," he argued. "It must be a whole and living part of the people's lives, their daily struggle to survive. To draw about revolutionary things, we must shoot and/or be ready to shoot when the time comes. . . . One must make strong roots among the masses of the people. . . . [O]nly then can a Revolutionary Artist renew this visual interpretation of Revolutionary Art indefinitely until liberation."[54]

Douglas practiced what he preached, participating regularly in BPP police patrols and at the BPP's interruption of proceedings at the California state capitol in May 1967. His primary role as minister for culture concerned the layout of the *Black Panther* and the production of the vast majority of the artwork that adorned its pages. Douglas's work rarely failed to appear on the back cover of the BPP's newspaper and survived the *Black Panther*'s frequent editorial changes.[55] His portraits of Black Power leaders were available for sale at BPP offices, and his art was posted in homes and shop windows as a sign of support. Even Eldridge Cleaver was keen to promote and contribute ideas for his work.[56]

Douglas combined "high" and "low" art. His work was displayed in galleries and exhibitions. Like Langston Hughes, he told "semple" stories of ordinary folk that carried profound underlying and implied meanings. He empowered the urban black community: rather than displaying outrage at police malpractice, Douglas depicted the community watching over the police. This was a subtle but crucial shift that suggested that the black community was in control of its destiny. Indeed, the unified black community was the central concern of Douglas's work. In a low-literacy area where large numbers of people had become alienated from the system, Douglas reached out to those who would have treated purely written propaganda with disdain. The BPP ensured that the newspaper did not distance itself from one of the organization's key support bases, and Douglas's artwork was central to this aim. This was an art with a political message that was firmly attuned to the urban ghettos.[57]

Douglas's pieces contained a message for the black community that complemented the words in the newspaper and that followed the BPP's changes in philosophy and direction. Douglas resisted the "poster and slogan" style through using dynamic imagery that needed little further explanation. His

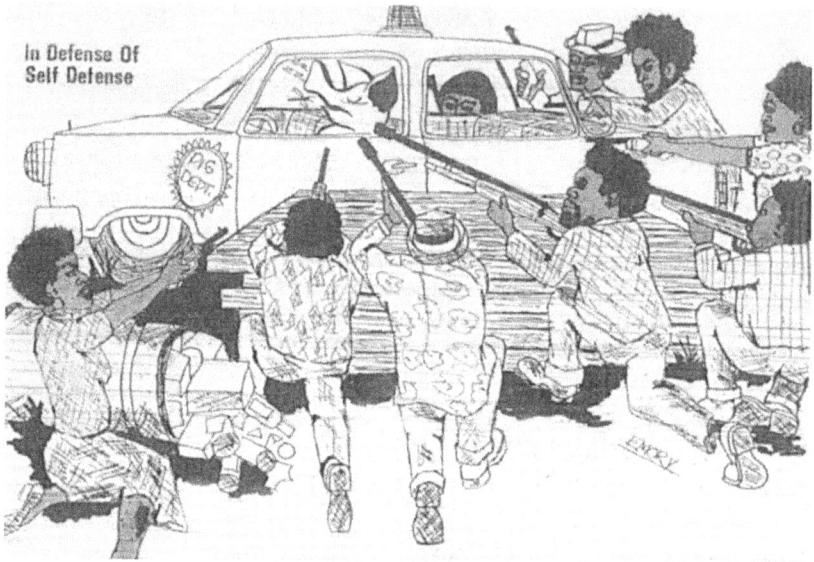

In Defense Of
Self Defense

Credit: Emory Douglas, *Black Panther*, 18 May 1968.

earliest work for the BPP relied on violent imagery and depicted the black community repelling the forces of white power, namely pig policemen and politicians (who later evolved into rats). Initially, the police were depicted simply as pigs but, with Douglas's increasing confidence, evolved human bodies, enabling Douglas to place them in realistic settings.[58]

Douglas also utilized Malcolm X's thought, depicting black American troops being sent into battle by the imperialist system before turning their guns on their oppressor, at once a reinterpretation of Malcolm X's chickens coming home to roost allegory and a dual critique of American foreign policy in Southeast Asia and the U.S. Army's recruitment of black soldiers in overwhelmingly unrepresentative numbers.[59]

Revolutionary art did not stop at Douglas's easel. The party encouraged members to write poetry, which was occasionally printed in the *Black Panther*. Most poems explicitly focused on the BPP's attitude toward violence, including Sheila Waldron's "For Many Years, but Now Today," which urged Black Panthers to make pigs dig their own graves before executing them. A number of poems addressed more cultural nationalist issues, such as Iris Wyse's "Because I'm Black," which equated blackness with beauty, boldness, and soulfulness. Poems by Sarah Webster Fabio and the black Cuban Nicolas Guillen were included to establish the widespread solidarity for the BPP. Although much of the poetry was simplistic, its presence indicates the breadth of the BPP's conception of revolutionary art and devotion to social realism. Fanon's assertion that mature revolutionary periods would inspire literary works from ordinary people that would "become the mouthpiece of a new reality in action" was particularly influential in this respect. This call to turn language into a weapon was a key characteristic of the Black Power movement, from Kwame Ture's chant of "Black Power" through Baraka's demand for "poems that kill." Extending the concept of revolutionary art, BPP members even barged into a Jimi Hendrix Experience recording session in the hope that Hendrix could be induced to declare his support for Black Power. Although a frequent purchaser of the *Black Panther*, Hendrix preferred not to declare himself an honorary Panther. Moreover, his interests were focused more on music and sex: Pat Hilliard, David Hilliard's wife and part of the BPP delegation, complained that Hendrix was only interested in an orgy and not a political discussion.[60]

The centrality of Douglas's work to the BPP's operations and the BPP's relationship with other art forms reveals that the BPP did not reject the use of culture as an organizing tool prior to its feud with US. This myth derives from Newton's and Seale's disagreements with the AAA. The term *cultural nationalist* became an all-encompassing term of abuse for frequent ad hominem attacks on African Americans who had not completely subsumed themselves within Black Panther philosophy. This public antipathy was deepened by the eruption of the feud with US, which resulted in the deaths of BPP organizers Alprentice "Bunchy" Carter and John Huggins and to the

Credit: Emory Douglas, *Black Panther*, undated, circa 1968.

BPP's insistence that cultural nationalism was a bastardized and dangerous aberration of black protest.[61]

US in fact had numerous similarities with the BPP. Like the BPP, it adopted a vanguard strategy, maintaining a black-only membership of fewer than 600. US members had to change many aspects of their former lives, from clothing and hairstyle to language, philosophy, and names. The BPP similarly required its members to undergo a process of self-redefinition. Both organizations used political education classes to indoctrinate youngsters and forged links with campus black student unions. Both organizations relied on internal discipline and unswerving devotion to the cause and the leader. Both initially advocated the development of a black co-operative economic system and laid claim to Malcolm X's legacy. Yet crucial differences remained: US rejected alliances with white radicals and dismissed Maoism, Marxism, and Fanonism since none could comprehend the reality of the African American revolution. Karenga rejected the concept of class struggle, arguing that race cut through class divisions: the black bourgeoisie was simply a philosophical construct, and all blacks were, by definition, oppressed by whites.[62]

US philosophy revolved around the seven principles of Nguzo Saba: unity, self-determination, collective work and responsibility, cooperative economics, purpose, creativity, and faith, all wrapped up in an ersatz African culture. To Karenga, black unity centered on the color, culture, and consciousness of blackness. His philosophical reference points were predominantly African. The Pan-African popularity of the language of Kiswahili encouraged Karenga to conceive of Africa as a pseudonation. From Sekou Toure, he took the concept of racial unity. Leopold Senghor's and Julius Nyerere's interpretations of socialism fed into Karenga's skeptical reading of Marxism and provided a framework for his political views. Their insistence that Africans need not follow rigid (text-based) doctrine reinforced Karenga's concept of African peoples as instinctively cultural. In this latter point, Karenga suggested that black people were more inclined to emotion, instinct, and folk wisdom than dispassionate intellectual rationality and a reliance on formal education for the accumulation of knowledge. Jomo Kenyatta's anthropological study of Kenya suggested that politics and economics were subdivisions of culture, an interpretation that directly influenced Karenga's belief that African Americans formed a cultural nation. Kenyatta's insistence that the tribe represented an extended family directly influenced Karenga's chauvinist interpretation of women's roles in the revolution and his adoption of polygamy. President of Indonesia and former independence campaigner

Sukarno's thoughts on nationalism also exerted an influence on Karenga's interpretation of collective responsibility, but Karenga missed Nyerere's assertion that socialism rejected racial essentialism. Indeed, Karenga's relationship with capitalism was filtered through a racialized prism. Although he deplored white capitalism, he was realistic enough to advocate what he termed *black economics*, a concept not dissimilar to black capitalism.[63]

Karenga termed himself a cultural revolutionary and approached community organizing as a cultural issue, arguing that the black community had to free itself culturally before it could succeed in organizing itself politically. His strong relationship with the Black Arts Movement developed from his view that art was vital to the creation of a cultural nation. Although he rejected Maoism, his conception of the role of art was suspiciously similar to Maoist cultural theory and might have been written by Emory Douglas: "Our creative motif must be revolution; all art that does not discuss or contribute to revolutionary change is invalid. . . . There is no better subject for Black artists than Black people, and the Black artist who doesn't choose and develop his subject will find himself unproductive. . . . All art must be revolutionary and in being revolutionary it must be collective, committing, and functional."[64] Art was the medium through which US philosophy could be spread to the black masses. A dance troupe was organized to perform African dances along with new routines fashioned to reflect US philosophy. Karenga was of the Senghorian opinion that black people were naturally infused with rhythm: the dance troupe would channel this into political expression. US's James Mtume also influenced pianist Herbie Hancock to give his sextet (which featured Mtume's uncle, Albert Heath) African names. Hancock's band experimented with African rhythms and recorded music for US before Hancock moved on to other projects.[65]

Karenga later argued that the BPP-US feud was essentially ideological. This myth is dispelled in part by Karenga's understanding of the hybrid nature of African American culture, which was farther from Pan-Africanism than he publicly accepted. His conception of the relationship between culture and politics echoed the BPP's Fanonist line on the development of oppositional culture in the colonial situation. Furthermore, initial relations between the BPP and US were cordial, perhaps as a result of their mutual rejection of the AAA. Huey Newton spoke alongside Karenga at US's first Uhuru Day rally. In early 1968, Karenga spoke at a rally in support of Newton, stating that the Newton defense campaign symbolized growing African American unity. His differences with the BPP at this point merely concerned the presence of Los Angeles Police Department security at the rally.

Credit: Emory Douglas, *Black Panther*, 2 February 1969.

Through 1968, an Emory Douglas portrait of Amiri Baraka, who was publicly supporting Karenga, was offered for sale as a BPP fund-raising tool.[66]

Much of the animus between the BPP and US stemmed from a basic argument over turf.[67] The rise of the BPP in Los Angeles appeared to threaten Karenga's seniority among the city's black activists. That these upstarts in the BPP were unafraid to criticize Karenga's tactics—not least his willingness to enter into dialogue with the white power structure—added to the interorganizational tension. His decision to meet with California governor Ronald Reagan in the wake of King's assassination was particularly provocative: Eldridge Cleaver was so disgusted at Reagan's actions as governor that he was soon to challenge Reagan to a duel, promising to beat the governor to death with a marshmallow if need be.[68] Karenga's dismissal of the BPP free breakfast and clinic programs, on the grounds that state welfare and Medicare already provided these services, was further proof to the BPP of his hypocrisy. Meanwhile, tensions were exacerbated by the FBI's distribution of counterintelligence, including fake cartoons depicting betrayals of the black community by both sides and a stream of forged memoranda designed to heighten animosity, which peaked in January 1969 with the shootout at UCLA that ended the lives of Carter and Huggins.[69]

In the immediate aftermath of the UCLA shootings, the *Black Panther* devoted much space to critiques of Karenga and cultural nationalists, whom the BPP now blamed for all the ills within the African American protest movement. A *Wall Street Journal* article suggesting that Karenga was in thrall to the white power structure was reprinted with a heavily satirical Douglas cartoon. (In the cartoon, Karenga appeared very keen to accept money from the white foundations. Like Baraka, he claimed that he was stealing from the white system to benefit the black community.)[70]

In February, George Murray, the BPP minister of education, reminded readers that a natural hairstyle was not as powerful as a gun and argued that black culture should be "anti-white, anti-capitalist [and] against imperialism." BPP member Linda Harrison cited Fanon in her denunciation of the political naïveté and capitalism of the cultural nationalists. One month later, Murray had moved further, asserting that cultural nationalism—a "bourgeois-capitalist scheme to confuse the masses"—had to be destroyed. Similarly, Bobby Seale snarled that "a cultural nationalist is a fool. The white

Credit: Emory Douglas, *Black Panther*, 23 August 1969.

racist power structure will holler 'black capitalism' and just because the word black is on the front of capitalism he relates to it." Soon afterward, Karenga was depicted in the *Black Panther* with a Sambo-like lolling tongue and outsize lips, grasping at morsels dangled by the power structure. The image, one of Douglas's most arresting, appeared on the front cover, giving clear indication of the BPP's animosity toward US.[71]

Fanon's influence warded the BPP away from the homogenization of Africa and black culture that was so important to Karenga. The party's fondness for the colonial analogy led it to view the African liberation struggle as a series of national struggles, which the BPP firmly believed to be an expression of an international clamor for socialism. During the height of the feud, the BPP took the opportunity to use this conception of Africa to denigrate cultural nationalism. Linda Harrison took particular exception to US's promotion of Swahili, arguing that the language was a construction of colonialism. Liberally peppered with quotes from Fanon, Harrison's article in the *Black Panther* relied on the invocation of an African revolutionary culture that developed out of the anticolonial situation as the only culture that could transcend national differences. In the next edition of the *Black Panther*, another article stressed that anticolonialism was the true African culture. Fanonist revolutionary culture was clearly still fundamental to the BPP's revolution.[72]

The BPP's rhetoric masks the fact that its cultural policy remained relatively close to cultural nationalism. It could not afford to place African American culture at the forefront of its propaganda campaign, since that would have handed Karenga the theoretical upper hand and rendered the deaths of Carter and Huggins even more pointless. Yet Harrison's attack on African hairstyles centered on their cost in black hair salons, suggesting that she was more offended by the close relationship between cultural nationalism and capitalism than by cultural nationalism per se. Music and art remained useful weapons in the struggle, as evinced by George Murray's approving quote of the Impressions' song "We're a Winner," which confirms the widespread appeal of Curtis Mayfield's work to the black political activists of the late 1960s. Murray was also rather close to cultural nationalists in San Francisco, having performed in one of Baraka's plays at San Francisco State. He had played a key role in the student strike at San Francisco State, which demanded that the college make a greater commitment to black studies, including black control of the program. Murray's first *Black Panther* article retained elements of cultural nationalism in its call for black unity and its acknowledgment that black culture was the singular element that elevated African Americans over white Americans. Essentially, it reiterated the Fanonist cultural stance, particularly in its suggestion that black Americans needed "a revolutionary culture, a fighting culture." His second, more strident article was less an assault on cultural nationalism than a denunciation of black capitalism and was generally approving of the recent "black is beautiful" impulse. Again, the willingness of certain cultural nationalists to buy into the capitalist system, rather than the deeper ramifications of cultural nationalist ideology, was the problematic issue. The close proximity between cultural nationalism and white capitalism was similarly central to Bobby Seale's 1969 critique of the cultural nationalists. In October 1969, the *Black Panther* published a long article by Earl Ofari on the competing tendencies of black revolutionary and cultural nationalism, in which he concluded that the latter had been a positive force in black America. Ofari was then vice president of the Black Student Union at California State College at Los Angeles and had clearly been aware of the roiling antagonisms at UCLA and San Francisco State. He maintained that cultural nationalism had been a "component part of the Black experience" since the first slaves arrived in North America. Cultural nationalism's crucial failing was predictably its mistaken reliance on capitalism and not its cultural politics. Ofari implied that US's failing was similarly its advocacy of "Buy Black" campaigns and its refusal to reject Western capitalism.[73]

The BPP was ultimately more concerned with the "nationalism" in cultural nationalism than it was with the "culture." It retained Emory Douglas as minister of culture, and his artwork remained prominently featured in the *Black Panther*. In September 1969, Douglas asserted that revolutionary culture was a natural outgrowth of the liberation struggle. Although he lambasted the hypocrisy of the Godfather of Soul, James Brown, extolling black pride while advertising beer, he seemed relatively positive about the former aspect of Brown's work. It was, rather, Brown's capitalist greed that caused offense, not his song's message of racial pride and unity.[74] Yet the BPP's position on the relationship between song and the struggle was no less compromised than Brown's. One month earlier, the *Black Panther* announced that an album of "Revolutionary Music" by Elaine Brown was to be released. Although the BPP maintained that Brown was first and foremost a revolutionary, it noted that Brown's songs were a useful addition to the revolutionary canon and saw no contradiction between them and the anticultural nationalist headlines of the preceding eight months. Somewhat ironically, the album included a song about Carter's and Huggins's deaths. The album's liner notes recapitulated the Maoist interpretation of the role of art, noting the relationship between artistic expression and revolutionary sentiment.[75] Brown was soon followed into the world of music by the Lumpen, the fittingly named revolutionary singing group of the BPP, who rejected the stimulation of emotion in favor of education and the stimulation of action. The Lumpen transformed "Old Man River" into "Old Pig Nixon," and erased the subtlety of Curtis Mayfield's "People Get Ready," asserting instead that "revolution's come." Aspects of BPP philosophy were set to music in original compositions such as "Revolution Is the Only Solution" and "Killing." Neither the Lumpen nor Elaine Brown fully appreciated the close relationship between form and content in popular music. In elevating the political message over the artistic statement, they fell into an agitprop trap, where their music could not transcend the political message. Where Douglas's art can be appreciated as art, as political statement, and as political art, Brown's and the Lumpen's work remains hamstrung by its artistic limitations. More significant, their work indicates that the BPP's critique of black capitalism was more rhetorical than real. Both released records on the BPP's Seize the Time label, in an attempt to generate an autonomous financial base for the party, linking the BPP to cultural nationalist economics and cultural production.[76]

There was little change in the BPP's stance on revolutionary culture in 1970. In June, Emory Douglas asserted that art was fundamental to the African American struggle and called for a united front of revolutionary artists and activists. Douglas was keen to demystify the art world, encouraging others to experiment with the form and including the work of other folk artists in the pages of the *Black Panther*.[77] As BPP ideology shifted in the early 1970s, so Douglas's art changed to reflect the party's new emphases. His posters lost the violent imagery in favor of a more celebratory style, which concentrated on the BPP's survival programs and occasionally included quotes from African American spirituals, suggesting that Douglas was moving deeper into black history.[78] Throughout the BPP's life, Douglas's art was a prominent feature of the party's propaganda. It faithfully reinterpreted BPP philosophy for Panther supporters in an imaginative and visceral manner. Where much of the BPP's other cultural productions elevated the message over the medium, Douglas's art maintained symbiosis, suggesting that art and politics could be afforded equal status.

In early 1971, Elaine Brown returned to the studio to record an album for Motown Records' subsidiary label, Black Forum. Motown, perhaps the archetypal black capitalist enterprise, became aware of the burgeoning market for records with an explicit political message. Through its subsidiary label, it cashed in on the cultural nationalist vogue with recordings by the Last Poets, Larry Neal, Baraka, and James Mtume. More concerned with the financial gains, the BPP found the association with some of the leading contemporary cultural nationalists of little consequence. The union, however, was a short-lived venture: Brown's album and accompanying single did not chart, and Motown declined to prolong the relationship.[79]

Revolutionary art also continued to appear in Huey Newton's thought, even during his downward spiral toward alcohol and cocaine dependence. An entire issue of the *Black Panther* was devoted to his lengthy interpretation of *Sweet Sweetback's Baadasssss Song*, an independent film written, produced, directed by, and also starring, the young black filmmaker Melvin Van Peebles. In spite of primitive direction and simplistic dialogue, the film, which was dedicated to "all the Brothers and Sisters who had enough of The Man," grossed over $15 million. An entire genre of so-called blaxploitation films followed in its wake.[80]

Newton was particularly taken with the film's suggestion that Sweetback came to maturity and freedom via sex and violence. He identified strongly with the film's message that black unity, consciousness, and power led to freedom. Significantly, he referred to "cultural cultists" in the film rather than cultural nationalists, directing his ire toward their invocation of Africa, rather than their nationalism, because the latter clashed with the film's insistence that black unity was the key to survival. He also endorsed Peebles's multimedia marketing, urging viewers to buy the book and the Earth, Wind and Fire–produced soundtrack LP to boost their understanding of the film. Only two months earlier, Newton had announced that the BPP was now no enemy of black capitalism. Since Peebles was using his money to take it to "The Man," Newton had no problem with his merchandising campaign.[81]

The BPP's faith in the blaxploitation cycle was short-lived. As the white studios realized that there was money in high-octane, low-budget films directed at the African American community, *Sweetback's* political message became subsumed within the sex, violence, and ghetto chic that were other salient features of the film. In 1972, concerned at the depiction of African Americans in movies such as *The Mack*, which was then being filmed in Oakland, the *Black Panther* ran an article demanding that the films truly reflect ghetto life and that the films' producers share their profits with the black community. The article took particular exception to the depiction of revolutionaries in other blaxploitation films, including *Shaft, Cotton Comes to Harlem*, and *Superfly* (unfortunately, and somewhat ironically given Huey Newton's troubles, the BPP did not take heed of Curtis Mayfield's *Superfly* soundtrack, which offers a majestic critique of the black community's drug culture). Ultimately, this opposition itself could not withstand the BPP's adoption of black capitalism: in April 1973, the *Black Panther* carried an advertisement for *The Mack*, signifying the BPP's increasing acceptance of the capitalist system rather than any approval of the film. This integration into the capitalist system extended to publishing agreements with Random House for George Jackson's *Blood in My Eye* and Newton's *Revolutionary Suicide*. The party also defended Oakland Athletics pitcher Vida Blue in his pay dispute with the baseball club's owner on orthodox capitalist lines.[82]

A full appreciation of the theoretical background to the BPP's dispute with US highlights how the various tributaries of Black Power thought evolved from similar source material. To caricature the dispute as a polarized argument between political and cultural nationalists is to underestimate these common bonds.

The zeal with which both organizations solidified and simplified their philosophies in the public sphere has led to an overemphasis on the tension between the BPP's philosophy and cultural nationalism. Thus the BPP becomes a virulently anticultural nationalist group, when it held a relatively subtle appreciation of the value of African American culture to the freedom struggle. Throughout this period, the BPP acknowledged that a revolutionary culture was fundamental to the successful conduct of a political revolution. The difference between the BPP and US was simply in terms of the use that could be made of this culture and the relative merits of an exceptional African American culture versus an all-encompassing African culture. Placing the BPP's philosophy within its praxis and specifically relating it to the US feud offer a more nuanced appreciation of the BPP's relationship with African American culture. The cultural thrust was a significant aspect of late-1960s black nationalist ideology, and the BPP was ultimately less concerned with the "culture" in cultural nationalism than the relationship between the nationalists and American capitalism.

Many historians accept William Van Deburg's assertion that Black Power was "essentially cultural," but few delve deeply into the nature of this attitude.[83] Rather than forcing the various radical Black Power groups into competing and separate traditions, it is better to view them as rival factions within one larger tradition of black cultural nationalism. Indeed, the examples of the BPP, the FST, Baraka, and US indicate that the cultural thrust grew to be a significant aspect of late-1960s black nationalist ideology. Although they came from different backgrounds, all understood that the freedom struggle was just as cultural as it was political.

7

African American Culture
in the Civil Rights Movement

The Free Southern Theater's (FST) performances of *Slave Ship* overcame the North-South divide that characterized much of the 1960s civil rights movement, illustrating the national appeal of black nationalist politics and culture. It signifies the confluence of many tributaries that filtered into the cultural politics of the civil rights movement during the 1960s. It confirms that there was a deep connection between the movement and African American cultural expressions, suggesting that this connection was in some respects a battleground between integrationist and separatist factions within the movement. It also reveals that integrationists like Martin Duberman and nationalists like Amiri Baraka could examine the same historical material yet come to diametrically opposed conclusions.

In a sense, the historical pageants of *In White America* and *Slave Ship* represent the civil rights movement's yin and yang. Where one presents the movement within an oppositional tradition set by the American Revolution, the other sets it within a purely African American tradition of accommodation and resistance. *In White America* suggests that white Americans remained capable of redemption; *Slave Ship* largely dispenses with notions of white American decency, honesty, and legality, instead denouncing white American morality as inhumane and debased, even perverted. Even their titles hint at their authors' views of the African American experience: *Slave Ship* offers a damning metaphor for the country and the behavior of its white inhabitants, whereas *In White America* offers a less inflammatory image. Duberman suggests that whites remain capable of change, that they can realize the moral quest of the nation's founders. For Baraka, white America should be destroyed; integration and assimilation are pointless goals. Of course, each play's time and place informed this aspect of its message. Duberman wrote during a period when hope still existed that integration could be achieved, when many activists retained faith in white America. By the time of *Slave Ship*, much of this hope had evaporated. Duberman was a white liberal who crafted his play to appeal to integrationists; Baraka was a black nationalist who by 1967 had little interest in speaking to whites, let alone addressing his work to them. Where *In White America* was designed for an integrated—or at least integration-sympathetic—audience, *Slave Ship* spoke to black audiences and explicitly excluded white audience members from participating in the catharsis.

Yet both playwrights understood the role of African American cultural forms in the liberation struggle. Duberman interspersed his narrative with freedom songs and spirituals, implying that the culture of black Americans could offer hope, succor, and the impetus for a freedom movement. For Duberman, this culture was inherently hybrid African and American: even during the episode on a slave ship, the slaves sing songs referring to a Christian God, reinforcing (if in an ahistorical fashion) the notion that integration was desirable and, indeed, achievable.[1] For Baraka, African culture provides the spark from which the black revolution takes flame and informs the final celebration of black spiritual freedom. He rejects the integrated culture of the civil rights movement in favor of an exclusive, homogenous black African culture. In *Slave Ship*, black Americans were not only cutting their ties of bondage but also their cultural ties with white America, heralding a new epoch in black history.

As these two plays suggest, the relationship between the civil rights organizations and African American culture is much more complex than a simple equation involving the freedom songs and African American Christianity, and confirms that the movement's parameters extended far beyond the struggle for social and political equality. An understanding of this relationship aids the investigation into the roots of Black Power and suggests that Black Power emerged not only as a critique of the civil rights movement but also out of that very same movement. For example, despite his avowal that he was no black nationalist, Robert F. Williams was hugely influential on late 1960s black nationalism.[2] Williams's militant posture developed partially out of his experiences in the movement. To ignore his close relationship with the National Association for the Advancement of Colored People (NAACP) and the southern protests of the late 1950s and early 1960s is to wrench him out of context. The Student Nonviolent Coordinating Committee's (SNCC) drift toward radicalism was similarly influenced by its organizing experience. The 1964 Summer Project was the crucible in which SNCC's disillusionment with liberalism was forged; the focus of the freedom school curriculum on black culture offers a glimpse of the future direction of black radicalism in the United States. The example of the FST is instructive in that it attempted to develop its black nationalist theater in Louisiana rather than in a northern urban center. This point urges further reconsideration of Black Power as a truly national phenomenon.

The issues raised by cultural organizing within the civil rights movement recall the debate concerning racial uplift at the start of the twentieth century. Most obviously, the Southern Christian Leadership Conference (SCLC), the Congress of Racial Equality (CORE), and the NAACP continued to insist that black leadership emerge from the ranks of the educated black middle class, and each of these organizations to a greater or lesser extent believed that education was crucial to the advancement of African Americans, whether it be through Negro History Week or citizenship education. SNCC's operations were often geared toward the creation of indigenous leaders. Where Du Bois envisioned the most educated blacks leading all other blacks, SNCC attempted to generate new leadership from among the ranks of the dispossessed. These indigenous new leaders would thus form a more organic leadership caste, one less likely to abandon kinship affinity for class identification. Advocates of uplift theory largely agreed that educated blacks held the most appropriate skills for leadership. Where Du Bois and others praised erudition and that which separated leaders from the masses, SNCC lauded ordinariness and that which united nominal "leaders" and "followers." For SNCC, an ability to bond with ordinary black southerners was vastly more useful than an expensive and therefore exclusive education. Where Du Bois thought that the talented tenth would guide the masses, SNCC believed that the race leaders should develop a more interactive style, one that was sensitive to the needs and desires of the masses. Crucially, where Du Bois saw the tenth emerging from the black middle class, SNCC believed that leadership should develop organically from the working class.

To focus on cultural organizing within the movement during its peak years deepens our understanding of the complex tensions between race and class that existed within the civil rights coalition. Highlander's fusion of black and white folk traditions in the freedom songs informed the mass movement's early years. Highlander's staff truly believed that a new culture of the oppressed could unite black and white America. The movement sang "black and white together" in "We Shall Overcome" not only to demonstrate the biracial identity of the movement's participants but also to establish its biracial culture and the long traditions of black and white song upon which it drew. While Highlander and Guy Carawan understood the importance of Christianity to black southerners, their ties to the Left turned them almost instinctively toward stressing the importance of a biracial working-class culture. Yet southern black Christianity eventually overwhelmed the leftist secular influence in the freedom songs. The Albany, Georgia, activists, perhaps thinking that the "whiteness" of the freedom songs as Carawan taught them did not truly reflect black southern culture, reconnected the freedom songs with their roots in the nineteenth-century slave spirituals and work songs. The Albany campaign was one of the key events in the movement, one that brought black cultural forms to the forefront of the movement's campaign. "You see why this is a singing movement?" asked James Forman soon after the demonstrations ceased. "The songs help. Without them, it would be ugly. Ugly." Forman is correct to emphasize the beauty that the freedom songs brought to the mass demonstrations and that they provided a valuable counterpoint to segregationist violence and brutality. The freedom songs undoubtedly offered an oasis of optimism for many protesters amid frequent beatings and jailing. Yet Forman misses the deeper meanings of the freedom songs. They incorporated and reflected the life of the black community, and were integral to the movement's conduct. As Bernice Reagon's substitution of the word *freedom* for *trouble* in "Over My Head (I See Trouble in the Air)" indicates, the freedom songs had an explicit political message that was clear to their singers. The songs not only beautified the movement, they also furnished it with a profound political expression. Furthermore, the freedom songs linked the movement with its heritage. Martin Luther King Jr. observed that "they are as old as the history of the Negro in America. . . . We sing the freedom songs today for the same reason the slaves sang them, because we too are in bondage and the songs add hope to our determination." Just as the 1964 Summer Project utilized the concept of a usable past, the freedom songs tapped into an African American heritage to emphasize the intergenerational bonds within the African American community. Yet in doing so, the songs implicitly rejected the white influence on the movement, suggesting that race overrode class. In the racializing of the freedom songs, activists such as Reagon placed racial identity at the center of the civil rights struggle. Through this process, they contributed (perhaps unwittingly) to a process that led to the expulsion of SNCC's white activists and the shift of the movement's focus from civil rights to black identity.[3]

King's statement might disguise the fact that the SCLC's attitude toward the movement's culture was suffused with religion. Even many of its explicitly secular acts were defined in terms of their religious aura: as Septima

Clark confessed, "voter registration is a ministerial act."[4] Throughout this period, even as the SCLC was coming to terms with the new mood that insisted on a psychological concept of freedom, the organization maintained that the Christian church was all the culture that black Americans needed. Psychological freedom could not be attained without Christianity. King aligned himself with Aretha Franklin's demand for respect in part because Franklin herself was steeped in the gospel tradition. For the SCLC, the black church *was* black culture. While it largely refrained from explicit cultural organizing, the SCLC understood the power of culture in the political sphere. Its use of the church's organizational structures went hand in hand with its use of the church's culture: the traditional role of the church within the black community, its network of committed individual activists, its preaching techniques, and, just as important, its songs. The freedom songs remain as one of the most evocative symbols of the civil rights movement, and the SCLC was aware of their power to unite activists and sympathizers. Yet once SCLC moved out of its heartland and into the North, it found its traditional methods to be inadequate. Its late 1960s plans reflect its loss of direction in the wake of its peak years.

For SNCC, the entire movement was more than simply a political or religious phenomenon. Field secretary Sandy Leigh recalled the organization adopting a principle in 1963 that "demonstrations shouldn't be mere marching up and down the street, clapping our hands and singing; that if a demonstration was going to be worth anything, it had to have an educational value." This educational aspect of SNCC's work was most vividly demonstrated in the 1964 Summer Project. One of the foundations of SNCC's freedom school curriculum was the knowledge and experience of black Mississippians, which would be used to extend discussions of history into the present. Fannie Lou Hamer always maintained that this educational focus, which encouraged poor, ill-educated southern blacks to see themselves as human beings, was SNCC's greatest success. SNCC's methods relied to a large extent on the pedagogic techniques pioneered at Highlander. Indeed, Highlander's techniques continued to inform African American political organizing for the duration of the civil rights movement's peak years. Highlander insisted that the key to overcoming oppression lay in trusting the decisions of the oppressed. It based its seminars on an existential approach, one that defined the pedagogy of SNCC's freedom schools. Highlander was also steeped in the singing tradition. Its music program was fundamental to the school's operation. Song transcended the intellectual and rational to access people's emotions and feelings, and was conducted as a group activity to engender a sense of community. For Highlander, such folk cultural forms and expressions played central roles in resisting oppression. African American history, for example, was presented as a living and usable history, with direct relevance to and parallels with the 1960s struggle. For Staughton Lynd, this experimental approach to learning, which acknowledged the worth of southern black culture, was one of the major legacies of the civil rights movement. This approach firmly validated the worth of the culture of the black South. Thanks to SNCC's work in Mississippi and elsewhere, these education programs ended up focusing exclusively on black southerners. One of the most important lessons that SNCC activists took from Highlander's citizenship education work was this reconnection of southern blacks with their heritage, history, and culture.[5]

Inevitably, white teachers were predominant in the freedom schools. This reinforcement of patriarchal notions of race in American society—blacks being taught about themselves by outsiders—caused numerous black southern activists to recoil at white involvement and thus must be implicated in the rise of black nationalist sentiment in SNCC. The subsequent organizing experience brought the issue of racial identity to the forefront of the movement, stymieing attempts at multiracial organizing, a process that seems to be confirmed by Bernice Reagon's journey. One of the activists who returned "We Shall Overcome" and other freedom songs to their African American roots, Reagon later abandoned Anne Romaine's attempt to resurrect the biracial alliance of the early 1960s. She clearly thought that she should focus her organizing energies on the black community at the expense of her commitment to biracial organizing. Romaine's suggestion that white folk culture remained central to southern history coincided with Reagon's departure from the Southern Folk Festival tours. Reagon surely would have baulked at Romaine's plan. Without Reagon's input, the way was paved for the Southern Folk Cultural Revival Project (SFCRP) to become even more "white" in outlook and for Romaine to move away from biracial interaction, into white folk revivalism. With committed integrationists like Reagon making such decisions, it is clear that integrationism was doomed by 1967. Cultural organizing initiatives could not hope to reverse its decline.[6]

The actors in the movement were fully aware of their roles in history and, like Martin Duberman and Amiri Baraka, were often at pains to remind other participants and observers of the close relationship between the present struggle and historical struggles for black freedom. Hence SNCC adviser Howard Zinn's study of the organization was suggestively subtitled *The New Abolitionists*. Similarly, the NAACP continued to promote Negro History

Week to enlighten the African American populace, even if enlightened self-interest was at the heart of this operation. More important, many of SNCC's initiatives were designed to raise awareness of African American history among movement participants, and to encourage them to understand that they were taking part in history. Thus SNCC sought both to empower African Americans politically (through voter registration and destroying segregation) and culturally (through opening blacks up to their heritage). In encouraging African Americans to consider themselves historical actors, SNCC was further empowering them and emphasizing the close relationship between their political lives and their cultural heritage. This was an extension of Highlander's ideas concerning the Citizenship Education Program (CEP). Along with its successful attempt to lay the foundations for large-scale registration of African American voters, Highlander hoped to develop political awareness through learning about historical events. Highlander was optimistic that the CEP students would become aware of the political benefits of educating themselves, of the necessity of standing firmly against oppression, and of the intrinsic benefits of bettering themselves in order that they might participate fully in American democracy. SNCC went one step further by suggesting that political awareness went hand in hand with cultural awareness: to know oneself and one's history was to *be* political. Thus history became a weapon that could be used in conjunction with the shared historical memory of oppression to ignite the dormant political passions of black southerners. History also operated as self-validation. In looking back to the past, activists saw historical precedents and were able to place themselves within a centuries-long continuum of resistance, thereby ennobling their own struggle and justifying its existence. For many activists, African American history was an ideal organizing tool.

The FST was the most important organization in the 1960s to stress the close relationship between the movement and African American cultural forms. The FST believed that political action could be stimulated by art, and that politics and art existed in such symbiosis that one could not exist without the other. Art, in John O'Neal's words, was "dominated by and is an expression of politics." The FST was also convinced that the African American population was instinctively cultural and that African American culture was inherently oral in nature. Theater, it thought, could reflect and transcend the orality of black culture. The black church and black music were the prime examples of this latent cultural element, and therefore the FST's task was to make black theater reflect black religious and musical traditions. Yet the FST was never able to come to terms with the value of

the church to the black population. Although the group declared its southern identity from its inception, many of its members were from the North,
and few held a Christian faith. Its early performances relied on civil rights
movement audiences both for interaction and support. This continued to
be the case even after the FST ended its formal relationship with the movement. Without the organizational apparatus that SNCC offered, the FST's
audiences began to dwindle. The group's failure to entice the support of the
black church created another vacuum in its support base. Coupled with the
group's increasing skepticism of integration—an attitude forged in Mississippi—the search for alternative sources of support and funds led the group
toward black nationalism and the departure of its white members, a process
that foreshadowed the racial mores of many black nationalist theater groups
that emerged in the late 1960s. As O'Neal proclaims, the FST demonstrates
both the utility of local organizing in the Black Power era and the potential
of theater as a political tool. Its retreat to New Orleans and its decision to
focus on organizing within the local community enabled it to prolong its life
long after the Black Power moment had passed.[7]

While there is scant evidence that Amiri Baraka was directly influenced
by the FST, his role as a champion of black artistic work in the community
was similar to that of the theater group. Just as the FST tried to establish
community theater in the South, Baraka tried to stimulate black theater in
the North. His organizational activities in Harlem and Newark helped to
pave the way for a national Black Arts Movement and sparked a renaissance
in black theater.[8] Ultimately, for him, cultural expressions were more than
simply vehicles for political sentiments. Black life and black art were one
and the same. His theatrical work gave clear indications as to his political
sensibilities. That his writing occasionally descended into crude hectoring
was less the point for Baraka than the fact that it was transmitting ideology
to the black masses. More important, Baraka firmly linked black politics,
history, and culture through his plays, presenting African American history as an inevitable progression toward black nationalist politics. In highlighting white depravity, mendacity, self-satisfaction, and brutality, Baraka
hoped to lead his audiences toward black nationalism and true freedom
from white oppression. The plays also act as a form of self-justification, ex-
plaining exactly why Baraka felt the need to dispense with his "white" life.
Dutchman and *The Slave* were in part designed to awaken black American
theatergoers to the necessity of casting off the white dominance over their
minds; *Slave Ship* almost completely so. Clay and Walker Vessels revealed
that black Americans were doomed unless they eliminated white thought

processes, white morals, and white behavioral traits from their minds and their bodies. The entire cast of *Slave Ship* revealed the possibilities for black Americans who were able to reject the white influence. Their incomplete revolution was to be completed by the audience.

Furthermore, Baraka's interpretation of music as a political expression emphasizes the symbiotic relationship between African American politics and culture. Baraka indicated throughout these plays that black cultural expressions were dominated by this political stance and acted as catharsis for black hatred of whites: as Clay told Lula in *Dutchman*, "If Bessie Smith had killed some white people she wouldn't have needed that music. She could have talked very straight and plain about the world."[9] Until the very late 1960s, Baraka argued that this black nationalist aesthetic was most perfectly realized by free jazz, which some listeners thought committed violence against white melodic and rhythmic traditions in a fashion that Baraka hoped black Americans would take to the outside world. Militants such as Baraka and Robert F. Williams looked to this music as a cultural articulation of the new black mood. Notwithstanding the integrated nature of many jazz groups and the jazz industry (which, since most record label owners and producers were white and most performers black, generally reflected the power differential inherent in American society), they considered jazz the quintessential musical articulation of black freedom. Jazz lay at the root of the liberation of black Americans in *Slave Ship*, and Baraka's jazz criticism was fueled by a similar notion. *Radio Free Dixie* was also steeped in the African American protest culture. As Williams later wrote, "the purpose of *Radio Free Dixie* was not for entertainment or escapism, it was to agitate and motivate."[10] He did not simply use music to assault his listeners but deliberately selected records that stimulated the minds of his audience. In highlighting the links between modern jazz, soul, and the spirituals, Williams reminded listeners of the intergenerational African American tradition of political and cultural protest that underpinned the 1960s movement. Alongside free jazz, Williams played freedom songs and politicized soul music. To punctuate and accentuate the message of these songs, he read slave spirituals and his own poetry and committed numerous verbal assaults on white America. Williams deliberately emphasized the political message of African American cultural expressions in order to increase the urgency of his words and suggest that all black Americans were straining at the leash for freedom. *Radio Free Dixie's* almost cacophonic mix often sounded like the start of the war on white America, and no listener could have failed to discern the political message at its heart.

Baraka went one step further by using jazz musicians to aid his organizing efforts, inventing a radical politics–jazz synthesis. This fusion did
not become a more powerful force in part because many of the musicians
were less inclined to politics than they were devoted to their art. Most desired critical acceptance as serious musicians, a quest that reshaped jazz in
numerous ways. Like many other musicians, Ornette Coleman found that
European audiences did not conceive of jazz concerts as a social event for
dancing, drinking, and conversing but instead believed them to be high
cultural events, akin to visiting the theater. When he returned to the United
States, he expected similar respect from his audiences. John Coltrane's experiments, where he pushed the register of his saxophone to its limits, demanded total concentration from his audience. This was not necessarily
music to dance to but music to inspire contemplation. While this music
emboldened black nationalist critics such as Baraka to political action, audiences were being encouraged (either explicitly by Coleman's admonish-
ments or implicitly by Coltrane's virtuosity) to sit and listen and to engage
via appreciation rather than through physical expression. Coltrane was reticent to make political statements beyond his desire for worldwide peace,
a position that was far from the political radicalism that Baraka heard in
Coltrane's music. Meanwhile, soul music, in the words of Motown Records,
was becoming the "sound of young America." Its accessibility and vivacity
rendered it more attractive to a mass audience. This was music for dancing,
and its message was transmitted verbally—more easily interpreted than an
instrumental solo. Jazz retreated into esoteric realms, while soul became
associated with a more popular constituency. Once soul's message became
more strident and transparent, it also seemed to have taken jazz's mantle as
African American protest music, hence Baraka's alienation from his former
heroes and his late-1960s conversion to soul.[11]

Class differentials remained salient features of the civil rights movement's
engagement with the emerging cultural mood in the wake of the 1964 Summer Project. The NAACP's rejection of Black Power was a reflection of the
organization's middle-class outlook. Its insistence that Black Power should
be equated with black capitalism corresponded to its class identity and accurately represented the beliefs of many middle-class black Americans. For
the NAACP, Black Power culture was a pointless diversion from the real
goal of political power. More troublingly, Black Power advocates frequently
adopted an essentialist and homogenized interpretation of black culture
alongside their fetishizing of racial difference. The 1964 Summer Project
and Judy Richardson's bisectional freedom school suggested that there were

huge regional variations within black America. Moreover, many activists in the pre–Black Power period noted that African American heroes were aplenty and, more to the point, were very different from African heroes. The early attempts at cultural organizing understood the heterogeneity that underpinned transnational bonds. Once Africa became such an important reference point for black activists searching for a deeper heritage than the one America offered, these transnational bonds became all-important. Yet certain Black Power–era organizations understood that Africa was little more than a symbol. Both the FST and the Black Panther Party (BPP) insisted that African Americans were firmly American and followed the NAACP in searching for African American heroes to celebrate. It is notable that when Tom Dent said "goodbye [to] *Godot*," he promised to "stick" to a potent symbol of African American manhood, Otis Redding, rather than an African icon. Similarly, the BPP had a cultural wing that stressed American cultural forms: soul music, American films, and a Western form of art. Emory Douglas looked to the social realism of Charles White and Elizabeth Catlett for inspiration, not that of African artists Ben Enwonwu or Gerard Sekoto. The BPP's war with US forced it to maintain a rhetorical anticultural nationalist stance, but its praxis was closer in application, if not in spirit, to many cultural nationalist groups and indicates that it would be wrong to reify a political nationalist–cultural nationalist divide.[12]

The BPP slowly denuded itself of Malcolm X's imprint in favor of closer identification with Frantz Fanon and Mao Tse-Tung. Maulana Ron Karenga and his supporters took much more notice of Malcolm X's interest in black culture, and as their feud escalated, both camps solidified and simplified their positions in order to differentiate themselves. Karenga's insistence that cultural unity took precedence over political unity was more in tune with Malcolm X's later sentiments. Following Malcolm X's lead, the West Coast cultural nationalists argued that to rebuild black self-identity, the black community needed to unite around its unique culture. The BPP instead stressed the importance of the colonial analogy to African American oppression and continued to argue that revolutionary groups should focus on developing the revolutionary credentials of the lumpen proletariat. Despite this, the BPP's supposed revolutionary nationalists certainly did not negate the utility of culture. Emory Douglas's position within the party is a clear indication that the BPP did not completely abandon its cultural focus. Indeed, as black artist Tom Feelings observes, the BPP was the only civil rights organization to use an artist to his or her full potential.[13] To define the BPP as a revolutionary nationalist organization imposes a reductive framework on the organization, overemphasizes Malcolm X's influence on the party, and underplays the party's rejection of black nationalism. Despite the fact that the BPP was not as forthcoming in promoting African American culture as a political weapon as was US, it certainly grasped the value of a cultural approach to the struggle. The BPP's quest for a revolution of values within the black community can be paralleled with the moderate civil rights movement's insistence that it was challenging not only white but also black Americans. Throughout the period, many civil rights organizations maintained that self-development, often through African American culture, was one of the central aims of the freedom struggle.

Cultural organizing in the civil rights movement reveals that seemingly disparate strands were entwined. Highlander pioneered citizenship education, convinced the SCLC of the efficacy of utilizing folk culture as an educational tool, and revealed the value of this organizing style to SNCC. The FST emerged from SNCC, and both organizations later incorporated black nationalist thought. Robert F. Williams profoundly influenced the BPP and encouraged Amiri Baraka to become involved in political activism; Baraka, in turn, influenced the FST. As the movement turned radical, even the SCLC came to the conclusion that African American cultural forms were useful tools in the fight for civil rights. The qualifying point is that there are certain limitations to the use of cultural expressions in a social movement. The civil rights movement was no different: cultural organizing was not as widespread or as deep as one might conclude and was not the overriding interest of most movement activists. Most obviously, the SCLC was restricted by its insistence that religion was all the culture that black Americans needed. Financial considerations also limited the organizations' work in this field. SNCC, in particular, was never able to reproduce the success of the 1964 freedom schools. Although many individual activists were committed to continuing the schools, without financial and organizational investment, few actually managed to do so. A focus on the use of cultural forms and expressions within the movement cannot provide the definitive answer as to why the organizations suffered such a loss of support and finances in the period after 1964. That the two went in tandem might suggest that the cultural focus was of little interest within the black community. The equation, however, is more complex and involves many other factors, such as the attitude of the black middle class, the white establishment, and white society in general.

The late 1960s focus on black culture did much to address psychological issues within the black community but did little to solve the economic problems that faced black Americans. Ultimately, all the major civil rights organizations were occupied with addressing political and social inequality. While all, to a greater or lesser degree, acknowledged that African American psychological and cultural freedom was important, few thought that this transcended other considerations. Thus the temptation to overemphasize the role that cultural organizing played in the 1960s freedom struggle should be resisted. Nevertheless, cultural organizing pervaded many aspects of the 1960s African American freedom struggle and provides a useful interpretative tool, for the movement was not solely concerned with political and social equality. The many forms of culture that interacted with the movement provided crucial adjuncts to civil rights protests. Dick Gregory's comedy is one example of African American cultural expressions becoming a pressure valve for the community in addition to its insistence on black equality. It also highlights that simply appreciating this expression was not going to end racial inequality, that cultural activity had to work alongside or encourage political activity. One of the central concerns of the freedom school curriculum was with normalizing black identity while attempting to boost black voter registration. That the 1964 Summer Project failed in the latter quest, though, does not negate the importance of the former. The very issue of identity became crucial to the development of the freedom struggle in the ensuing years. To understand the civil rights movement fully, African American culture, identity, history, and heritage must be appreciated as part of the movement's weaponry. Studying the civil rights movement's cultural organizing also illustrates how change occurs within a social movement. Partially as a consequence of its use during the mid period of the movement, cultural organizing became a rallying cry for the Black Power generation, even as the cultural turn arguably diverted energies from the political job at hand.

Notes

Introduction

1. SCLC press release, 2 August 1967, Records of the Southern Christian Leadership Conference, Library of Congress, microfilm, part 3, reel 10, frame 0530 (hereafter cited as SCLC); Franklin and Ritz, *Aretha*, 118; Smith, *Dancing in the Street*, 209–12; Ward, *My Soul Responding*, 400.

2. Franklin, *I Never Loved a Man*; Phyl Garland, "Aretha Franklin—'Sister Soul'" *Ebony*, October 1967, 47 (quote).

3. Stokely Carmichael rejected his given name in favor of a chosen name, Kwame Ture. He will be referred to by this name, although references to his given name as author will remain unchanged. Carmichael, *Ready for Revolution*, 4, 627–28.

4. Werner, *Change Is Gonna Come*, 116.

5. Rolontz, quoted in Hirshey, *Nowhere to Run*, 241.

6. Franklin, quoted in "Lady Soul: Singing It Like It Is," *Time*, 28 June 1968, 66 (first quote); Franklin and Ritz, *Aretha*, 150 (second quote); Franklin, "Respect," on Franklin, *I Never Loved a Man* (third quote). See also comments from the Reverend C. L. Franklin on Franklin, *Amazing Grace*, disc 2, track 11: "If you wanna know the truth, she has never left the church!" For Detroit's religious geography, see Smith, *Dancing in the Street*, 56; Salvatore, "Reverend C. L. Franklin."

7. Hall, "Gramsci's Relevance," 26; Hoare and Smith, *Prison Notebooks*, 165, 324–33. Grace Elizabeth Hale, in *Making Whiteness*, illustrates how white southerners perpetuated Jim Crow through the cultural apparatus of the South.

8. Vietnam veteran "Hobie," quoted in Hirshey, *Nowhere to Run*, 242.

9. Guralnick, *Sweet Soul Music*, 344; David Nathan, liner notes to Franklin, *I Never Loved a Man*. Detroiter Ronny Shannon wrote "I Never Loved a Man." For country-soul, see Hoskyns, *Say It One Time*, esp. 89–121, 187–203; Franklin, *I Never Loved a Man*; Franklin, *Aretha Now*, esp. "Think."

10. As Adam Fairclough has written of the pitfalls of local history, "[e]mphasis on the purely local can lead to insularity and incoherence. . . . [N]or is national history simply local history writ large. The two approaches are two sides of the same coin." Fairclough,

Race and Democracy, xx. See also Lemann, *Promised Land*; and Guralnick, *Feel Like Going Home*.

11. Led by Van Deburg, *New Day in Babylon*, historians have emphasized the close relationship between political protest and African American culture in the Black Power movement.

12. The prefix "African American" fixes the identity of the author(s), not the racial roots of the form or expression; that is, "African American cultural forms" refers to cultural forms produced by African Americans but does not suggest that these cultural forms are only produced by African Americans.

13. A white university student from Wales visited the United States in 1969 and was introduced to various members of the Black Panther Party. He found the variety and complexity of the handshakes that greeted friends and comrades impenetrable. For the student, these handshakes served as a badge of membership and a means of exclusion. Edward Street, interview by author, Cardiff, 12 March 2004; also Baugh, "Black Power Handshakes," 32–36.

14. Mills, *Michel Foucault*, 16, 29, 33–35, 47–49; Rabinow, *Foucault Reader*, 57–58, 60, 293–95; Hall, "Gramsci's Relevance"; Hoare and Smith, *Prison Notebooks*, 165, 324–33.

15. LeRoi Jones, "The Revolutionary Theatre," in Jones, *Home*, 210, 212.

16. Glaude, *Exodus!* 19–23; Torres, *Black, White and in Color*; Smith, *Dancing in the Street*.

17. Anonymous (probably Staughton Lynd), untitled document, July 1964, 3, Howard Zinn papers, State Historical Society of Wisconsin (SHSW), box 2, folder 2 (hereafter cited as ZP); Jones, "Revolutionary Theatre"; Hilliard and Cole, *This Side of Glory*, 150.

18. Cohen, *Rainbow Quest*.

19. Hoare and Smith, *Prison Notebooks*, 247, 258–59, 350.

20. Clarke, *Styron's Nat Turner*; Campbell, "Profile"; Van Deburg, *New Day in Babylon*, 255–56; Scot French, "Mau-Mauing the Filmmakers: Should Black Power Take the Rap for Killing Nat Turner, the Movie?" in Ward, *Modern African American Freedom Struggle*, 233–54. For black studies, see Van Deburg, *New Day in Babylon*, 63–82; and Anderson, *Movement and the Sixties*, 294–99.

21. To prevent this study becoming too focused on Baraka, there will be no assessment of his poetry and his fiction. Although both reflect Baraka's political development and are clearly autobiographical, they tend not to address themselves as directly to issues surrounding cultural organizing.

Chapter 1. Singing for Freedom

1. Adams, *Unearthing Seeds of Fire*, 28; Tjerandsen, *Education for Citizenship*, 143 (quote).

2. Bernice Reagon, interview by Therese Spaude, 27 January 1982, SHSW, cassette 1303A, side 1.

3. Forman, *Black Revolutionaries*, 282; Lewis, *Walking with the Wind*, 81, 82; Branch, *Parting the Waters*, 163–64, 290, 486–87; Carson, *In Struggle*, 28, 41, 50–51, 77; Zinn, *SNCC*, 58–59; Payne, *Light of Freedom*, 71–77.

4. Tjerandsen, *Education for Citizenship*, 142.

5. Glen, *Highlander*, 42–43; Adams, *Unearthing Seeds of Fire*, 73; Zilphia Horton, "Music Isn't Trimming," n.d., Highlander Research and Education Center (hereafter cited as HREC), SHSW, box 65, folder 6 (quote); Zilphia Horton, "People Like to Sing," *Food for Thought*, March 1948, 17, HREC, box 64, folder 14.

6. "I Shall Not Be Moved," at http://www.simusic.com/worship/ishallno.htm; movement version in Carawan and Carawan, *Sing for Freedom*, 25.

7. Hoare and Smith, *Prison Notebooks*, 418; Myles Horton, "Random Notes," undated fragment, HREC, box 13, folder 31.

8. "Highlander Folk School Statement of Purpose, Program and Policy," 3 April 1950 (quote), HREC, box 1, folder 2; Glen, *Highlander*, 46–47; Highlander Folk School 23rd Annual Report, 1955, HREC, box 1, folder 6, 2–3; "This We Believe at Highlander," 1955, HREC, box 1, folder 2.

9. Horton, "People Like to Sing," 17, 19–20.

10. Glen, *Highlander*, 125, 127; Honey, *Southern Labor*, 183–84, 210, 218, 229–30, 236; Sullivan, *Days of Hope*, 235. For the relationship between Highlander and the CIO, Glen, *Highlander* 116–27, 141–46.

11. Adams, *Unearthing*, 78; Highlander 27th Annual Report, September 1959, 2, HREC, box 1, folder 6; Glen, *Highlander*, 43, 164–65.

12. Guy Carawan, form letter to "friends of Highlander," ca. 1959, 1, HREC, box 37, folder 11; Cohen, *Rainbow Quest*, 4–5, 75; Ling, "Spirituals," 220; Guy Carawan to Myles [Horton] and Connie [Conrad Browne of Highlander], 1965, 3, HREC, box 37, folder 11. Recent research indicates that Ledbetter was originally known as "Lead Belly," and that the single-word spelling emerged in the 1940s. Filene, *Romancing the Folk*, 51, 246n15.

13. "Sing for Freedom—In the Community and on the Campus" workshop program, HREC, box 64, folder 16; Highlander 28th Annual Report, 1960, 2–3, HREC, box 1, folder 6; Carawan and Carawan, *Sing for Freedom*, 15; Brown, *Ready from Within*, 55–59; Carawan to Myles and Connie, 4; Cohen, *Rainbow Quest*, 185.

14. Carawan to Myles and Connie, 2; Litwack, *Trouble in Mind*, 69–73, 88–94, 107–9. Myrdal, *American Dilemma*, 645, 879–903, 904–7, highlighted this process in 1944.

15. Pete Seeger to Al Brackman, 10 June 1967, Highlander Research and Education Center records, University of Nottingham, microfilm, reel 35, frame 883 (hereafter cited as HREC-UN); Guy Carawan notes for "We Shall Overcome," in Carawan and Carawan, *Sing for Freedom*, 15; Filene, *Romancing the Folk*, 198; Johnson Reagon, "Songs," 64–80; Brown, *Ready from Within*, 57; Carawan and Carawan, *Tree of Life*, 208–9.

16. Sanger, *"When the Spirit Says Sing!"* 108; Reagon, interview, side 1; Johnson Reagon, "Songs," 85.

17. Contract for "We Shall Overcome," July 1960; We Shall Overcome royalty memo, 14 June 1965; "We Shall Overcome" memo, ca. 1966, all in HREC-UN, reel 35, frames 866, 873, 881; Bernice Reagon to Myles Horton, 21 February 1966, HREC, box 65, folder 3; Lewis, *Walking with the Wind*, 353–54; Sanger, *"When the Spirit Says Sing!"* 29; Johnson Reagon, "Songs," 86–88.

18. Levine, *Black Culture*; Cobb, *Southern Culture*, 92–124.

19. Guy Carawan, "Report of Work with Adult School Program in the South Carolina Sea Islands 1960–1961," 2, HREC, box 8, folder 9; Carawan to Myles and Connie, 2; Brown, *Ready from Within*, 43–44; Carawan and Carawan, *Tree of Life*, 140–69.

20. Carawan to Myles and Connie, 5; Joyner, *Shared Traditions*, 234; Carawan and Carawan, *Sing for Freedom*, 111; Carawan and Carawan, *Tree of Life*, 195; see HREC, box 67, folder 7, for the first Johns Island music festival. At Greenwood, the SNCC Freedom Singers performed alongside Pete Seeger and Bob Dylan. SNCC press release, 8 July 1963, ZP, box 2, folder 3; Heylin, *Dylan*, 74; Dittmer, *Local People*, 174–75; Lyon, *Memories*, 110.

21. Guy Carawan and Candie Carawan, "Introduction to *We Shall Overcome*," in Carawan and Carawan, *Sing for Freedom*, 12 (quote); Highlander Three-Year Report, 1961–1964, 6, HREC, box 1, folder 7.

22. "Highlander Folk School Statement of Purpose."

23. Tjerandsen, *Education for Citizenship*, 149.

24. Myles Horton, report on trip to Johns Island, 17–20, October 1955, quoted in Tjerandsen, *Education for Citizenship*, 153; Carawan and Carawan, *Tree of Life*, 140–69.

25. "Experimental Workshop on Adult Education," 21 January 1961, HREC Audio Collection, cassette 206, side 2; Tjerandsen, *Education for Citizenship*, 174, 179; Septima P. Clark, "Literacy and Liberation," *Freedomways* 4, no. 1 (first quarter 1964): 120.

26. See, for example, Brown, *Ready from Within*; Payne, *I've Got the Light of Freedom*, 70–77; Branch, *Parting the Waters*, 263–64, 381–82, 576–78, 588, 646, 899.

27. Brown, *Ready from Within*, 48; Final Report of the Edisto Adult School for 1959–1960, quoted in Tjerandsen, *Education for Citizenship*, 168.

28. "The Citizenship School Program: A Proposal for South-wide Voter Education," August 1961, 1, HREC, box 38, folder 2; Horton, quoted in Carawan and Carawan, *Tree of Life*, 198 (emphasis added); also "Training Leaders for Citizenship Schools," n.d., timetable for citizenship school students, 1, HREC, box 38, folder 2.

29. Highlander 27th Annual Report, September 1959, 3.

30. SCLC Citizenship Workbook, n.d., SCLC, microfilm, part 4, reel 12, frames 0364–0365; Septima Clark, interview by Eugene Walker, 7, Southern Oral History Collection, University of North Carolina–Chapel Hill; Septima Clark, interview by anonymous interviewer, SHSW.

31. SCLC Citizenship Workbook, SCLC, part 4, reel 12, frames 0382–0386.

32. Clark, interview by Walker, 3–4.

33. Highlander 27th Annual Report, 2–3; Glen, *Highlander*, 231–33; Brown, *Ready from Within*, 56–59; Adams, *Unearthing Seeds of Fire*, 121–41; "Citizenship School Program," 3.

34. Many texts suggest that the transfer of the CEP to the SCLC was straightforward: Adams, *Unearthing Seeds of Fire*, 118; Branch, *Parting the Waters*, 381–82; Fairclough, *Soul of America*, 69–70, 95; Garrow, *Bearing the Cross*, 149–51. Tjerandsen, *Education for Citizenship*, 181; Glen, *Highlander*, 203, suggest otherwise.

35. James R. Wood to Highlander staff, 23 November 1960, SCLC, part 4, reel 2, frame 0532; Martin Luther King Jr., "Leadership Training Program and Citizenship Schools," post–October 1960 memo, in Tjerandsen, *Education for Citizenship*, 203.

36. CEP Progress Report June–November 1963, SCLC, part 4, reel 3, frame 0002; Maxwell Hahn, Executive Vice-President of the Field Foundation, to Dr. Wesley Hotchkiss (American Missionary Association), 9 April 1963, SCLC, part 4, reel 2, frame 0486; Myles Horton states that the average monthly cost of each citizenship school was $113.12. Horton to Wyatt Walker, 22 August 1961, 1, HREC, box 38, folder 3. The CEP was active in eleven states.

37. Victoria Gray, Report to SCLC Board Meeting, 1966, SCLC, part 3, reel 9, frame 0571.

38. CEP Annual Report to SCLC Board Meeting, 29–30 March 1967, SCLC, part 3, reel 10, frame 0212 (quote); Septima Clark, CEP proposal for 1965–1970, ca. 1965, SCLC, part 4, reel 11, frames 0250–0252; Septima Clark, Report on CEP at Highlander Board of Directors meeting, 14 May 1965, HREC, box 2, folder 3; Leslie Dunbar, Executive Director, Field Foundation, to Dorothy Cotton, 22 November 1967, SCLC, part 2, reel 11, frame 0837. Clark has claimed that some 95,000 voters registered in the same period. According to Frank Adams, Clark estimated in 1970 that 100,000 African Americans had been educated in citizenship schools. Septima Clark, CEP proposal, ca. 1965, SCLC, part 4, reel 11, frame 0252; Adams, *Unearthing Seeds of Fire*, 118.

39. Martin Luther King to Maxwell Hahn, 13 February 1962, SCLC, part 4, reel 2, frame 0488.

40. Hosea L. Williams, "History and Philosophy of the Southeastern Georgia Crusade for Voters," n.d., 1, SCLC, part 4, reel 4, frame 0416; Officers of the SGCV to Wiley Branton, 14 August 1962, Southern Regional Council Papers, Library of Congress, microfilm, reel 179, frames 0183–0185 (hereafter cited as SRC); Tuck, *Beyond Atlanta*, 128–29; Fairclough, *Soul of America*, 94–95.

41. John Due memo to Wiley Branton, 1 September 1964, SRC, reel 176, frames 1644–1645.

42. Williams, "History," 3, frame 0418 (quotes).

43. Jack Minnis memo to Wiley A. Branton, 12 February 1963, 4, SRC, reel 178, frame 0127; Adams, *Unearthing Seeds of Fire*, 114–15; "Experimental Workshop on Adult Education."

44. "Experimental Workshop," side 2.

Chapter 2. Cultural Organizing in the Integrationist Movement, 1961–1964

1. Martin Luther King Jr., "Love, Law, and Civil Disobedience," address, 16 November 1961, in Washington, *Testament of Hope*, 52.

2. Andrew Young to Septima Clark, 20 July 1964, SCLC, microfilm, part 4, reel 12, frames 0729–0730 (hereafter cited as SCLC).

3. Andrew Young oral history in Hampton and Fayer, *Voices of Freedom*, 113.

4. Vincent Harding and Staughton Lynd, "Albany, Georgia," *Crisis* 70, no. 2 (February 1963): 73–78 (quote 77); King, *Freedom Song*, 92–97, 158, 167–68; Sanger, *"When The Spirit Says Sing!"*; Tuck, *Beyond Atlanta*, 147–53; Zinn, *Albany*.

5. Carson, "SNCC," 18, 23; Forman, *Black Revolutionaries*, 260; Watters, *Down to Now*, 158.

6. Zinn, "Albany," 3.

7. Carson, "SNCC," 16–8; Zinn, *Albany*, 3; Branch, *Parting the Waters*, 524–25; William G. Anderson oral history in Hampton and Fayer, *Voices of Freedom*, 103; Zinn, *SNCC*, 125–28; "Survey: Current Field Work, Spring 1963," 3–4, ZP, box 2, folder 9.

8. Sherrod, quoted in Zinn, *SNCC*, 129; Branch, *Parting the Waters*, 532–33, 544–45; Johnson Reagon, "Songs," 84.

9. Carson, "SNCC," 23; Reagon, interview, side 1; Branch, *Parting the Waters*, 532; Carawan and Carawan, *Sing for Freedom*, 62, 77; interview with unidentified female protester in Albany campaign, Guy Carawan Collection, Southern Folklife Collection, University of North Carolina–Chapel Hill, cassette FT3696: Civil Rights Material; Bernice Reagon oral history in Hampton and Fayer, *Voices of Freedom*, 108.

10. See, for example, Gaines, *Uplifting the Race*; and Gilmore, *Gender and Jim Crow*.

11. Robert Mants Jr., "Report: Americus Georgia," 5 October 1963, Records of the Student Nonviolent Coordinating Committee, Library of Congress, reel 17, frame 0067 (hereafter cited as SNCC).

12. Ward, *My Soul Responding*, 295, 320; Reagon, interview, side 2; Johnson Reagon, "Songs," 140. By 1964, the group's personnel had changed, with Emory Harris replacing his sister, Rutha. James Peacock, Rafael Bentham, Matthew Jones, and Marshall Jones joined the group, with the two Reagons departing. Neblett remained until he joined the Black Panther Party. SNCC press release re: the Freedom Singers, n.d., SNCC, reel 19, frame 0681; SNCC press release re: Freedom Singers tour, July 1965, SNCC, reel 37, frame 0599; Emory Douglas, interview by author, 28 June 2001, San Francisco; Johnson Reagon, "Songs," 146.

13. Reagon, interview, side 2.

14. Ibid.; Johnson Reagon, "Songs," 22.

15. See SNCC, reel 5, frames 0874–0886, for lists of contributors and sponsors to SNCC's "Salute to Southern Students" benefit concert at Carnegie Hall on 1 February 1963; Forman, *Black Revolutionaries*, 350. See also *Down Beat*, 28 March 1964, 45.

16. Ward, *My Soul Responding*, 304, 308–9; Branch, *Parting the Waters*, 718, 887; Marqusee, *Wicked Messenger*, 8–15, 52, 79–83; Josephine Baker benefit concert advertisement, 12 October 1963; C. Howard Burney to Val Coleman, 25 November 1963, both in Records of the Congress of Racial Equality, SHSW, series 5, box 28, folder 8 (hereafter cited as CORE).

17. Gregory, *Nigger*, 85; Gregory, *Callus*, 19–20. Gregory's other autobiographical work is the well-titled *Up from Nigger*.

18. Gregory, *Nigger*, 85, 126–45, 148 (quotes), 168.

19. Gregory, *Callus*, 47.

20. Rickford and Rickford, *Spoken Soul*, 65.

21. Gregory, *Nigger*, 172–75; Gregory, *Callus*, 52–53.

22. Dick Gregory, performance at evening meeting in Greenwood, ca. 1963, Guy Carawan collection, Southern Folklife Collection, University of North Carolina–Chapel Hill, cassette 3690: Civil Rights Material—Greenwood documentary, side B.

23. Ibid.

24. Bakhtin, *Rabelais*, 89–95; Levine, *Black Culture*, 298–366, stresses the orality and communality of black humor.

25. Gregory, *Nigger*, 176 (quote); Gregory, *Callus*, 62.

26. Branch, *Parting the Waters*, 713, 722 (quote); Ivanhoe Donaldson oral history in Hampton and Fayer, *Voices of Freedom*, 151; Payne, *Light Of Freedom*, 198–99; Gregory, *Callus*, 67–68; "Dick Gregory Defies Police in South," *New York Times*, 3 April 1963.

27. Gregory, *Nigger*, 188.

28. Gregory, *Callus*, 69; Payne, *Light of Freedom*, 260.

29. Gregory, *Callus*, 71–75 (quote 71), 83; Branch, *Parting the Waters*, 722. "I asked one guy when was the good old days," said Gregory in Birmingham. "He said, '10 BC and 15 BC.' I said, 'Baby, you're not that old.' 'I mean 10, 15 years before Bull Connor.'" Dick Gregory, speech on release from Birmingham jail, n.d., tape 15, Highlander Tape Collection, SHSW.

30. SNCC staff meeting minutes, 9–11 June 1964, 27, 29, ZP, box 2, folder 7; Larry Still, "Comedian Doubts Freedom Fight Will Hurt Show Business Career" *Jet*, 19 March 1964, 14–20 (first quote 16); Gregory, *Nigger*; *Jet*, 31 December 1964, 43 (second quote).

31. Gregory, *Callus*, 83 (quote). Branch, *Parting the Waters*, 722, claims that Gregory's presence jolted the Justice Department into action. Gregory's reticence to discuss the depth of his involvement has obscured exactly how much he contributed, but the historical record is very long: Robert E. Johnson, interview by John Britton, Ralph J. Bunche Oral History Collection, Moorland-Spingarn Research Center, Howard University, RJB33 28, 30–31 (hereafter cited as RJBOHC); Anderson, *Movement and the Sixties*, 50, 70; Branch, *Parting the Waters*, 758, 765, 770, 808–9, 898; Branch, *Pillar of Fire*, 67, 71; Farber, *Chicago '68*, 122–23; Forman, *Black Revolutionaries*, 303–4; Horne, *Fire This Time*, 184; Lyon, *Memories*, 129; Pearson, *Shadow of the Panther*, 60; Van Deburg, *New Day in Babylon*, 84, 126, 128; Terry Francois, interview by Robert Wright, 13 November 1968, 35, RJB341, RJBOHC; Woodard, *Nation within a Nation*, 141, 148; Malcolm X, "At the Audubon," speech, 13 December 1964, in Breitman, *Malcolm X Speaks*, 98–100; Zinn, *SNCC*, 150–51.

32. Tom Hayden, "Revolution in Albany," 8 January 1962, SNCC, reel 37, frame 0295; Carson, *In Struggle*, 74.

Chapter 3. Jazz and Radical Politics, 1960–1964

1. Baraka, *Autobiography*, 246. Baraka changed his name from LeRoi Jones to Amiri Baraka in 1965; he will be referred to by his chosen name. Citations will use his name at the time of publication.

2. Tyson, *Radio Free Dixie*, 150–52, 154–57, 160–64; Robert F. Williams, interview by Robert C. Cohen, July 1968, 108–9, 514, 627, Robert C. Cohen papers, SHSW, box 1, folders 6, 9 (hereafter cited as RCP).

3. LeRoi Jones, "Cuba Libre," in Jones, *Home*, 42. For Baraka's Beat period, see Baraka, *Autobiography*, 218–41; and Watts, *Amiri Baraka*, 27–42.

4. Jones, "Cuba," 13; Baraka, *Autobiography*, 243; Polsgrove, *Divided Minds*, 126–27; Tyson, *Radio Free Dixie*, 224–26. For the FPCC, see Gosse, *Where the Boys Are*, 108–10, 137–73, 207–11, 216–22, 240–45.

5. Young, "Havana"; Baraka, *Autobiography*, 244–45; Jones, "Cuba," 42, 55, 56 (quote); Cruse, *Crisis*, 357.

6. Tyson, *Radio Free Dixie*, 232 (quote); Jones, "Cuba," 11, 62–63; Baraka, *Autobiography*, 248–50, 267.

7. Kelley, "New Monastery," 137; Don DeMichael, review of Ornette Coleman, *This Is Our Music*, *Down Beat*, 11 May 1961, 25; Leroi Jones, "The Jazz Avant-Garde" (1961), in Jones, *Black Music*, 69–80.

8. Baraka, *Autobiography*, 261; Charles Mingus, "Fables of Faubus" (*Mingus Ah Um*); Charles Mingus, "Original Faubus Fables" (*Charles Mingus Presents Charles Mingus*); Rollins, *Freedom Suite*; John Coltrane Quartet, "Alabama" (*Classic Quartet*); Kahn, *Love Supreme*, 78–79.

9. Malcolm X, *Autobiography*, 174–80, 181 (first quote); LeRoi Jones, "Jazz and the White Critic," in Jones, *Black Music* 15 (second quote).

10. LeRoi Jones, "New Black Music: A Concert in Benefit of the Black Arts Repertory Theatre/School Live," in Jones, *Black Music*, 172–76. Impulse was part of ABC-Paramount. Kahn, *Love Supreme*, 50, 52–53. Baraka wrote liner notes for the Impulse albums John Coltrane, *Live at Birdland*, and Archie Shepp, *Four for Trane* and *New Black Music*. Jones, *Black Music*, 63, 156, 172.

11. Jones, *Blues People*; Watts, *Amiri Baraka*, 117–26; Ralph Ellison, "Blues People," in Ellison, *Shadow and Act*, 247–58; Don DeMichael, review of *Blues People*, *Down Beat*, 2 January 1964, 34.

12. LeRoi Jones, "The Myth of a Negro Literature" (1962), in Jones, *Home*, 105 (quote), 115; Jarab, "Black Aesthetic," 59.

13. Kofsky, *Black Nationalism*, 251, 256; West, *Race Matters*, 101, 102; Malcolm X, *Autobiography*, 187 (quote), 192; DeCaro, *On the Side of My People*, 67, 69; Perry, *Malcolm*, 73.

14. Ingrid Monson, "Miles Politics, and Image" in Early, *Miles Davis*, 86–97; Miles Davis, "*Playboy* Interview with Alex Haley," ibid., 199–207; Santoro, *Myself*, 132–33, 140, 204; Ward, *My Soul Responding*, 303–6.

15. Malcolm X, speech at OAAU founding rally, 28 June 1964, in Breitman, *By Any Means Necessary*, 53, 63–64; Malcolm X, comments at Harvard Law School Forum, 16 December 1964, in Epps, *Malcolm X*, 160 (quote).

16. Jones, *Blues People*, 214; LeRoi Jones, "'Black' Is a Country," in Jones, *Home*, 82–86.

17. Watts, *Amiri Baraka*, 135–36; Cruse, *Crisis*, 485–86. Jones, *The Baptism* and *The Toilet* are, by comparison with his other plays, minor works that center on the Christian church and homosexuality.

18. Art Sears Jr., "Realistic Play Dramatizes Growing Negro-White Split," *Jet*, 9 April 1964, 64 (quote); Jones, *Dutchman*, 9–21.

19. Jones, *Dutchman*, 22–37 (first and second quotes 31, other quotes 35).

20. Ibid., 43–88 (quote 66); Benston, *Baraka*, 183.

21. Jones, "In The Ring."

22. Watts, *Amiri Baraka*, 84.

23. LeRoi Jones, "LeRoi Jones Talking," in Jones, *Home* 180, 186 (quote).

24. Baldwin, *Blues for Mister Charlie*.

25. Baldwin, "Notes for Blues," introduction to Baldwin, *Blues for Mister Charlie*, 9, 11; Weatherby, *James Baldwin*, 247, 250; Leeming, *James Baldwin*, 233.

26. Weatherby, *James Baldwin*, 237–38.

27. Advertisement for *Blues for Mr. Charlie*, *Jet*, 30 April 1964, 63; "*Blues for Mr. Charlie*: Baldwin Drama Roars with the Spirit of America's Current Negro Revolution," *Ebony*, June 1964, 188; Allan Morrison, "James Baldwin's Play 'Boils' with Fury, but It Is Realistic," *Jet*, 7 May 1964, 61; "Rockefeller Daughters Give $10,000 to Aid Baldwin's Play," *Jet*, 11 June 1964, 61; Campbell, *Talking at the Gates*, 174, 197; Weatherby, *James Baldwin*, 248–49, 251.

28. Roy Wilkins memo to NAACP members, 9 June 1963; NAACP press release, "NAACP Urges Members to See 'Blues for Charlie,'" Records of the National Association for the Advancement of Colored People, Special Collections, Library of Congress, Manuscripts Division, III box A242, Plays: "Blues for Mr. Charlie" (hereafter cited as NAACP); Campbell, *Talking at the Gates*, 197, 253–54; Leeming, *James Baldwin*, 238–39; "Rockefeller Daughters," 60–61.

29. Watts, *Amiri Baraka*, 129.

30. Tyson, "Robert F. Williams," 551–56.

31. Timothy B. Tyson, introduction to Williams, *Negroes with Guns*, xxi; Williams, *Negroes with Guns*, 23; Tyson, *Radio Free Dixie*, 90–136, 195–96, 262–85; Robert F. Williams, interview by James Mosby, 22 July 1970, Detroit, RJB588 76, RJBOHC; editorial, *Crusader*, 18 February 1961, 1.

32. Robert F. Williams, interview by Cohen, 31, 67, RCP, box 1, folder 6; "Violence and Freedom," *Crusader*, 31 December 1960, 3–4; "Centennial of Shame," *Crusader*, 4 March 1961, 4 (quote). Williams estimates that the *Crusader's* print run peaked at 40,000 copies, with reproductions boosting the figure in the United States. Williams, interview by Cohen, 623, RCP, box 1, folder 9.

33. Williams, interview by Cohen, 514, 627, RCP, box 1, folder 9; Robert F. Williams to Mae Mallory, 18 July 1962, Robert Franklin Williams papers, box 1, Bentley Historical Library, University of Michigan–Ann Arbor (hereafter cited as RFW); *Crusader*, August 1962, 5 (following Williams's exile, the pamphlet became a monthly publication); Williams, interview by Cohen, July 1968, 108–9, RCP, box 1, folder 6, and 516, 625, RCP, box 1, folder 9.

34. Williams, interview by Cohen, 626, RCP, box 1, folder 9 (quote); LeRoi Jones to Robert F. Williams, 18 December 1962, RFW, box 1; Williams, interview by Cohen, 623, 625, RCP, box 1, folder 9; Roach, *We Insist!*; Blakey and the Jazz Messengers, *Moanin'.*

35. Robert F. Williams to Richard Elman of WRAI Radio, 26 February 1963, RFW, box 1. A listener in Kentucky reported that "though the signal was weak and fading, *the message was not.*" Williams also claimed to have received letters from navy officers, Canadians, and Britons who heard the show. James H. Williams to Robert F. Williams, 12 October 1962, RFW, box 1; Williams, interview by Cohen, 622–27, RCP, box 1, folder 9; Tyson, *Radio Free Dixie*, 287–88.

36. Undated broadcast cassette of *Radio Free Dixie*, courtesy of Tim Tyson. *Radio Free Dixie* always featured the same spoken introduction. Monty Kelly's "I Can't Sit Down"

from *Porgy and Bess* was normally used as the theme, although in its first broadcasts, *Radio Free Dixie* began with a ragtime song entitled "Dixieland." Both titles illustrate the satirical humor that runs through much of Williams's work. I want to thank Tim Tyson for granting access to the recordings.

37. Transcript of *Radio Free Dixie*, 27 July 1962, 1, courtesy Tim Tyson; Hughes, "When a Man Sees Red."

38. Broadcast cassette, transcript of *Radio Free Dixie*, 27 July 1962; undated broadcast cassette, transcript of *Radio Free Dixie*, 10 August 1962, both in RFW; *Radio Free Dixie* broadcast transcript, 14 June 1964, 2 (second quote), 3 (first quote), Johns Committee Papers, Florida State Archives, Tallahassee, series 1486, carton 18, "Radio Free Dixie" file.

39. See, for example, transcript of *Radio Free Dixie*, 10 August 1962, 4–5.

40. Williams, interview by Mosby, 200.

41. Williams, interview by Cohen, 516, 523, 527, 546, 580–82, RCP, box 1, folder 9; Robert F. Williams to Fidel Castro, 28 August 1966, 5, RCP, box 1, folder 5.

42. *Crusader*, April–May 1965, 7; Horne, *Fire This Time*, 265, 268; Williams, interview by Cohen, 846–47, RCP, box 1, folder 11; "Exiled Williams Flies Back to U.S. in Special Plane," *Jet*, 25 September 1969, 8; Tyson, *Radio Free Dixie*, 293–99, 304–7; Robert F. Williams, "USA: The New Auction Block," *Crusader*, March 1968, 4–5; Robert F. Williams, "Africa and the African-American," *Crusader*, November 1968, 9–11; Williams, interview by Robert Cohen, 23 July 1968, 16, 22–26, RCP, box 1, folder 4; Williams, interview by Cohen, n.d., 39–40, RCP, box 1, folder 12; Williams, interview by Cohen, cassette 4, track B, part 2, 21–22, 24–25, RCP, box 2, folder 1.

43. Malcolm X, "Message to the Grass Roots," speech, Detroit, 10 November 1963, in Breitman, *Malcolm X Speaks*, 9.

44. Cook, *Sweet Land of Liberty*, 139–42.

45. Williams, *Negroes*, 76 (quote), 83. Gendered language was a salient feature of Malcolm X's rhetoric: Malcolm X, untitled speech, December 1962; Malcolm X, "The Ballot or the Bullet," 3 April 1964; "The Black Revolution," 8 April 1964; "With Mrs. Fannie Lou Hamer," 20 December 1964, all in Breitman, *Malcolm X Speaks* 29–30, 49, 53–54, 107.

46. Gosse, *Where the Boys Are*, 138–47. Note the absorption of OYM, by On Guard for Freedom, dismissed in Cruse, *Crisis*, 368–71; Watts, *Amiri Baraka*, 85–86; also Baraka, *Autobiography*, 248–51.

47. Malcolm X, speech at OAAU Founding Rally, 54, 55 (quote); Sales, *Black Liberation*, 120–22.

Chapter 4. The 1964 Mississippi Summer Project

1. Only recently has the Summer Project been renamed (by historians) Freedom Summer. SNCC workers simply referred to it as "the Summer Project." Belfrage, *Freedom Summer*, xx.

2. Minutes of NAC meeting, 21–23 February 1964, 4, CORE, series 4, box 2, folder 1 (quote; emphasis added); Dave Dennis, interview by Tom Dent, 8 October 1983, Mississippi Oral Histories, Amistad Research Center, Tulane University, cassette #46; Dave Dennis memo to Jim McCain, "Mississippi in Motion," 19 October 1963, 2–3, Floyd B.

McKissick papers, University of North Carolina–Chapel Hill, folder 6955 (hereafter cited as McKP).

3. "SCLC Citizenship Education Program (Mississippi)," ca. 1964, Sandra Hard papers, SHSW.

4. Minutes of SNCC Executive Committee, 27–31 December 1963, SNCC, microfilm, reel 3, frames 0305–0324; Liz Fusco, "Freedom Schools in Mississippi, 1964," 1 (quote), SNCC, reel 39, frame 0005. See also "Mississippi: Structure of the Movement, Present Operations, and Prospectus for This Summer," 1964, 3, SNCC, reel 6, frame 0049.

5. Anonymous (probably Mendy Samstein), "Outline for Maureen Murphy," December 1963, 5, 7, Mendy Samstein papers, SHSW.

6. Staughton Lynd, "Mississippi Freedom Schools: Retrospect and Prospect," July 1964, 1, ZP, box 2, folder 2. Clayborne Carson grants the freedom schools less than five pages in his history of SNCC; Howard Zinn's history of SNCC is similarly brief on the freedom schools. Doug McAdam focuses on the Summer Project's effects on SNCC activists and the white volunteers. Nicolaus Mills similarly focuses on the teachers. Carson, *In Struggle*, 109–11, 119–21; Zinn, *SNCC*, 247, 249; McAdam, *Freedom Summer* 66–115; Mills, *Holy Crusade*, 122–28. For gender issues, see Minutes of 5th District COFO staff meeting, 14–17 April 1965, 11, Social Action Vertical File, SHSW, box 47 (hereafter cited as SAVF); Payne, *Light of Freedom*, 305; Dittmer, *Local People*, 260–61.

7. "Prospectus for the Summer," ca. 1964, 2, ZP, box 2, folder 12; Charles Cobb, "Prospectus for a Summer Freedom School Program" (December 1963), reprinted in *Radical Teacher* 40 (Fall 1991): 36; Dittmer, *Local People*, 258; Payne, *Light of Freedom*, 42; Carmichael, *Ready for Revolution*, 302.

8. Jane Stembridge, "Freedom Schools Teaching Guide," 2, Papers of the Mississippi Freedom Democratic Party (SNCC appendix A), reel 67, frame 0316 (hereafter cited as SNCC-MFDP); COFO publication, "Adopt a Freedom School," n.d., 4, SNCC, reel 6, frame 0054 (quote). See also "Mississippi: Structure," 3, reel 6, frame 0049; John O'Neal and Lois Chaffee to Myles Horton, March 1964, HREC, box 41, folder 6.

9. "Outline for Maureen Murphy," December 1963, 7, Mendy Samstein papers; Cobb, "Prospectus" (quote). See also "Mississippi: Structure," 5, reel 6, frame 0050; "Overview of the Community Centers," n.d., SNCC, reel 38, frame 0106; Lois Chaffee memo "to everybody interested in or working in the community center program," n.d., 1, Stuart Ewen papers, SHSW, box 1, folder 1.

10. Joseph Ellin "to Gazette," 10 July 1964, 3, Elizabeth Sutherland papers, SHSW, microfilm, reel 1, frame 158 (hereafter cited as ESP); "Freedom School Data," 1, SNCC-MFDP, reel 67, frame 0208; Carson, *In Struggle*, 119. See also "Freedom Schools Mississippi," *Student Voice*, 5 August 1964, Carson and Staff, *Student Voice*, 181.

11. "White America's Blind Spot: Negro History," n.d., 2, SNCC-MFDP, reel 64, frame 1207 (quote); "Curriculum Planning for Summer Project," n.d., 1, ZP, box 2, folder 2; "Mississippi Freedom School Curriculum—1964," *Radical Teacher* 40 (Fall 1991): 6–34; "Freedom Schools Mississippi," 181; Novick, *Noble Dream*, 426, 428, 431–33.

12. Marcia Hall, "Canton, Mississippi Freedom School Report," July 1964, 4–5, SNCC-MFDP, reel 67, frames 0236–0237; profiles in SNCC-MFDP, reel 67, frames 0822–0829; "Books Needed in the Mississippi Freedom Schools and Libraries," n.d., SNCC, reel 38,

frame 1266, lists over 100 books that SNCC wanted for freedom school libraries. See also list of history texts in Council of Federated Organizations, Panola County papers, SHSW, box 1, folder 7 (hereafter cited as COFO-Panola).

13. Transcript of SNCC staff meeting, 9–11 June 1964, 15, ZP, box 2, folder 7; Tyson, *Radio Free Dixie*, 290; Payne, *Light of Freedom*, 114, 204–5, 279; Robert Cooper Howard, Lee Mae Howard, Bee Jenkins, and Leola Blackmon oral histories in Youth of the Rural Organizing and Cultural Center, *Minds Stayed on Freedom*, 93–95, 99, 138–40, 175; Carmichael, *Ready for Revolution*, 303.

14. Transcript of *Radio Free Dixie* broadcast, 7 August 1964, 2, 9, Johns Committee papers, Florida State Archives, Tallahassee, series 1486, carton 18, "Radio Free Dixie" file; Nina Simone, "Mississippi Goddam" (recorded March or April 1964), *Nina Simone in Concert*.

15. Ira Landess, "Freedom School Report: McComb," 1, SNCC-MFDP, reel 68, frame 0486; Lois Chaffee to Beryle Banfield, 29 May 1964, SNCC-MFDP, reel 67, frame 0262.

16. CORE Southern Office, "Relation of Southern Program to National Program," September 1964, 1, Alan Gartner papers, SHSW, box 1, folder 10 (hereafter cited as AGP); Eric Morton memo to NAC, ca. September 1964, CORE, series 5, box 22, folder 3. See also Mike Lesser, "Field Report: Oachita Parish," 9–12 December 1963, 4, CORE Monroe, Louisiana, chapter, box 3, folder 2, (hereafter cited as CORE-Monroe); unnamed project director, "COFO Project in Meridian, Mississippi summer 1964," 17 August 1964, 1, 3–4, CORE, series 5, box 15, folder 3.

17. Monroe CORE, "Freedom School Program," n.d., 2, CORE-Monroe, box 3, folder 10; minutes of Western Regional Action Council meeting, 17 January 1964, additional paper for discussion, CORE Western Regional Office papers, SHSW, box 2, folder 11 (hereafter cited as CORE-WRO); Rita Schwerner, "Meridian Community Center," 19 October 1964, 1, Scholarship Education and Defense Fund for Racial Equality papers, SHSW, box 1, folder 14; Meier and Rudwick, *CORE*, 276.

18. Zoya Zeman, "Clarksdale Community Center," 7 September 1964, 1, SNCC-MFDP, reel 67, frame 0374.

19. "SNCC Freedom Schools Art Curriculum," 1–2 (quote), SNCC-MFDP, reel 67, frames 1167–1168; "Negro History Curriculum, chapter 8—The Negro in Culture, Art and Literature," 4, COFO-Panola, box 1, folder 7.

20. "Report of a Subgroup of the Leadership Development and Current Issues Committee at the Mississippi Summer Project Curriculum Conference," 21–22 March 1964, SNCC, reel 38, frame 1257; Lois Chaffee to Barbara Jones, 26 April 1964, SNCC-MFDP, reel 67, frame 0255.

21. SNCC handout, "Basic Question: What Are Freedom Schools For and What Do You Want from Them," n.d., 4, Lise Vogel papers, SHSW.

22. Liz Fusco, "Deeper Than Politics," *Liberation*, November 1964, 17 (quote); Florence Howe, "Mississippi's Freedom Schools: The Politics of Education," in Howe, *Myths of Coeducation*, 13; Belfrage, *Freedom Summer*, 91.

23. Howard Zinn, "Schools in Context: The Mississippi Idea," SNCC pamphlet, 5 (*Nation*, 23 November 1964), Linda Gordon papers, SHSW, "SNCC, 1964–1965" folder; Freedom school students of Hattiesburg, "Declaration of Independence," ZP, box 2, folder 2.

24. Myles Horton to Liz Fusco, 21 October 1964; Fusco to Horton, 25 October 1964, both in HREC, box 9, folder 23; Holt, *Summer That Didn't End*, 109–11; Mae Alice Matthews, "President Kennedy," *Benton County Freedom Train* 1, no. 2 (28 July 1964): 3, ZP, box 2, folder 2; Arelya J. Mitchell, "Nov. 22, 1963," in *Freedom News* 1, no. 2 (10 July 1964): 1, ZP, box 2, folder 2.

25. Beulah Mae Ayers, "What a Woman Can Do," *Benton County Freedom Train* 1, no. 2 (28 July 1964): 3, ZP, box 2, folder 2.

26. See, for example, "Homesick Blues" and "Bound No'th Blues," in *Fine Clothes to the Jew*; "I, Too" in Hughes, *Selected Poems*, 275 (originally in *The Weary Blues* [1926]). For the use of Hughes's poetry in the freedom schools, see "Gluckstadt Freedom School," ca. July 1964, 2, SNCC-MFDP, reel 67, frame 0240; Holt, *Summer That Didn't End*, 109; Etta Forbes, "A Gypsy," *Pratt Freedom Press* 1, no. 1 (21 August 1964): 4, ZP, box 2, folder 2; Lillie Mae Powell, "The Negro Soldier," in Zinn, "Schools in Context," 5.

27. Documents in HREC, box 41, folder 6, refer to the COFO conference; Howe, "Mississippi's Freedom Schools," 7–8; Mississippi Summer Project Fact Sheet, 1 August 1964, 2, ZP, box 2, folder 2; Bob Cohen, "The Mississippi Caravan of Music," *Broadside* 51 (20 October 1964), HREC-UN, microfilm, reel 35, frame 0960; "Freedom School Data," 5, SNCC-MFDP, reel 67, frame 0210; Carawan and Carawan, *Sing for Freedom*, 175; Lester, *Search for the New Land*, 69.

28. "Seeds of Freedom" cast list, SNCC-MFDP, reel 68, frame 0436. The cast later performed in New York City. SNCC press release, "Miss. 'Freedom School' Players to Act in NY," n.d., SNCC, reel 37, frame 0601; see also Sandy Siegel, "Clarksdale Freedom School," 17 July 1964, SNCC-MFDP, reel 67, frame 0372; and Chilcoat and Ligon, "Theatre," 515–43.

29. Richard Schechner, a white drama professor from Tulane University and editor of the *Tulane Drama Review*, joined soon after the FST's formation. Doris Derby, Gilbert Moses, and John O'Neal, "The Need for a Southern Freedom Theatre," *Freedomways* 4, no. 1 (first quarter 1964): 111; Stuart W. Little, "Fulfilling a Deep Need in the Deep South," *New York Herald Tribune*, 16 August 1964; SNCC press release, 10 April 1964, SAVF, box 19; John O'Neal, "At the Heart of the Matter in Jackson," ca. March or April 1964, 1, Free Southern Theater Records 1963–1978, Amistad Research Center, Tulane University, microfilm, reel 2, box 6, folder 12 (hereafter cited as FST). Biographical detail: Dent, Schechner, and Moses, *Free Southern Theater*, 3; Harris, "Mirror of the Movement," 12–13; Little, "Fulfilling" 29; Zinn, *SNCC*, 103.

30. Derby, Moses, and O'Neal, "Need," 111; Doris Derby, Gilbert Moses, John O'Neal, and William Hutchinson, "A General Prospectus for the Establishment of a Free Southern Theater," SCLC, microfilm, part 4, reel 5, frame 0647; Duberman, *White America*, x (quote); Martin Duberman to Staughton Lynd, 8 July 1964; Carolyn Amussen (Houghton Mifflin) to Lynd, 8 July 1964, both in FST, reel 17, box 54, folder 10. For Duberman and the New Left, see Duberman, "Abolitionists," 183–91; Wiener, "Radical Historians," 413.

31. Duberman, *White America*, 4 (quote), 81, 83–112; Gilbert Moses, "Notes on *In White America*," 11 July 1964, 2, FST, reel 17, box 54, folder 10.

32. Gilbert Moses, John O'Neal, Denise Nicholas, Murray Levy, Richard Schechner, "Dialog: The Free Southern Theatre," (1965), in Bean, *Sourcebook*, 106.

33. Clayborne Carson, John Dittmer, Seth Cagin, and Philip Dray make only fleeting references to the FST. Charles Payne, Doug McAdam, Nicolaus Mills, and Howard Zinn ignore it. Carson, *In Struggle*, 120; Dittmer, *Local People*, 261; Cagin and Dray, *We Are Not Afraid*, 386; Payne, *Light of Freedom*; McAdam, *Freedom*; Mills, *Holy Crusade*; Zinn, *SNCC*.

34. Cagin and Dray, *We Are Not Afraid*, 386; Lynd, "Retrospect," 3; "Freedom School Data," 4, SNCC-MFDP, reel 67, frame 0209; Belfrage, *Freedom Summer*, 232; Howe, "Mississippi's Freedom Schools," 8; Kirsty Powell, "Report Mainly on Ruleville Freedom School, Summer Project, 1964," 9–10, SNCC-MFDP, reel 68, frame 0586; "Mississippi Negro," quoted in Little, "Fulfilling," 29; Holt, *Summer That Didn't End*, 83; David Gelford to "people," 11 August 1964, 1, ESP, reel 1, frame 0208.

35. Fabre, "Free Southern Theatre," 55; Elizabeth Sutherland, "Theater of the Meaningful," *Nation*, 19 October 1964, in Dent, Schechner, and Moses, *Free Southern Theater*, 25, 28–29; Erika [Teer of SNCC] to Joy, 19 August 1964, FST, reel 17, box 54, folder 10; Moses et al., "Dialog," 112; Belfrage, *Freedom Summer*, 232; anonymous Mississippian, quoted in Holt, *Summer That Didn't End*, 83.

36. "Special Report—Community Centers," September 1964, 1, 2; "Freedom Centers—What's Happening," September 1964, both in COFO-Panola, box 1, folder 3; Payne, *Light of Freedom*, 304–5; Dittmer, *Local People*, 390–91, 425. We know little of what happened to many Mississippians who encountered SNCC in 1964. The University of Southern Mississippi has taken testimony from a wide variety of activists, but only one freedom school pupil, Lodie Marie Robinson-Cyrille. Dittmer, *Local People*, 261; University of Southern Mississippi Center for Oral History and Cultural Heritage oral histories; Payne, *Light of Freedom*, 409–11.

37. Various field reports for West Helena freedom school (Phillips County), June–July 1965, SNCC Arkansas Project papers, SHSW, box 1, folder 15; "Gould 'Freedom School' Primarily Teaches Pride," *Arkansas Gazette*, 27 March 1966, SNCC Arkansas, box 8, folder 6 (Laura Foner papers); Nancy Stoller, "Freedom School Workshop [at Highlander]," ca. April 1965, SNCC Arkansas, box 2, folder 1.

38. SNCC press release, 27 August 1965, SAVF, box 48; "Albany Georgia Nursery School: A Pilot Program for Southern Nursery Schools," post–summer 1964, 3–4, SNCC, reel 37, frames 0405–0406; "SNCC Programs for 1965," 23 February 1965, 3, 5, SAVF box 47; SNCC press release, "Mississippi Summer Project: One Year Later," 25 May 1965, SAVF, box 29; John Lewis, statement to SNCC staff meeting, February 1965, 2–3, SAVF, box 47.

39. Judy Richardson memo to SNCC Executive Committee "re: Residential Freedom School," September 1964, SNCC, reel 3, frame 0367; "Prospectus for Residential Freedom School," n.d., attachment to memo to SNCC staff, 29 May 1965, 1, SAVF, box 47; "Southwest Georgia SNCC Newsletter," 28 February 1965, 2, SNCC, reel 37, frame 0352; Judy Richardson, Report on Residential Freedom School, August 1965, SNCC, reel 35, frames 0077–0082.

40. The visitors were Lewis, Forman, Bob Moses, Dona Richards, Fannie Lou Hamer, Prathia Hall, Julian Bond, Ruby Doris Robinson, Bill Hansen, Don Harris, and Matthew Jones. Lewis, statement to SNCC staff meeting, 1; Carson, *In Struggle*, 134–35; Lewis, *Walking with the Wind*, 235; Harry Belafonte oral history in Hampton and Fayer, *Voices of Freedom*, 146–48.

Chapter 5. Integrationist Cultural Organizing in the Black Power Era, 1965–1969

1. Cook, *Sweet Land of Liberty*, 195; Phyl Garland, "The Natural Look: Many Negro Women Reject White Standards of Beauty," *Ebony*, June 1966, 143–44, 146, 148; David Llorens, "Natural Hair: New Symbol of Race Pride," *Ebony*, December 1967, 139–44.

2. Andrew Young address to Black Is Beautiful meeting, 16 August 1967, SCLC, microfilm, part 3, reel 4, frame 0449.

3. SCLC press release, 28 April 1965, SCLC, part 3, reel 2, frame 0398; King concert program, SCLC, part 3, reel 2, frames 0400–0401; Coretta Scott King, *My Life*, 133–34, 230 (quote), 231; SCLC 1966 Board Meeting reports, SCLC, part 3, reel 9, frame 0389.

4. King concert program.

5. SCLC press release, 28 April 1965; King, *My Life*, 231 (quote).

6. King, *Where Do We Go*, 38–45, 50.

7. "*Playboy* Interview: Martin Luther King, Jr.," in Washington, *Testament of Hope*, 364; King, 'Hammer on Civil Rights' (9 March 1964), ibid., 169–70; King, *Why We Can't Wait*, 22 (quote), 33, 81, 87; *SCLC Newsletter* 2, no. 7 (June 1964), 10, SCLC, part 3, reel 4, frame 0342; S. O. Adebo, address to SCLC annual convention, 10 August 1965, SCLC, part 3, reel 8, frame 0661.

8. King, *Where Do We Go*, 61–62, 70, 131–32; "MLK's Tropic Interlude," *Ebony*, June 1967, 112, 118; Martin Luther King Jr., "The State of the Movement," presentation to SCLC staff retreat, 28 November 1967, SCLC, part 1, reel 21, frames 0086, 0093 (quotes).

9. *Jet*, 9 April 1964, 61; "Top Actor of Year," *Ebony*, March 1964, 125; "America's 100 Most Influential Negroes," *Ebony*, September 1963, 228–32; Louie Robinson, "Academy's Oscar Brings Sidney More Money, Boost in Career," *Jet*, 30 April 1964, 60–61 (first quote, 61); Sidney Poitier, address to SCLC annual conference, 14 August 1967, SCLC, part 3, reel 10, frames 0507–0509 (second quote, frame 0509).

10. SCLC press release, 2 August 1967, SCLC, part 3, reel 10, frame 0530 (first quote); Garland, "Aretha Franklin," 47, 52; Martin Luther King Jr., "Annual Report of the President," 16 August 1967, SCLC Annual Convention 1967 program, SCLC, part 3, reel 10, frames 0514–0523, 0536; Black Is Beautiful program, 16 August 1967, SCLC, part 3, reel 4, frame 0444; Lerone Bennett Jr., address to SCLC Convention, 16 August 1967, SCLC, part 3, reel 4, frames 0445–0446; Andrew Young, address to Black Is Beautiful meeting, 16 August 1967, SCLC, part 3, reel 4, frames 0449–0450 (subsequent quotes).

11. Carawan and Carawan, *Sing for Freedom*, 288–93, 308–9; Pruter, *Chicago Soul*, 136–42.

12. SCLC Ford Foundation proposal, 1 March 1967, SCLC, part 1, reel 2, frames 0851 (quote), 0861; SCLC press release, 17 July 1967, SCLC, part 2, reel 11, frames 0010–0012. The program received a $109,000 grant from the U.S. Office of Education.

13. "A Big Angry Man Turns Nonviolent," *Washington Post*, 17 June 1968; Poor People's Campaign press release, 3 June 1968, 1, SCLC, part 4, reel 27, frame 0494; Hill, *Deacons for Defense*, 162, 254.

14. "We'll Never Turn Back" song sheet, 1968, HREC, box 106, folder 5; Diane Suggs, "There Is Peace in Blackness," *True Unity*, June 1968, SCLC, part 4, reel 28, frame 0578; Martin Luther King Jr. speech, 19 March 1968, cited in Cone, *Martin and Malcolm*, 230; "Singing and Discussion in Resurrection City," *Highlander Reports*, Fall 1968, 5, HREC, box 1, folder 7.

15. Poor People's Campaign press release, 3 June 1968, 2, SCLC, part 4, reel 27, frame 0495; Mariette Wickes, "Cultural Program: Poor People's Campaign," 30 May 1968, SCLC, part 4, reel 28, frames 0446–0449; Conrad Browne to Guy Carawan, 9 May 1968, 2, HREC, box 109, folder 10; "Singing and Discussion in Resurrection City," 5; untitled notes on Highlander's role at Resurrection City; Myles Horton to Bernard Lafayette (SCLC), 1 May 1968, HREC, box 109, folder 10; Mike Clark, "Resurrection City Comments," December 1968, 4, HREC, box 105, folder 12.

16. Guy Carawan, Report on Poor People's Cultural Workshop, Resurrection City, 20 May–29 June 1968, esp. 5–6, HREC, box 109, folder 10; Fairclough, *Soul of America*, 386; Hampton and Fayer, *Voices of Freedom*, 475–83; McKnight, *Last Crusade*, 107–39.

17. Field Report on SCLC Many Races Culture program, n.d., SCLC, part 2, reel 12, frame 0283.

18. Alan Lomax, "Folk Music Workshop at Highlander Center," *Southern Patriot*, n.d., enclosure with Highlander fund-raising letter, October 1965; "Report on the Conference for Southern Community Cultural Revival" at Highlander, 1–3 October 1965, 4, both in HREC, box 65, folder 2.

19. "East Kentucky Mountain Project," 1 June–15 December 1967, HREC, box 37, folder 11; Bernice Reagon to Myles Horton, 21 February 1966, HREC, box 65, folder 3; Julius Lester, Report on Greenwood, Mississippi, Festival and Proposals for the Negro Community Cultural Revival Project, February 1966; Report on Field Trip March 1–May 22 1966; Report from Newport Folk Festival, July 1966, all in HREC, box 71, folder 3; Willie B. Peacock, "Folk Song Festivals," ca. 1965–1966, 1–2, SNCC, reel 40, frame 0050.

20. Julius Lester to Myles Horton, received 4 April 1966, HREC, box 104, folder 18; SSOC Workshop agenda, 17 September 1965; Anne Cook Romaine, "Proposal for SSOC," 1 September 1965, HREC, box 81, folder 4; finding aid, Records of the Southern Folk Cultural Revival Project, Southern Folklife Collection, University of North Carolina–Chapel Hill (hereafter cited as SFCRP); Michel, *Struggle*, 54, 56–58, 102.

21. Reagon, interview, side 1; Anne Romaine, "Southern Folk Festival," n.d., 1, HREC, box 71, folder 2; Anne Romaine, "Southern Folk Cultural Revival Project," 1982, 1–2, SFCRP, box 2.

22. Romaine, "Southern Folk Cultural," 2–4; Anne Romaine, "Southern Grassroots Revival Project—Narrative Script," ca. 1981, 2–3, SFCRP, box 3; Anne Romaine and Bernice Reagon, SFCRP Foundation Proposal, 1967, 7–8, SFCRP, box 3; Michel, *Struggle*, 118.

23. Anne Romaine to Conrad Browne, 30 October 1966, HREC, box 104, folder 18; SSOC Music Workshop agenda and report, November 1966, HREC, box 104, folder 18;

Romaine, "Southern Folk Cultural," 1. See also Anne Romaine to Conrad Browne, 5 August 1966; Conrad Browne to Anne Romaine, 28 September 1966; Guy Carawan to Myles Horton, Conrad Browne, Anne Romaine, 9 October 1966; Romaine to Browne, 22 October 1966, all in HREC, box 104, folder 18.

24. Anne Romaine to members of the Board of the Newport Folk Foundation, 3 January 1968, 1, SFCRP, box 3; Romaine, "Southern Folk Cultural," 4, 6; Anne Romaine, "1967 Southern Folk Festival," April 1967, HREC, box 106, folder 11; Romaine and Reagon, SFCRP Foundation Proposal, 3.

25. "Singers Teach History," *Atlanta Journal*, 4 June 1968; Anne Romaine to "Martha," 25 October 1968, 1, Papers of Anne Romaine, Southern Folklife Collection, University of North Carolina–Chapel Hill, folder 1; "Afro-American Cultural Program," ca. 1966, SNCC, reel 17, frame 0390. See also Bernice Reagon to Myles Horton, 21 February 1966, HREC, box 65, folder 3; Bernice Reagon, "Penny Festival Evaluation Report," February 1967, 1, HREC, box 104, folder 19.

26. Bernice Reagon to Conrad Browne, 12 February 1967, HREC, box 104, folder 19 (quote); Reagon, "Penny Festival Evaluation Report"; "The Penny Festival: Documentary of Afro-American History," ca. 1967, SNCC, reel 17, frame 0391; Bernice Reagon, "The Penny Festival: A Report for Two Years 1967–1968," 4–5, HREC, box 104, folder 19; Bernice Reagon, "Remarks," in Reagon, "Report for Two Years," 15; Bernice Reagon, introduction to Bruce Stewart with Lynn Shapiro, "Oh, What a Time," enclosure with SFCRP long-playing record *Oh, What a Time*, 1982, 32 galleys, SFCRP, box 4.

27. Michel, *Struggle*, 50, 83–85, 115, 192–93; Anne Romaine to Leslie Dunbar (Field Foundation), 17 May 1967, and reply, 6 June 1967, SFCRP, box 3; Romaine to Martha, 1; Romaine, "Southern Folk Cultural," 4–5; "Times Are Changing—Slowly—for Folk Revival Project" *Tennesseean*, 15 July 1979, SFCRP, box 12.

28. Romaine, "Southern Folk Cultural," 4; Reagon, introduction, 31–32.

29. Berg, "*Ticket*," 157–65; "Resolutions Adopted by the Forty-seventh Annual Convention of the NAACP at San Francisco, California June 26, 1956," 2, 4, 12–13, NAACP, III box A2, folder 1956 Resolutions Adopted; "1958 Convention Work Shop Manual," NAACP, III box A2, 1958 Workshops.

30. Ruby Hurley, Report for March meeting of NAACP Board of Directors, 24 February 1965, 5, NAACP, III box C175, Southeastern Regional Office Reports 1965; "Community Action Workshop Supplementary Notes" for 1965 National Convention, NAACP, III box A20, 1965 Workshops.

31. Executive Director's Report: Departmental Reports, July, August 1965, 7, NAACP, III box A32, Secretary's Reports 1965; Executive Committee meeting minutes, 8 February 1965, 12, NAACP, III box A26, Minutes 1964–1965; Director of Branches memo to Alabama State Conference, 11 February 1965, 1 (quote); Executive Director's Report: Departmental Reports, April 1965, 2; Executive Director's Report: Departmental Reports, May 1965, 1–2, both in NAACP, III box A32, Secretary's Reports 1965; NAACP press releases, 7 and 19 May 1965; "1965 Voter Registration Summer Projects," May 1965, NAACP, III box A267, Register and Vote: NAACP Summer Project 1964–1965 May; "1965 Voter Registration Summer Projects in Alabama, Mississippi, and South Carolina," ca. September 1965, NAACP, III box A268, Register and Vote: NAACP Summer Project 1965, n.d. (cost fig-

ure); Minutes of NAACP Board of Directors meeting, 12 September 1965, 3, NAACP, III box A26, Minutes 1964–1965; Executive Director's Report: Departmental Reports, July, August 1965, 11; "Coahoma County Branch NAACP 'Cryer,'" 6 March 1965, NAACP, III box C73, Coahoma County MS 1964–1965; Executive Director's Report: Departmental Reports, October 1965, 4, NAACP, III box A32, Secretary's Reports 1965; NAACP press release, 7 August 1965 NAACP, III box A268; Rowland Evans and Robert Novak, "Inside Report: Mississippi Summer 1965," *New York Herald Tribune*, 26 August 1965, NAACP, III box A268, Register and Vote: NAACP Summer Project, 1965 June–August. Approximately 17,000 black Mississippians attempted to register in 1964, with 1,600 being successful. Carson, *In Struggle*, 117.

32. Rhea, *Race Pride*, 107–8; John Morsell to Charles Pine, 3 November 1966, NAACP, IV box A18, Black Power; Gloster Current, address at NAACP Texas State Conference, 3 November 1966, 6, NAACP, IV box C56, Current, Gloster B., Speeches 1966. James Ivy even conceded that Frantz Fanon's prescription for the racial crisis was "in many respects . . . unanswerable." James W. Ivy, review of Frantz Fanon, *Wretched of the Earth*, *Crisis* 72, no. 9 (November 1965): 597.

33. List of publications and newspapers, 9 October 1929; Walter White memo to Herbert Sligmann, 15 October 1929, NAACP I box C222, Capital "N" for Negro 1929, 1930; *New York Times*, 7 March 1930; NAACP press release, 28 March 1930, NAACP, I box C222, Capital "N" for Negro, 18–30 March 1930; James Ivy, review of Richard B. Moore, *The Name "Negro": Its Origin and Evil Use*, *Crisis* 67, no. 10 (December 1960): 680–81 (quote). Moore, a prominent Harlem bookstore owner, black nationalist, and former Communist Party USA member, was stung enough by Ivy's barbs to note sarcastically that if Ivy's contention were true, then the *Crisis* should not exist. Richard B. Moore to *Crisis* 68, no. 3 (March 1961): 185–86.

34. Lerone Bennett Jr., "Stokely Carmichael: Architect of Black Power," *Ebony*, September 1966, 28; Jane Stembridge, "Notes About a Class," Minor, *Stokely Speaks*, 3–8; Stokely Carmichael, "Who Is Qualified?," ibid., 14; Stokely Carmichael, "Toward Black Liberation," ibid., 32; Stokely Carmichael, "Berkeley Speech," ibid., 58.

35. Lerone Bennett Jr., "What's In a Name?: Negro vs. Afro-American vs. Black," *Ebony*, November 1967, 46–54; Wilkins, *Standing Fast*, 330–31; Fairclough, *Race and Democracy*, 434; Cook, *Sweet Land of Liberty*, 206; Berg, *Ticket*, 238–39; John A. Morsell, "The Name 'Negro,'" NAACP, IV box A7, Speeches 1968 (quotes); John Morsell to *Nevada State Journal*, 4 June 1968, NAACP, IV box A58, "Negro" the word 1966–1968. See also Roy Wilkins, interview by Stan Scott and Jack Smee, 14 July 1968, 1–3, NAACP, IV box A80, Staff: Wilkins, Roy Interviews 1966–1969.

36. Roy Wilkins, Keynote Address to NAACP 59th Annual Convention, 28 June 1968, 1, NAACP, IV box A7, Speeches 1968; "Resolutions Adopted by the Fifty-ninth Annual Convention of the NAACP," 38; "NAACP Annual Report 1968," 135, NAACP, IV box A15, Annual Report 1968; *NAACP Newsletter*, July–August 1968, 1, NAACP, IV box J2, Printed Matter: National Office Newsletter 1966–1969.

37. Luther Jackson memo to Roy Wilkins, Henry Moon, and John Morsell, 10 July 1968, NAACP, IV box A45, Leagues and Organizations: CORE; Stephen Gill Spottswood, Keynote Address to NAACP 59th Annual Convention, 24 June 1968, NAACP, IV box

A7, Speeches 1968. For the NAACP and black capitalism, see also Robert Easley, "The National Afro-American Builders Corp.," NAACP, IV box A9, Speeches 1969.

38. Roy Wilkins, Keynote Address to NAACP 57th Annual Convention, 5 July 1966, 2, NAACP, IV box A3, Speeches 1966; Jean White, "Wilkins Opposes Black Separatism," *Washington Post*, 6 July 1968; Roy Wilkins to Adam Clayton Powell, 30 August 1966, NAACP, IV box A18, Black Power; Wilkins memo to Henry Lee Moon, 25 August 1966, NAACP, IV box A60, Powell, Adam Clayton, Black Power 1966. See also Wilkins to NAACP members and friends, 17 October 1966, NAACP, IV box A18, Black Power.

39. John Hope Franklin, "The Negro in History Textbooks," *Crisis* 72, no. 7 (August–September 1965): 427.

40. "NAACP 60th Annual Convention Resolutions," 10–12, NAACP, IV box A9, Resolutions 1969; "Crisis on Campus," *Journal of the Annual Convention of the NAACP* (1969), 9–16, NAACP, IV box A9, Souvenir Booklet; Doxey A. Wilkerson, address at NAACP Convention, 1 July 1969, NAACP, IV box A9, Speeches 1969; Spottswood, Keynote Address, 5; Roy Wilkins, address to 60th NAACP Annual Convention, 3 July 1969, 3, NAACP, IV box A9, Speeches 1969. See also Wilkins's remarks at California State College, Hayward, 22 April 1969, NAACP, IV box A76, Speakers: Wilkins, Roy, Speeches Texts 1966–1971. Two NAACP officials from Sacramento—close to the black studies epicenter at San Francisco State—had already resigned in protest at Wilkins's rejection of black studies. Virna Canson to NAACP members, ca. January 1969, NAACP, IV box C37, West Coast Regional Office Virna Canson Correspondence and Memoranda 1968–1970; "NAACP Dispute," *San Francisco Chronicle*, 17 January 1969.

41. Jonas, *Freedom's Sword*, 333–35; Roy Wilkins to editor, *New York Times*, 17 February 1969, NAACP, IV box A59, New York Times 1966–1969.

42. Arlene Howell memo to Gloster Current, 27 June 1966, NAACP, IV box C24, Branches: New York State Conference 1966; Leonard Carter memo to Gloster Current, 18 March 1966, NAACP, IV box A66, Riots: Watts; Norman B. Houston (president, Los Angeles branch) to Lucille Black, 18 February 1968, NAACP, IV box C3, Branches: Los Angeles, Cal.: Central 1966–1968; Loring D. Emile, Annual Report, 28 February–23 November 1966, 2, 8, NAACP, IV box C40, West Coast Regional Office: Loring D. Emile 1966–1967; Jesse D. Scott, Monthly Report, November 1967, 1, NAACP, IV box C41, West Coast Regional Office: Jesse D. Scott 1966–1968; various San Francisco field reports, July–October 1967, NAACP, IV box C40, West Coast Regional Office: Joseph L. Howerton Jr. 1967.

43. Michel, *Struggle*, 155; Carmichael, "Toward Black Liberation," 32.

44. King in Cone, *Martin* 230.

Chapter 6. Black Cultural Nationalism, 1965–1969

1. Jones, *Revolutionary Plays*.

2. LeRoi Jones, "The Legacy of Malcolm X, and the Coming of the Black Nation," in Jones, *Home*, 248. At this point, Malcolm X's religion was of little importance to Baraka. Baraka, *Autobiography*, 302.

3. LeRoi Jones, "The Revolutionary Theatre," in Jones, *Home* 210 (quote); Amiri Baraka, "Black Arts" undated fragment, Amiri Baraka papers, Moorland-Spingarn Re-

search Center, Howard University, box 12 (hereafter cited as BP); LeRoi Jones, "Black-hope," transcript of undated speech given as director of BARTS, in Jones, *Home*, 235–37; Hoyt W. Fuller, "Up in Harlem: New Hope," *Negro Digest*, October 1965, 49–50, 83; Bill Hall, "What's Happening in Harlem?" Report for SNCC, 24 November 1965, 2, SAVF, box 47; Thomas, "Shadow World," 68; Woodard, *Nation within a Nation*, 66; LeRoi Jones, liner notes to Various Artists, *The New Wave in Jazz*, in Jones, *Black Music* 175; Gilbert Erskine, review of Various Artists, *The New Wave in Jazz*, *Down Beat*, 27 January 1966, 29; Amiri Baraka, speech at the Hip-Hop Generation Conference, University of Wisconsin–Madison, 22 April 2001, notes in author's collection; Baraka, *Autobiography*, 298–99, 306–9.

4. Watts, *Amiri Baraka*, 156–60; Baraka, *Autobiography*, 325–28; Woodard, *Nation within a Nation*, 66; "Police Raid LeRoi Jones' Theatre: Find Guns, Bomb," *Jet*, 31 March 1966, 65; Allan Morrison, "Hope for Harlem," *Ebony*, October 1964, 168–78; Black Arts Repertory Theater, "Long Range Community Programs and 'Summer Crash Program,'" 25 June 1965, 1, 4–6, BP, box 12.

5. "Newark Afro-American Festival of the Arts," 1966, BP, box 35; Woodard, *Nation within a Nation*, 66–67; Watts, *Amiri Baraka*, 291–92, 367–68; Baraka, quoted in Stephen Schneck, "LeRoi Jones: Or, Poetics and Policemen or, Trying Heart, Bleeding Heart," *Ramparts*, 29 June 1968, 16; Amiri Baraka, liner notes to Baraka, Sun Ra, and the Myth Science Arkestra, *Black Mass*.

6. Amiri Baraka, untitled notebook, 1967, f.12.1 (quote), Imamu Amiri Baraka papers, Bancroft Library, folder 1; Amiri Baraka, "Work Notes—'66," in Baraka, *Raise Race*, 11–15.

7. "Proposal—Education in Newark," ca. 1967, 13–15, BP, box 16; Committee for Unified Newark, "Method," ca. 1970, BP, box 12; Amiri Baraka, "Summer Project Philosophy," June 1968, BP, box 22; David Llorens, "Ameer (LeRoi Jones) Baraka," *Ebony*, August 1969, 82–83; see also Amina Baraka, "Proposal for Experimental Class at Robert Treat School," n.d., BP, box 22.

8. Baraka in Llorens, "Ameer," 82 (first quote); Baraka, "7 Principles of US, Maulana Karenga and the Need for a Black Value System," Baraka, *Raise Race*, 146; Baraka, "The Need for a Cultural Base to Civil Rites and Bpower Mooments," ibid., 43 (second quote), 44; Baraka, "Black Art, Nationalism, Organization, Black Institutions," ibid., 98; Marvin X and Faruk, "Islam and Black Art: An Interview with LeRoi Jones," *Negro Digest*, January 1969, 4–10, 77–80; Amiri Baraka, "Simba Doctrine," BP, box 35.

9. LeRoi Jones, "The Changing Same (R&B and New Black Music)," in Jones, *Black Music*, 210 (first quote), 205–6 (second quote).

10. LeRoi Jones, interview by Robert L. Allen (ca. 1967), transcript 9–10, BP, box 9; Jones, "Changing," 208; Baraka, "What Is Black Art?" *Black NewArk* radio editorial, 24 November 1969, transcript 1, 2 (quote), BP, box 22; Brown, *James Brown*, 200; James Brown "Say It Loud—I'm Black and I'm Proud," "I Don't Want Nobody to Give Me Nothing (Open Up the Door I'll Get It Myself)" (Brown's paean to bootstrap capitalism), in Brown, *Foundations*. Baraka warned jazz players not to abandon the blues in 1965, which contextualizes his later position, in LeRoi Jones, "Apple Cores #2," in Jones, *Black Music*, 124.

11. Sidran, *Black Talk*, 144–46; Ward, *My Soul Responding*, 410–11.

12. Amiri Baraka, "The Fire Must Be Permitted to Burn Full Up: Black 'Aesthetic,'" in Baraka, *Raise Race*, 120; Impressions, *People Get Ready*; Impressions, *This Is My Country*; Mayfield, *Curtis/Live!*

13. Imamu Amiri Baraka, interview by Mike Coleman, transcript, n.d. (ca. 1969–1970), 1, BP, box 9 (quote); McAlister, *Epic Encounters*, 103.

14. LeRoi Jones, *Experimental Death Unit #1*, in Jones, *Revolutionary Plays*, 1–15. The play was written in 1964, but is included in the revolutionary plays anthology, suggesting that he considered it to represent a new phase in his development; LeRoi Jones, *A Black Mass*, in Jones, *Revolutionary Plays*, 21–39; Baraka, Sun Ra, and the Myth Science Arkestra, *Black Mass*; Essen-Udiom, *Black Nationalism*, 124–25; Baraka, "Why No J-E-L-L-O?" in Jones, *Revolutionary Plays*, 89; Watts, *Amiri Baraka*, 265–66.

15. LeRoi Jones, *Great Goodness of Life: A Coon Show*, in Jones, *Revolutionary Plays*, 45–63 (quote 61); LeRoi Jones, *Madheart*, in Jones, *Revolutionary Plays*, 69–87. In his eulogy at Malcolm X's funeral, Ossie Davis referred to Malcolm X as "a Prince—our own black shining Prince!" Alex Haley, foreword to Malcolm X, *Autobiography*, 77.

16. McAlister, *Epic*, 106; Baraka, *Autobiography*, 321.

17. "A Report on Black Theater in America," *Negro Digest*, April 1970, 25; Watts, *Amiri Baraka*, 273; Benston, *Baraka*, 242, 243.

18. Amiri Baraka, *Slave Ship: A Historical Pageant*, in Baraka, *Motion of History*, 132–42 (quotes 137, 142).

19. Ibid., 142.

20. Ibid., 143.

21. Ibid., 144 (first quote), 145 (second quote).

22. Jones, "Changing," 182 (quote), 184–85, 191–92; Benston, *Baraka*, 250–51.

23. Gioia, *History of Jazz*, 202–4, 245–46, 299–300, 304, 344; Kahn, *Love Supreme*, 92–93; Kahn, *House That Trane Built*, 52, 125–27, 134–37; Porter, *John Coltrane*, 199–200, 212–13, 232–33, 263, 276. Miles Davis provided only brief outlines for the tracks that became *Kind of Blue*. Bill Evans and Robert Palmer, liner notes to Davis, *Kind of Blue*.

24. Val Ferdinand in "Report on Black Theater," 28–29; Moses cited in Watts, *Amiri Baraka*, 217.

25. Dent, Schechner, and Moses, *Free Southern Theater*, 14, 16; Stephanie Harrington, "Free Southern Theatre: Speech for the Speechless," *Village Voice*, 11 February 1965, 13, 17; Sandra Schmidt, "Trying Theater in the Rough," *Christian Science Monitor*, 16 April 1965, Samuel Walker papers, SHSW, box 1, folder 11; Moses et al., "Dialog," 105–9; John O'Neal, "Motion in the Ocean: Some Political Dimensions of the FST," in Dent, Schechner, and Moses, *Free Southern Theater*, 178; Beckett, *Waiting for Godot*, esp. 21–25. Baraka also experimented with whiteface. Baraka, *Autobiography*, 309.

26. "Progress Report: Free Southern Theater," summer 1965, 2, 5, FST, reel 2, box 6, folder 12; Free Southern Theater program, n.d., 3 (first quote), SAVF, box 19; Free Southern Theater program, 1965, 3, 7, 9 (second quote), SAVF, box 19.

27. Robert Costley diary entry, 22 August 1965, in Dent, Schechner, and Moses, *Free Southern Theater*, 88.

28. "Progress Report," 2, 5; Free Summer Theater press release, 19 October 1965,

FST, reel 30, box 93, folder 10; Dent, Schechner, and Moses, *Free Southern Theater*, 80; Costley diary entries, 1, 16, 21, 22 August 1965, ibid., 85–88; Richard Schechner to board members, 5 June 1965; Schechner to Margaret Hellbach, 14 June 1965, both in FST, reel 1, box 2, folder 19; Denise Nicholas, "View from the Free Southern Theater," *Liberator*, July 1966, 20.

29. Moses to O'Neal, 14 November 1965, in Dent, Schechner, and Moses, *Free Southern Theater*, 93–97; Nicholas, "View," 20; Tom Dent, "A Look Ahead," in Dent, Schechner, and Moses, *Free Southern Theater*, 232; ya Salaam, "Paper Trail," 331–33; Richard Schechner, "The FST and Me," in Dent, Schechner, and Moses, *Free Southern Theater*, 221; Tom Dent, journal of summer 1967, FST tour, 14 June 1967, in Dent, Schechner, and Moses, *Free Southern Theater*, 149. Dent leaves no record as to whether the departure of the FST's last remaining white member, Murray Levy, was of Levy's own volition. Soon after Levy's departure, Dent made a number of sarcastic remarks about white applicants for FST apprenticeships in *Negro Digest*, which suggests that opinion within the FST was opposed to the continued presence of whites. Tom Dent, "The Free Southern Theater," *Negro Digest*, April 1967, 41

30. Dent, "Free Southern Theater," 42–43; Tom Dent, "The Free Southern Theater: An Evaluation," *Freedomways* 6, no 1. (first quarter 1966): 27, 29 (quote); Harris, "Mirror of the Movement," 44–46.

31. Moses to O'Neal, 14 November 1965; anonymous Mississippian, quoted in Holt, *Summer That Didn't End*, 83.

32. Dent to Denise Nicholas, 13 June 1966, in Dent, Schechner, and Moses, *Free Summer Theater*, 115; Dent, "Evaluation," 29–30; Free Summer Theater Statement of Receipts, 1966, 1967, 1968, 1969, FST, reel 19, box 27, folder 2. In December 1969, O'Neal told the Rockefeller Foundation of the FST's intention to apply for $225,000 to be spread over three years, to be augmented with $450,000 from the Ford Foundation. O'Neal to Norman Lloyd, 15 December 1969, FST, reel 8, box 25, folder 15.

33. Tom Dent memo to FST Board of Directors, 4 June 1967, 2, FST, reel 1, box 3, folder 1; David W. Payne, "The Free Southern Theatre: A Report on Its Promises and Problems as Seen in New Orleans," July 1967, 1, FST, reel 2, box 6, folder 17.

34. Between 1966 and 1967, O'Neal and Moses were forced out of the FST, the former by the draft and the latter by his own frustration with the company's direction. Although both later returned, their departures left Dent in effective control. O'Neal moved to New York, where he helped to solidify funding for the FST through contacts in the city. Moses moved north to study and teach drama. Dent, Schechner, and Moses, *Free Summer Theater*, 61; Moses to O'Neal, March 1967, in Dent, Schechner, and Moses, *Free Summer Theater*, 102; Harrington, "Speech"; Harris, "Mirror of the Movement," 74–75, 85–89.

35. Patricia Brooks, "Free Southern Theater: An Experiment in Art," *National Guardian*, 18 September 1965, 12, SNCC, reel 38, frame 190; Tom Dent, journal of summer 1967 Free Summer Theater tour, FST, reel 18, box 56, folder 24; Tom Dent, "Progress Report: Workshop Program," November 1967, FST, reel 1, box 3, folder 1; FST Newsletter, 18 March 1968, FST, reel 1, box 3, folder 2; Free Summer Theater press release, 7 March 1969, FST, reel 30, box 93, folder 13; Thomas C. Dent to John [O'Neal], 19 July 1967, 1, FST, reel 4, box 1, folder 21 (quote).

36. Williams, *Black Theatre*, 62–63; Dent, Schechner, and Moses, *Free Summer Theater*, 9; Dent, "Look Ahead," 233 (quote). Dent's invocation of Redding is a misreading of Redding's relationship with black and white culture. Redding's frequent writing partner Steve Cropper was a white Missourian whose musical background was as much white country as black rhythm and blues. Redding recorded almost all of his hit records with the integrated group Booker T and the MGs (which included Cropper). Bowman, *Soulsville U.S.A.*, 20; Guralnick, *Sweet Soul Music*, 128–31, 142–51.

37. Williams, *Black Theatre*, 63, 91; Bogle, *Prime Time Blues*, 243; Martinez, Martinez, and Chavez, *What It Is*, 62–63. In 1973, Orman joined the Children's Television Workshop cast for its groundbreaking and resolutely integrated television show, *Sesame Street*. He is known to, and admired by, millions (including the author) as Gordon. Borgenicht, *Sesame Street*, 122.

38. Dent, Schechner, and Moses, *Free Summer Theater*, 67. For race in Louisiana, see Fairclough, *Race and Democracy*, 1–20, 382–84.

39. Val Ferdinand in "Report on Black Theater," 28–29; LeRoi Jones, "To Survive 'The Reign of the Beasts,'" *New York Times*, 16 November 1969; Watts, *Amiri Baraka*, 217; Dent to John, 19 July 1967, 1.

40. Schechner, "FST and Me," 214.

41. Henderson, "Lumpen Proletariat," 171–99; Doss, "Imaging the Panthers," 483–516; Erika Doss, "'Revolutionary Art Is a Tool for Liberation': Emory Douglas and Protest Aesthetics at the *Black Panther*," in Cleaver and Katsiaficas, *Liberation*, 175–87; Brian Ward, "Jazz and Soul, Race and Class, Cultural Nationalists and Black Panthers: A Black Power Debate Revisited," in Ward, *African American Freedom Struggle*, 161–96; Clayborne Carson, foreword to Foner, *Black Panthers Speak*, xiv, xvi; Horne, *Fire This Time*, 187, 200–2; Pinkney, *Red, Black, and Green*, 98–108, 122–24; Pearson, *Shadow of the Panther*; Van Deburg, *New Day in Babylon*, 152–70, 174. The essays in Jones, *Black Panther Party Reconsidered*, emphasize the ideological differences between the BPP and US.

42. Donald Warden, interview by Robert Martin, 25 July 1969, RJB426, 32, RJBOHC; Newton, *Revolutionary Suicide*, 63; Crowe, *Prophets of Rage*, 99–100, 154, 163–68, 185; Welton Smith, interview by Malaika Lumumba, 30 January 1970, RJB347, 3, 11, RJBOHC; Fred Lewis, interview by Malaika Lumumba, 20 January 1970, RJB494, 6, 8, 9, 11, RJBOHC; Warden, interview, 34, 40, 42, 44; Ernie Allen, interview by Robert Wright, 15 November 1968, RJB347, 1, 5, 7, RJBOHC.

43. Brown, "US," 58; Ron Everett-Karenga, interview by Clayborne Carson, 4 October 1977. I want to thank Clayborne Carson for granting access to this recording.

44. Lane, "Huey Newton Speaks," interview, 4 July 1970, 62–64, Dr. Huey P. Newton Foundation Collection, Stanford University, series 1, box 57, folder 7 (hereafter cited as NFC); Newton, *Revolutionary Suicide*, 3–7, 64–65, 72–73, 108, 111–12; Seale, *Seize the Time*, 34; Leo Bizell, interview by James Mosby, 29 August 1969, 7–15, RJBOHC; Huey P. Newton, "To the Black Movement," *Black Panther*, 15 May 1968, in Morrison, *To Die for the People*, 92–93; Fanon, *Wretched of the Earth*, 109.

45. In November 1970, the newspaper changed its name to the *Black Panther Intercommunal News Service*. It will be referred to as the *Black Panther*.

46. Huey P. Newton, "In Defense of Self-Defense II," *Black Panther*, 3 July 1967, in

Morrison, *To Die for the People*, 90; Huey P. Newton, Bobby Seale, "Black Panther Party Platform and Program: What We Want, What We Believe," in Foner, *Black Panthers Speak*, 2, 3; *Black Panther*, 7 December 1968, 7; Newton, "Black Movement," 93–94.

47. Hampton and Fayer, *Voices of Freedom*, 364–66; Seale, *Seize the Time*, 139–59; Newton, *Revolutionary Suicide*, 130–33; Eldridge Cleaver, "The Courage to Kill: Meeting the Panthers," in Scheer, *Eldridge Cleaver*, 27–36.

48. Williams, *Negroes with Guns*, 9–12; Newton, *Revolutionary Suicide*, 112; Seale, *Seize the Time*, 107–22; Bobby Seale oral history in Hampton and Fayer, *Voices of Freedom*, 365, 366; Pearson, *Shadow of the Panther*, 145–47; Isserman and Kazin, *America Divided*, 266; Tyson, *Radio Free Dixie*, 286–89, 357n7. There is no evidence that the BPP acknowledged Williams's later Fanonist-Maoist concept of the role of culture in the liberation struggle.

49. Malcolm X, *Autobiography*, 481–501. Of the collections of Malcolm X's speeches, only Breitman's *Malcolm X Speaks* was published at the time of the BPP's foundation. There are no references to it in the *Black Panther*. For references to Malcolm X, see "Black Panther Party Book List," *Black Panther*, 14 September 1968, 6; George Murray, "For a Revolutionary Culture," *Black Panther*, 2 February 1969, 7; "The Week of the Heroic Guerilla," *Black Panther*, 9 October 1971, 13. Articles citing Guevara, Mao, and Fanon are too numerous to cite in their entirety.

50. Fanon, *Wretched of the Earth*, 163 (quote).

51. Newton, *Revolutionary Suicide*, 111; Seale, *Seize the Time*, 42, 51–52; Fanon, *Wretched of the Earth*, 166–200; Karenga, "Kawaida," 130; Huey P. Newton and Bobby Seale, "Platform and Program," in Foner, *Black Panthers Speak*, 2–3; Seale, *Seize the Time*, 211; Pearson, *Shadow of the Panther*, 196.

52. Emory Douglas, interview by author, 28 June 2001, San Francisco; Baraka, *Autobiography*, 352. Catlett was to take inspiration from the BPP in her 1969 work, *Negro es Bello II (Black Is Beautiful)*: a neat feedback circuit. Powell, *Black Art*, 5.

53. Douglas, interview; Seale, *Seize the Time*, 209; Hilliard and Cole, *This Side of Glory*, 150; Mao Tse-Tung, *Quotations*, 172–73 (quotes); Emory Douglas, "Revolutionary Art/Black Liberation," *Black Panther*, 18 May 1968, 20. For comparison, see Fanon, *Wretched of the Earth*, 174, 179, 187.

54. Emory Douglas, "Position Paper #1 On Revolutionary Art," *Black Panther*, 20 October 1968, 5.

55. Douglas, interview; Hilliard and Cole, *This Side of Glory*, 129; Doss, "Imaging," 495. Newton, Seale, and Eldridge Cleaver edited the newspaper until November 1967, when Newton and Seale were replaced by Kathleen Cleaver. Elbert "Big Man" Howard and Bobby Heron succeeded the Cleavers in March 1969. Raymond Lewis and Frank Jones were editors between 1969 and mid-1970, when Elaine Brown took over. David Du Bois was editor between 1972 and 1976. U.S. House Committee on Internal Security, "Black Panther Party," 1; Christian A. Davenport, "Reading the "Voice of the Vanguard": A Content Analysis of *The Black Panther Intercommunal News Service, 1969–1973*," in Jones, *Black Panther Party Reconsidered*, 200–1.

56. Hilliard and Cole, *This Side of Glory*, 150; "Revolutionary Posters," *Black Panther*, 10 June 1968, 28; Douglas, interview; Ward, "Jazz," 179–80; Charles Pinderhughes to Jen-

nifer Wood Nangombe, 1 May 2000, author's collection; Lane, "Huey Newton Speaks," 3–4; Sonia Sanchez and Eldridge Cleaver oral histories in Hampton and Fayer, *Voices of Freedom*, 363–64.

57. Douglas, interview; Phineas Israeli, "Emory Grinds Down the Pigs," *Black Panther*, 22 November 1969, 6; Dugald Stermer, "The Agit Pop Art of Cuba," *Ramparts*, 14–28 December 1968, 34. Significantly, the only white face in Douglas's work is a bearded peace demonstrator (inevitably being beaten by a pig/ police officer), *Black Panther*, 29 November 1969, back cover.

58. All illustrations by Emory Douglas printed in the *Black Panther* on the date and page noted.

59. Reproduced in Foner, *Black Panthers Speak*, 221 (unknown date and page of the *Black Panther*).

60. Sheila (Zidiska) Waldron, "For Many Years, but Now Today," *Black Panther*, 12 October 1968, n.p.; Iris Wyse, "Because I'm Black," *Black Panther*, 7 September 1968, 13; Nicolas Guillen, "It's All Right," *Black Panther*, 7 September 1968, 13; Sarah Webster Fabio, "Free by Any Means Necessary," *Black Panther*, 18 May 1968, in Foner, *Black Panthers Speak*, 20–21; Fanon, *Wretched of the Earth*, 179, Amiri Baraka, "Black Art," in Jones and Neal, *Black Fire*, 302; Murray, *Crosstown Traffic*, 93; Douglas, interview.

61. Brown, "US," 151–52, 160–64; Douglas, interview; Carson, *In Struggle*, 283; Everett-Karenga, interview; Clayborne Carson, foreword to Brown, *Fighting for US*, viii.

62. Brown, *Fighting for US*, 4, 69–70, 76–77; Huey P. Newton, "The Correct Handling of a Revolution," *Black Panther*, 18 May 1968, in Foner, *Black Panthers Speak*, 41–45; Brown, "US," 26–39, 50, 144–45.

63. Halisi, *Quotable Karenga*, 9, 12, 13, 14, 16, 19, 21, 22, 24–25, 26; "Karenga, Black Panthers Speak Out," *Los Angeles Sentinel*, 6 March 1969 (first quote); Brown, "US," 55–56; Allen, *Guide to Black Power*, 140; Baraka, *Autobiography*, 357, for Karenga's selective use of white philosophy; Kenyatta, *Facing Mount Kenya*; Nyerere, *Ujamaa*, esp. 1–12, 38–44; Senghor, *On African Socialism*; Childs and Williams, *Post-Colonial Theory*, 39–41; Weisbrot, *Freedom Bound*, 229 (second quote). The anonymous introduction to *The Quotable Karenga* asserts that Karenga saved the writer from having to wear "some shark skin suit I had to buy from a Jew," suggesting that US had not transcended anti-Semitism. Halisi, *Quotable Karenga*, 6.

64. Halisi, *Quotable Karenga*, 29, 31.

65. Ibid., 10, 31; Brown, *Fighting for US*, 132–36, 137–42; Hancock, *Mwandishi*.

66. Horne, *Fire This Time*, 201; Brown, "US," 151–52, 160–64; Douglas, interview; Everett-Karenga, interview; Halisi, *Quotable Karenga*, 4; Brown, *Fighting for US*, 78–79; *Black Panther*, 10 June 1968, 28; *Black Panther*, 14 September 1968, 6; Thomas Kilgore Jr., "Black Leadership in Los Angeles," oral history, n.d., 149–50, UCLA Oral History Program transcripts, Bancroft Library.

67. Brown, *Taste of Power*, 142–43; Hilliard and Cole, *This Side of Glory*, 163. Emory Douglas and Karenga believe that Elaine Brown made no small contribution to US-BPP tension through her provocative actions and rhetoric. Brown's memoirs are silent on her role. Douglas, interview; Everett-Karenga, interview; Brown, *Taste of Power*.

68. "The Wall Street Journal Exposes Karenga," *Black Panther*, 2 February 1969, 3;

"Cleaver Challenges Reagan to 'Weapon Duel,'" *Jet*, 24 October 1968, 4; Eldridge Cleaver, "An Aside to Ronald Reagan," in Scheer, *Eldridge Cleaver*, 112. Horne, *Fire This Time*, 199–204, asserts that Karenga was happy to work with governmental agencies, including the Los Angeles Human Relations Commission, to maintain the peace and his own position within the community.

69. Brown, *Fighting for US*, 94–95, 108, 120–27; Newton, "Black Movement," 93; Lockwood, *Conversation with Eldridge Cleaver* 112; Churchill and Vander Wall, *Agents of Repression*, 42–43, 63, 80; Brown, *Taste of Power*, 144; Brown, "US," 300. The BPP tried to use the assassinations to embroil Robert F. Williams in the feud. Robert Cohen to Robert F. Williams, 13 April 1969; Robert F. Williams to Robert Cohen, 26 April 1969, 2, both in RCP, SHSW, box 1, folder 3.

70. "Wall Street," 3; Everett-Karenga, interview; Horne, *Fire This Time*, 199–204; Brown, *Fighting for US*, 94–95, 108.

71. Murray, " Revolutionary Culture," 7 (first quote); Linda Harrison, "On Cultural Nationalism," *Black Panther*, 2 February 1969, in Foner, *Black Panthers Speak*, 151–54; George Murray, "Cultural Nationalism," *Black Panther*, 3 March 1969, 4 (second quote); Bobby Seale interview, *Black Panther*, 3 March 1969, 10.

72. Harrison, "Cultural Nationalism"; "The True Culture of Africans," *Black Panther*, 17 February 1969, 15–18.

73. Harrison, "Cultural Nationalism"; Murray, "Revolutionary Culture"; Murray, "Cultural Nationalism"; Baraka, *Autobiography*, 352; "Blacks Set to Strike at S.F. State," *San Francisco Chronicle*, 5 November 1968; Seale, interview; Earl Ofari, "Cultural Nationalism vs. Revolutionary Nationalism," *Black Panther*, 11 October 1969, 9 (quote). Ofari extended his critique of cultural nationalism in Hutchinson, *Black Liberation*.

74. Emory Douglas, "On Revolutionary Culture," *Black Panther*, 13 September 1969, 6; Israeli, "Emory," 6. Brown was singled out for criticism during the 1972 campaign for his endorsement of Richard Nixon. "'Stars' That Shine in the White House, Fall in the Black Community," *Black Panther*, 4 November 1972, 4.

75. Liner notes reprinted in "Revolutionary View on Music," *Black Panther*, 18 October 1969, 8; Brown, *Taste of Power*, 185. Bobby Seale was not impressed, claiming that "he knew what singing was about—and she couldn't." Maycock, "Seize the Time," 19.

76. Ward, *My Soul Responding*, 413–14; James Mott, Michael Torrence, and Clark Bailey, "Old Pig Nixon" NFC, series 2, box 27, folder 12; Bill Calhoun, reinterpretation of "People Get Ready" (Mayfield) NFC, series 2, box 27, folder 12; Bill Calhoun, "Killing," "Revolution Is the Only Solution" lyrics, NFC, series 2, box 27, folder 12. Emory Douglas claims that Torrence went on to work with Marvin Gaye. Douglas, interview.

77. All references here from *Black Panther*: 3 January 1970, 7; 24 January 1970, 5; Emory Douglas, "Revolutionary Art: A Tool for Liberation," 4 July 1970, 13; 17 April 1971, 9; 21 October 1972, 4–5. Art by other BPP artists: 9 May 1970, 18; 24 October 1970, 17. See also Monk Teba, "A Message to Black Entertainers," 14 December 1970, 5; "Progress, Progress?" 3 July 1971, 10–12.

78. See, for example, *Black Panther*, 20 March 1971, back cover, entitled "Survival Pending Revolution"; untitled, *Black Panther*, 3 March 1972, back cover, which quotes "This Little Light of Mine."

79. Brown, *Taste of Power*, 305–6, 311–12; Smith, *Dancing in the Street*, 231, 235–36; Ward, *My Soul Responding*, 396, 511n24.

80. By comparison, the top-grossing films of 1970 and 1971 (*Love Story*, *M*A*S*H*, *Patton*, *The French Connection*, *Fiddler on the Roof*) yielded between $25 million and $50 million. Thompson and Bordwell, *Film History*, 522; Martinez, Martinez, and Chavez, *What It Is*, 58.

81. Huey Newton, "He Won't Bleed Me: A Revolutionary Analysis of *Sweet Sweetback's Baadasssss Song*," *Black Panther*, 19 June 1971, in Morrison, *To Die for the People*, 112–47. Newton also approved of the size of the black prostitutes' breasts in the opening scene, insisting that they represented Africa's potential as "the breadbasket of the world" (115). Newton's other cinematic choice was *The Godfather*, which he apparently watched repeatedly while high on cocaine. Newton's acceptance of the Mafia operation in *The Godfather* relates to his reconceptualization of black capitalism and his control of the Cal-Pak Boycott. Huey P. Newton, "Black Capitalism Re-Analyzed," in Morrison, *To Die for the People*, 101–11; Pearson, *Shadow of the Panther*, 234, 240–46.

82. "Blaxploitation," *Black Panther*, 7 October 1972, 2, 9, 11; *The Mack* advertisement, *Black Panther*, 14 April 1973, 10; advertisements for BPP–Random House books in the *Black Panther*, 23 August 1972, 11, and 9 September 1972, 13; "How Come I'm So Black and Blue," *Black Panther*, 6 May 1972, 7.

83. Van Deburg, *New Day in Babylon*, 9, 306–8.

Chapter 7. African American Culture in the Civil Rights Movement

1. Duberman, *White America*, 6.

2. Williams, *Negroes with Guns*, 82.

3. Forman, quoted in John Poppy, "The South's War against Negro Votes," *Look*, 21 May 1963, SCLC, part 3, reel 2, frame 0269; Reagon, interview, side 1; Martin Luther King Jr., *Why We Can't Wait*, 61.

4. Septima Clark to Ralph Abernathy, 31 April 1965, SCLC, part 2, reel 17, frame 0199.

5. Sandy Leigh, interview by Anne Romaine, Washington, D.C., November 1966, 98, Papers of Anne Romaine, Southern Folklife Collection, University of North Carolina–Chapel Hill, folder 54 (quote); Fannie Lou Hamer, interview in Stoper, *Student Nonviolent Coordinating Committee*, 308; Lynd, *Living*, 5–6, 33.

6. Ed Brown, interview by Tom Dent, 2 July 1979; Dave Dennis, interview by Tom Dent, 8 October 1983, both in Mississippi Oral Histories, Amistad Research Center, Tulane University, cassettes 25, 46; Carson, *In Struggle*, 142–45; Don Harris, interview in Stoper, *Student Nonviolent Coordinating Committee*, 169.

7. O'Neal, "As a Weapon Is to Warfare . . . ," 66 (quote); Thomas C. Dent to John [O'Neal], 19 July 1967, 2, FST, reel 4, box 11, folder 21; Tom Dent, interview by Robert Wright, 12 August 1969, RJB480, 5, 14, 19, RJBOHC; John O'Neal, "A Road through the Wilderness," in Bean, *Sourcebook*, 98.

8. Smethurst, *Black Arts Movement*, 150–53, 176–77.

9. LeRoi Jones, *Dutchman*, in Jones, *Dutchman and The Slave*, 35.

10. Kofsky, *Black Music*, 18–24; Robert F. Williams, "And God Lay Sleeping," 198. I wish to thank Tim Tyson for granting access to this latter source.

11. Martin Williams, "No Work in U.S. for Ornette?" *Down Beat*, 30 June 1966, 12; Ornette Coleman, "To Whom It May Concern," *Down Beat*, 1 June 1967, 19; Kofsky, *Black Nationalism*, 224–25, 239–40. Porter, *John Coltrane*, 262–92, examines the complexity of Coltrane's final recordings.

12. Dent, "Look Ahead," 233; Enwezor, *Short Century*, 52–55.

13. Emory Douglas, interview by author, 28 June 2001; Tom Feelings, interview by Malaika Lumumba, 29 January 1970, RJB496, 6, RJBOHC; "Negro Art Theme Winning—Successful Brooklynite," *Crisis* 70, no. 4 (April 1963): 228–30; Michele P. Allen, interview by Robert Wright, 16 November 1968, RJB345, 31–32, RJBOHC.

Selected Bibliography

Archival Sources

Amiri Baraka, speech at Hip-Hop Generation Conference, University of Wisconsin–Madison, 22 April 2001, notes in author's collection

Imamu Amiri Baraka papers, Bancroft Library, University of California–Berkeley

Amiri Baraka papers, Moorland-Spingarn Research Center, Howard University, Washington, D.C.

Ralph J. Bunche Oral History Collection, Moorland-Spingarn Research Center, Howard University, Washington, D.C.

Guy Carawan Collection, Southern Folklife Collection, Manuscripts Department, University of North Carolina–Chapel Hill (UNC)

Septima Clark, interview by anonymous interviewer, Manuscripts Department, State Historical Society of Wisconsin (SHSW), Madison

Robert C. Cohen papers, SHSW

Records of the Congress of Racial Equality (CORE), SHSW

CORE Brooklyn, New York, chapter papers, SHSW

CORE Madison County papers (microfilm), SHSW

CORE Monroe, Louisiana, chapter papers, SHSW

CORE Oakland, California, chapter papers, SHSW

CORE Southern Regional Office papers, SHSW

CORE Western Regional Office papers, SHSW

Council of Federated Organizations, Panola County papers, SHSW

Robert Curvin papers, SHSW

Emory Douglas, interview by author, 28 June 2001, San Francisco, transcript and audio recording in author's collection

Ron Everett-Karenga, interview by Clayborne Carson, 4 October 1977, collection of Clayborne Carson

Stuart Ewen papers, SHSW

FBI file 100–446080: Stokely Carmichael

David Feingold papers, SHSW

Free Southern Theater Records, 1963–1978 (microfilm), Amistad Research Center, Tulane University, New Orleans

Alan Gartner papers, SHSW

Linda Gordon papers, SHSW

Fannie Lou Hamer papers (microfilm), UNC

Sandra Hard papers, SHSW

Highlander Research and Education Center records, SHSW

Highlander Research and Education Center records (microfilm), University of Nottingham

"I Shall Not Be Moved," song lyrics at www.simusic.com/worship/ishallno.htm

Johns Committee papers, Florida State Archives, Tallahassee

Kim Lacy-Rogers–Glenda Stevens Collection, Amistad Research Center, Tulane University, New Orleans

Ellen Lake papers, SHSW

Staughton Lynd papers, SHSW

Floyd B. McKissick papers, UNC

Meier-Rudwick Collection of CORE papers, SHSW

Mississippi Oral Histories, Amistad Research Center, Tulane University, New Orleans

Papers of the National Association for the Advancement of Colored People (microfilm), Cambridge University

Records of the National Association for the Advancement of Colored People, Manuscripts Department, Library of Congress, Washington, D.C.

Dr. Huey P. Newton Foundation collection, Manuscripts Department, Stanford University, Stanford, California

Charles Pinderhughes, letter to Jennifer Wood Nangombe and author, 1 May 2000, in author's collection

Radio Free Dixie broadcast recordings, collection of Timothy B. Tyson

Bernice Reagon, interview by Therese Spaude, 27 January 1982, SHSW cassette 1303A

Faith Rich papers, SHSW

Papers of Anne Romaine, Southern Folklife Collection, UNC

Mendy Samstein papers, SHSW

Scholarship Education and Defense Fund for Racial Equality papers, SHSW

Social Action Vertical File, SHSW

Records of the Southern Christian Leadership Conference (microfilm), Manuscripts Department, Library of Congress, Washington, D.C.

Records of the Southern Folk Cultural Revival Project, Southern Folklife Collection, UNC

Southern Oral History Collection, UNC

Records of the Southern Regional Council (microfilm), Manuscripts Department, Library of Congress, Washington, D.C.

Edward Street, interview by author, Cardiff, 12 March 2004, notes in author's collection.

Records of the Student Nonviolent Coordinating Committee (SNCC) (microfilm), Manuscripts Department, Library of Congress, Washington, D.C. (incorporating papers of the Mississippi Freedom Democratic Party)

SNCC Arkansas Project papers, SHSW

SNCC Vine City Project papers, SHSW

Elizabeth Sutherland papers (microfilm), SHSW

UCLA Oral History Program transcripts, Bancroft Library, University of California–Berkeley

University of Southern Mississippi Center for Oral History and Cultural Heritage oral histories at www.lib.usm.edu/~spcol/crda/index

Lise Vogel papers, SHSW

Samuel Walker papers, SHSW

Robert Franklin Williams papers, Bentley Historical Library, University of Michigan–Ann Arbor

Malcolm X, untitled speech, December 1962, at http://www.malcolm-x.organisation/speeches/blackhistory.htm

Howard Zinn papers, SHSW

Published Sources

Adams, Frank, with Myles Horton. *Unearthing Seeds of Fire: The Idea of Highlander.* Winston Salem, N.C.: John F. Blair, 1975.

Allen, Robert L. *A Guide to Black Power in America: An Historical Analysis.* London: Gollancz, 1970.

Anadolu-Okur, Nilgun. *Contemporary African American Theater: Afrocentricity in the Works of Larry Neal, Amiri Baraka, and Charles Fuller.* New York: Garland, 1997.

Anderson, Terry H. *The Movement and the Sixties: Protest in America from Greensboro to Wounded Knee.* New York: Oxford University Press, 1995.

Angelou, Maya. *I Know Why the Caged Bird Sings.* Reprint, London: Virago, 1984.

———. *All God's Children Need Travelling Shoes.* London: Virago, 1986.

Anthony, Earl. *Picking Up the Gun: A Report on the Black Panthers.* New York: Dial, 1970.

Bakhtin, Mikhail. *Rabelais and His World.* Translated by Hélène Iswolsky. Bloomington: Indiana University Press, 1985.

Baldwin, James. *Go Tell It on the Mountain.* New York: Dell, 1953.

———. *Notes of a Native Son.* New York: Bantam, 1955.

———. *The Fire Next Time.* New York: Dell, 1963.

———. *Nobody Knows My Name: More Notes of a Native Son.* London: Penguin, 1964.

———. *Blues for Mister Charlie.* London: Corgi, 1965.

———. *No Name in the Street.* New York: Dell, 1972.

Baraka, Imamu Amiri. *Raise Race Rays Raze: Essays since 1965.* New York: Random House, 1971.

Baraka, Amiri (LeRoi Jones). *The Motion of History and Other Plays.* New York: William Morrow, 1978.

———. *The Autobiography of LeRoi Jones.* Rev. ed. Chicago: Lawrence Hill, 1997.

Baraka, Amiri (LeRoi Jones), Sun Ra, and the Myth Science Arkestra. *A Black Mass*. Washington, D.C.: Son Boy Records CD, 1999.

Barbour, Floyd B., ed. *The Black Power Revolt*. New York: Collier, 1969.

Baskerville, John D. "Free Jazz: A Reflection of Black Power Ideology." *Journal of Black Studies* 24, no. 4 (1994): 484–97.

Baugh, John. "The Politics of Black Power Handshakes." *Natural History* 87 (1978): 32–36.

Bean, Annemarie, ed. *A Sourcebook of African-American Performance: Plays, People, Movements*. New York: Routledge, 1999.

Beckett, Samuel. *Waiting for Godot*. London: Faber and Faber, 1956.

Belfrage, Sally. *Freedom Summer*. Charlottesville: University of Virginia Press, 1990.

Bell, Inge Powell. *CORE and the Strategy of Nonviolence*. New York: Random House, 1968.

Benston, Kimberly W. *Baraka: The Renegade and the Mask*. New Haven, Conn.: Yale University Press, 1976.

Berg, Manfred. *"The Ticket To Freedom": The NAACP and the Struggle for Black Political Integration*. Gainesville: University Press of Florida, 2005.

Billings, Dwight B. "Religion as Opposition: A Gramscian Analysis." *American Journal of Sociology* 96, no. 1 (July 1990): 1–31.

Blakey, Art, and the Jazz Messengers. *Moanin'.* New York: Blue Note LP, 1958.

Bloom, Alexander. *Long Time Gone: Sixties America Then and Now*. Oxford: Oxford University Press, 2001.

Bogle, Donald. *Toms, Coons, Mulattoes, Mammies, and Bucks: An Interpretive History of Blacks in American Films*. 3rd ed. Oxford: Roundhouse, 1994.

———. *Prime Time Blues: African Americans on Network Television*. New York: Farrar, Straus and Giraux, 2001.

Borgenicht, David. *Sesame Street Unpaved: Scripts, Stories, Secrets, and Songs*. New York: Hyperion, 1998.

Bowman, Rob. *Soulsville U.S.A.: The Story of Stax Records*. London: Books with Attitude, 1997.

Boyer, Horace Clarence, and Lloyd Yearwood. *The Golden Age Of Gospel*. Chicago: University of Illinois Press, 2000.

Branch, Taylor. *Parting the Waters: America in the King Years 1954–1963*. New York: Simon and Schuster, 1988.

———. *Pillar of Fire: America in the King Years, 1963–1965*. New York: Simon and Schuster, 1998.

Breitman, George. *The Last Year of Malcolm X: The Evolution of a Revolutionary*. New York: Merit, 1967.

———, ed. *Malcolm X Speaks: Selected Speeches and Statements*. New York: Grove, 1965.

———, ed. *By Any Means Necessary: Speeches, Interviews and a Letter by Malcolm X*. New York: Pathfinder, 1970.

Brick, Howard. *Age of Contradiction: American Thought and Culture in the 1960s*. Ithaca, N.Y.: Cornell University Press, 1998.

Brown, Cynthia Stokes, ed. *Ready from Within: Septima Clark and the Civil Rights Movement*. Trenton, N.J.: Africa World Press, 1990.

Brown, Elaine. *A Taste of Power: A Black Woman's Story*. New York: Anchor, 1992.

Brown, H. Rap. *Die Nigger, Die!* New York: Dial, 1969.

Brown, James. *Foundations of Funk: A Brand New Bag: 1964–1969*. London: Polygram CD, 1996.

Brown, James, with Bruce Tucker. *James Brown: The Godfather of Soul*. Glasgow: Fontana, 1987.

Brown, Scot. "The US Organization: African-American Cultural Nationalism in the Era of Black Power, 1965 to the 1970s." Ph.D. diss., Cornell University, 1999.

———. *Fighting for US: Maulana Karenga, the US Organization, and Black Cultural Nationalism*. New York: New York University Press, 2003.

Cagin, Seth, and Philip Dray. *We Are Not Afraid: The Story of Goodman, Schwerner and Chaney and the Civil Rights Campaign for Mississippi*. New York: Macmillan, 1988.

Calloway, Carolyn R. "Group Cohesiveness in the Black Panther Party." *Journal of Black Studies* 8 (1977): 55–74.

Campbell, James. *Talking at the Gates: A Life of James Baldwin*. London: Faber and Faber, 1991.

———. "Profile: William Styron." *Guardian* (London), 22 March 2003, Review Section, 20–23.

Carawan, Guy, and Candie Carawan. *Freedom Is a Constant Struggle: Songs of the Freedom Movement*. New York: Oak, 1968.

———, eds. *Ain't You Got a Right to the Tree of Life?: The People of Johns Island, South Carolina—Their Faces, Their Words and Their Songs*. Rev. and exp. ed. Athens: University of Georgia Press, 1989.

———, eds. *Sing for Freedom: The Story of the Civil Rights Movement through Its Songs*. Bethlehem, Pa.: Sing Out, 1990.

Carmichael, Stokely, and Charles V. Hamilton. *Black Power: The Politics of Liberation in America*. Harmondsworth, England: Penguin, 1967.

Carmichael, Stokely, with Ekwueme Michael Thelwell. *Ready for Revolution: The Life and Struggles of Stokely Carmichael Kwame Ture*. New York: Scribner, 2003.

Carson, Clayborne. *In Struggle: SNCC and the Black Awakening of the 1960s*. Cambridge, Mass.: Harvard University Press, 1981.

———. "SNCC and the Albany Movement." *Journal of Southwest Georgia History* 2 (Fall 1984): 15–25.

———. "Martin Luther King, Jr.: Charismatic Leadership in a Mass Struggle." *Journal of American History* 74 (1987): 448–54.

Carson, Clayborne, Stewart Burns, Susan Carson, Peter Holloran, and Dana L. H. Powell, eds. *The Papers of Martin Luther King, Jr*. Vol. 3, *Birth of a New Age, December 1955–December 1956*. Berkeley: University of California Press, 1997.

Carson, Clayborne, and Staff of the Martin Luther King, Jr. Papers Project, eds. *The Student Voice 1960–1965: Periodical of the Student Nonviolent Coordinating Committee*. Westport, Conn.: Meckler, 1990.

———, eds. *The Movement 1964–1970*. Westport, Conn.: Greenwood, 1993.

Chafe, William H. *Civilities and Civil Rights: Greensboro, North Carolina, and the Black Struggle for Freedom.* New York: Oxford University Press, 1980.

Chilcoat, George W., and Jerry A. Ligon. "Theatre as an Emancipatory Tool: Classroom Drama in the Mississippi Freedom Schools." *Journal of Curriculum Studies* 30 (1998): 515–43.

Childs, Peter, and R. J. Patrick Williams. *An Introduction to Post-Colonial Theory.* London: Prentice Hall, 1997.

Chrisman, Robert, "The Formation of a Revolutionary Black Culture." *Black Scholar* 1, no. 8 (June 1970): 2–9.

Churchill, Ward, and Jim Vander Wall. *Agents of Repression: The FBI's Secret Wars against the Black Panther Party and the American Indian Movement.* Boston: South End, 1988.

Clark, Steve, ed. *Malcolm X, February 1965: The Final Speeches.* New York: Pathfinder, 1992.

Clarke, John Henrik, ed. *William Styron's Nat Turner: Ten Black Writers Respond.* Boston: Beacon, 1968.

Cleaver, Eldridge, *Soul on Ice: Selected Essays.* London: Jonathan Cape, 1969.

Cleaver, Kathleen, and George Katsiaficas, eds. *Liberation, Imagination, and the Black Panther Party: A New Look at the Panthers and Their Legacy.* New York: Routledge, 2001.

Cobb, James C. *Redefining Southern Culture: Mind and Identity in the Modern South.* Athens: University of Georgia Press, 1999.

Cohen, Ronald D. *Rainbow Quest: The Folk Music Revival and American Society, 1940–1970.* Amherst: University of Massachusetts Press, 2002.

Colburn, David R. *Racial Change and Community Crisis: St. Augustine, Florida, 1877–1980.* Gainesville: University Press of Florida, 1985.

Collier, Peter, and David Horowitz. *Destructive Generation: Second Thoughts About the '60s.* New York: Free Press, 1996.

Cone, James H. *Martin and Malcolm and America: A Dream or a Nightmare.* London: Fount, 1991.

Cook, Robert. "UnFurl That Banner: The Response of White Southerners to the Civil War Centennial of 1961–1965." *Journal of Southern History* 68, no. 4 (November 2002): 879–912.

———. *Sweet Land of Liberty: The African-American Struggle for Civil Rights in the Twentieth Century.* New York: Longman, 1998.

Crawford, Vicki L., Jacqueline Anne Rouse, and Barbara Woods. *Women in the Civil Rights Movement: Trailblazers and Torchbearers 1941–1965.* New York: Carlson, 1990.

Cripps, Thomas. *Making Movies Black: The Hollywood Message Movie from World War II to the Civil Rights Era.* New York: Oxford University Press, 1993.

Crowe, Daniel. *Prophets of Rage: The Black Freedom Struggle in San Francisco, 1945–1969.* New York: Garland, 2000.

Cruse, Harold. *The Crisis of the Negro Intellectual: From Its Origins to the Present.* London: W. H. Allen, 1967.

Daniel, Pete. *Lost Revolutions: The South in the 1950s*. Chapel Hill: University of North Carolina Press, 2000.

Davis, Miles. *Kind of Blue*. New York: Columbia CD reissue, 1997.

DeCaro, Louis A., Jr. *On the Side of My People: A Religious Life of Malcolm X*. New York: New York University Press, 1996.

D'Emilio, John. *Lost Prophet: The Life and Times of Bayard Rustin*. New York: Free Press, 2003.

Denisoff, R. Serge. *Great Day Coming: Folk Music and the American Left*. Urbana: University of Illinois Press, 1971.

Denning, Michael. *The Cultural Front: The Laboring of American Culture in the Twentieth Century*. London: Verso, 1997.

Dent, Thomas C., Richard Schechner, and Gilbert Moses, eds. *The Free Southern Theater by the Free Southern Theater*. Indianapolis, Ind.: Bobbs-Merrill, 1969.

Dickstein, Morris. *Gates of Eden: American Culture in the Sixties*. Cambridge, Mass.: Harvard University Press, 1977.

Dittmer, John. *Local People: The Struggle for Civil Rights in Mississippi*. Urbana: University of Illinois Press, 1994.

Doss, Erika. "Imaging the Panthers: Representing Black Power and Masculinity, 1960s-1990s." *Prospects* 23 (1998): 483–516.

Draper, Theodore. *The Rediscovery of Black Nationalism*. New York: Viking, 1969.

Duberman, Martin B. "The Abolitionists and Psychology." *Journal of Negro History* 47 (1962): 183–91.

———. *In White America*. Boston: Houghton Mifflin, 1964.

———. *Paul Robeson*. London: Pan, 1989.

Du Bois, W. E. B. *The Souls of Black Folk*. Norton Critical Edition, ed. Henry Louis Gates Jr. and Terry Hume Oliver. New York: Norton, 1999.

Dudziak, Mary L. *Cold War Civil Rights: Race and the Image of American Democracy*. Princeton, N.J.: Princeton University Press, 2000.

During, Simon, ed. *The Cultural Studies Reader*. London: Routledge, 1993.

Dyson, Michael Eric. *Reflecting Black: African-American Cultural Criticism*. Minneapolis: University of Minnesota Press, 1993.

———. *Making Malcolm: The Myth and Meaning of Malcolm X*. New York: Oxford University Press, 1995.

———. *I May Not Get There with You: The True Martin Luther King, Jr*. New York: Touchstone, 2000.

Eagleton, Terry. *The Idea of Culture*. Oxford: Blackwell, 2000.

Early, Gerald. *Tuxedo Junction: Essays on American Culture*. New York: Ecco, 1989.

———. *One Nation Under a Groove: Motown and American Culture*. Hopewell, N.J.: Ecco, 1995.

———, ed. *The Muhammad Ali Reader*. Hopewell, N.J.: Ecco, 1998.

———, ed. *Miles Davis and American Culture*. St. Louis: Missouri Historical Society Press, 2001.

Eckman, Fern Marja. *The Furious Passage of James Baldwin*. London: Michael Joseph, 1968.

Edwards, Harry. *The Revolt of the Black Athlete*. New York: Free Press, 1969.

Ellison, Ralph. *Invisible Man*. London: Penguin, 1952.

———. *Shadow and Act*. New York: Random House, 1964.

Enwezor, Okwui, ed. *The Short Century: Independence and Liberation Movements in Africa, 1945–1994*. London: Prestel, 2001.

Epps, Archie, ed. *Malcolm X: Speeches at Harvard*. New York: Paragon House, 1991.

Essen-Udiom. E. U. *Black Nationalism: The Rise of the Black Muslims in the U.S.A.* Harmondsworth, England: Penguin, 1966.

Fabre, Genevieve. "The Free Southern Theatre, 1963–1979." *Black American Literature Forum* 17, no. 2 (Summer 1983): 55–59.

Fairclough, Adam. *To Redeem the Soul of America: The Southern Christian Leadership Conference and Martin Luther King, Jr.* Athens: University of Georgia Press, 1987.

———. "Historians and the Civil Rights Movement." *Journal of American Studies* 24 (1990): 387–98.

———. *Race and Democracy: The Civil Rights Struggle in Louisiana, 1915–1972*. Athens: University of Georgia Press, 1995.

———. "'Being in the Field of Education and Also Being a Negro . . . Seems . . . Tragic': Black Teachers in the Jim Crow South." *Journal of American History* 87 (2000): 65–91.

———. *Better Day Coming: Blacks and Equality, 1890–2000*. New York: Penguin, 2001.

Falkner, David. *Great Time Coming: The Life of Jackie Robinson from Baseball to Birmingham*. New York: Simon and Schuster, 1995.

Fanon, Frantz. *The Wretched of the Earth*. Harmondsworth, England: Penguin, 1965.

Farmer, James. *Freedom—When?* New York: Random House, 1965.

———. *Lay Bare the Heart: An Autobiography of the Civil Rights Movement*. Fort Worth: Texas Christian University Press, 1985.

Fergus, Devin. "Federally Subsidized Black Nationalism: Soul City, Statist Liberalism, and the Menace of Black Republicanism, 1968–1980." Paper delivered at Southern Historical Association annual conference, Baltimore, 6 November 2002. Copy in author's collection.

Filene, Benjamin. *Romancing the Folk: Public Memory and American Roots Music*. Chapel Hill: University of North Carolina Press, 2000.

Fitzgerald, Jon. "Motown Crossover Hits 1963–1966 and the Creative Process." *Popular Music* 14 (1995): 1–11.

Fleming, Cynthia Griggs. *Soon We Will Not Cry: The Liberation of Ruby Doris Smith Robinson*. Lanham, Md.: Rowman and Littlefield, 1998.

Foner, Philip S., ed. *The Black Panthers Speak*. Rev. ed. New York: Da Capo, 1995.

Forman, Jame. *The Making of Black Revolutionaries*. Seattle: University of Washington Press, 1985.

Frady, Marshall. *Jesse: The Life and Pilgrimage of Jesse Jackson*. New York: Random House, 1996.

Franklin, Aretha. *Aretha Now*. Los Angeles: Rhino CD reissue, 1993.

———. *I Never Loved a Man (The Way I Love You)*. Los Angeles: Rhino CD reissue, 1995.

———. *Amazing Grace: The Complete Recordings*. Los Angeles: Rhino CD, 1999.

Franklin, Aretha, and David Ritz. *Aretha: From These Roots*. New York: Villard, 1999.

Franklin, John Hope, and Alfred A. Moss Jr. *From Slavery to Freedom: A History of African Americans*. 8th ed. Boston: McGraw-Hill, 2000.

Gaines, Kevin K. *Uplifting the Race: Black Leadership, Politics, and Culture in the Twentieth Century*. Chapel Hill: University of North Carolina Press, 1996.

Gaffney, Floyd. "Black Theatre: Commitment and Communication." *Black Scholar* 1, no. 8 (June 1970): 10–15.

Garrow, David J. *Bearing the Cross: Martin Luther King, Jr. and the Southern Christian Leadership Conference*. London: Vintage, 1988.

Gates, Henry Louis, Jr. *Loose Canons: Notes on the Culture Wars*. Oxford: Oxford University Press, 1992.

Gayle, Addison, Jr., ed. *The Black Aesthetic*. Garden City, N.Y.: Doubleday, 1971.

Geertz, Clifford. *The Interpretation of Cultures*. London: Fontana, 1973.

George, Nelson. *Blackface: Reflections on African-Americans and the Movies*. New York, HarperCollins, 1994.

Gibson, Donald P., ed. *Five Black Writers: Essays on Wright, Ellison, Baldwin, Hughes, and LeRoi Jones*. New York: New York University Press, 1970.

Gilmore, Glenda Elizabeth. *Gender and Jim Crow: Women and the Politics of White Supremacy in North Carolina, 1896–1920*. Chapel Hill: University of North Carolina Press, 1996.

Gilroy, Paul. *The Black Atlantic: Modernity and Double Consciousness*. London: Verso, 1993.

Gioia, Ted. *The History of Jazz*. New York: Oxford University Press. 1997.

Glaude, Eddie S., Jr. *Exodus!: Religion, Race, and Nation in Nineteenth-Century Black America*. Chicago: University of Chicago Press, 2000.

Glen, John M. *Highlander: No Ordinary School*. Knoxville: University of Tennessee Press, 1996.

Goggin, Jaqueline. *Carter G. Woodson: A Life in Black History*. Baton Rouge: Louisiana State University Press, 1993.

Goldman, Peter. *The Death and Life of Malcolm X*. Urbana: University of Illinois Press, 1979.

Gosse, Van. *Where the Boys Are: Cuba, Cold War America and the Making of a New Left*. London: Verso, 1993.

Greenberg, Cheryl Lynn, ed. *A Circle of Trust: Remembering SNCC*. New Brunswick, N.J.: Rutgers University Press, 1998.

Gregory, Dick, with Robert Lipsyte. *Nigger: An Autobiography*. New York: E. P. Dutton, 1964.

Gregory, Dick, with James M. McGraw. *Up from Nigger*. Greenwich, Conn.: Fawcett, 1976.

Gregory, Dick, with Sheila P. Moses, *Callus on My Soul: A Memoir*. Atlanta: Longstreet, 2000.

Griffith, Barbara S. *The Crisis of American Labor: Operation Dixie and the Defeat of the CIO*. Philadelphia: Temple University Press, 1988.

Guillory, Monique, and Richard C. Green, eds. *Soul: Black Power, Politics, and Pleasure*. New York: New York University Press, 1998.

Guralnick, Peter. *Feel Like Going Home: Portraits in Blues and Rock 'n' Roll*. New York: Outerbridge and Dienstfrey, 1971.

———. *Sweet Soul Music: Rhythm and Blues and the Southern Dream of Freedom*. London: Penguin, 1986.

Hale, Grace Elizabeth. *Making Whiteness: The Culture of Segregation in the South, 1890–1940*. New York: Pantheon, 1998.

Haley, Alex. "Alex Haley Interviews Malcolm X." *Playboy*, May 1963, at http://members.dencity.com/ccblack/shabazz/playboy.html.

Halisi, Clyde, ed. *The Quotable Karenga*. Los Angeles: US Organization, 1967.

Hall, James C. *Mercy, Mercy Me: African-American Culture and the American Sixties*. Oxford: Oxford University Press, 2001.

Hall, Simon. "The NAACP, Black Power, and the African American Freedom Struggle, 1966–1969." *Historian* 69 (2007): 49–82.

Hall, Stuart. "Gramsci's Relevance for the Study of Race and Ethnicity." *Journal of Communication Inquiry* 10 (Summer 1986): 5–27.

———. "What Is This 'Black' in Black Popular Culture?" In *Black Popular Culture: A Project by Michele Wallace*, ed. Gina Dent, 21–33. Seattle: Bay Press, 1992.

Hampton, Henry, and Steve Fayer. *Voices of Freedom: An Oral History of the Civil Rights Movement from the 1950s through the 1980s*. London: Vintage, 1990.

Hancock, Herbie. *Mwandishi*. New York: Warner Bros. LP, 1971.

Harris, Clarissa Myrick. "Mirror of the Movement: The History of the Free Southern Theater as a Microcosm of the Civil Rights and Black Power Movements 1963–1978." Ph.D. diss., Emory University, 1988.

Harris, Fredrick C. "Something Within: Religion as a Mobilizer of African-American Political Activism." *Journal of Politics* 56, no. 1 (February 1994): 42–68.

Harris, William J., ed. *The LeRoi Jones/Amiri Baraka Reader*. New York: Thunder's Mouth, 1991.

Hauser, Thomas. *Muhammad Ali: His Life and Times*. London: Pan, 1991.

Hebdige, Dick. *Subculture: The Meaning of Style*. London: Methuen, 1979.

Henderson, Errol. "The Lumpen Proletariat as Vanguard?: The Black Panther Party, Social Transformation, and Pearson's Analysis of Huey Newton." *Journal of Black Studies* 28 (1997): 171–99.

Henry, Charles P. *Culture and African American Politics*. Bloomington: Indiana University Press, 1990.

Hernton, Calvin. "Umbra: A Personal Recounting." *African American Review* 27, no. 4 (Winter 1993): 579–84.

Heylin, Clinton. *Dylan: Behind the Shades*. London: Penguin, 1991.

Higginbotham, Evelyn Brooks. "African-American Women's History and the Metalanguage of Race." *Signs* 17 (1992): 251–74.

———. *Righteous Discontent: The Women's Movement in the Black Baptist Church, 1880–1920*. Cambridge, Mass.: Harvard University Press, 1993.

Hill, Lance. *The Deacons for Defense: Armed Resistance and the Civil Rights Movement*. Chapel Hill: University of North Carolina Press, 2004.

Hilliard, David, and Lewis Cole. *This Side of Glory: The Autobiography of David Hilliard and the Story of the Black Panther Party*. Boston: Little, Brown, 1993.

Hirshey, Gerri. *Nowhere to Run: The Story of Soul Music*. London: Pan, 1984.

Hoare, Quintin, and Geoffrey Nowell Smith, eds. *Selections from the Prison Notebooks of Antonio Gramsci*. London: Lawrence and Wishart, 1971.

Holt, Len. *The Summer That Didn't End: The Story of the Mississippi Civil Rights Project of 1964*. New York: Da Capo, 1992.

Honey, Michael K. *Southern Labor and Black Civil Rights: Organizing Memphis Workers*. Urbana: University of Illinois Press, 1993.

Horne, Gerald. *Fire This Time: The Watts Uprising and the 1960s*. New York: Da Capo, 1995.

Hoskins, Barney. *Say It One Time for the Brokenhearted: Country Soul in the American South*. London: Bloomsbury, 1987.

Howe, Florence. "Mississippi's Freedom Schools: The Politics of Education." In *Myths of Coeducation: Selected Essays 1964–1983*, 1–17. Bloomington: Indiana University Press, 1984.

Hughes, Langston. "When a Man Sees Red" (1943), at http://eblackstudies.organisation/intro/chapter7.htm.

———. *Fine Clothes to the Jew*. New York: Alfred A. Knopf, 1927.

———. *Selected Poems*. London: Pluto, 1986.

Hutchinson, Earl Ofari. *Black Liberation Cultural and Revolutionary Nationalism*. Ann Arbor, Mich.: Radical Education Project, ca. 1969.

The Impressions. *People Get Ready: The Best of the Impressions Featuring Curtis Mayfield, 1961–1968*. London: Universal CD, 1997.

———. *This Is My Country and The Young Mods' Forgotten Story*. London: Charly CD, 1996.

Isserman, Maurice, and Michael Kazin. *America Divided: The Civil War of the 1960s*. New York: Oxford University Press, 2000.

Jarab, Josef. "Black Aesthetic: A Cultural or Political Concept?" *Callaloo* 25 (Autumn 1985): 587–93.

Jennings, Regina. "Poetry of the Black Panther Party: Metaphors of Militancy." *Journal of Black Studies* 29 (1998): 106–29.

The John Coltrane Quartet. *The Classic Quartet—The Complete Impulse! Studio Recordings*. New York: GRP Recordings CD, 1998.

Johnson Reagon, Bernice. "Songs of the Civil Rights Movement 1955–1965: A Study in Culture History." Ph.D. diss., Howard University, 1975.

Jonas, Gilbert. *Freedom's Sword: The NAACP and the Struggle against Racism in America, 1909–1969*. New York: Routledge, 2005.

Jones, Charles E., ed. *The Black Panther Party Reconsidered*. Baltimore: Black Classic, 1998.

Jones, LeRoi. *Dutchman and The Slave*. New York: William Morrow, 1964.

——. "In the Ring." *Nation*, 29 June 1964, at http://www.thenation.com/historic/bhm2000/19640629jones.shtml.

——. *Home: Social Essays.* New York: William Morrow, 1966.

——. *The Baptism and The Toilet.* New York: Grove, 1967.

——. *Four Black Revolutionary Plays.* Indianapolis, Ind.: Bobbs-Merrill, 1969.

——. *Blues People: The Negro Experience in White America and the Music That Developed from It.* 2nd ed. Edinburgh: Payback, 1995.

Jones, LeRoi (Amiri Imamu Baraka). *Black Music.* New York: Da Capo, 1968.

Jones, LeRoi, and Larry Neal, eds. *Black Fire: An Anthology of Afro-American Writing.* New York: William Morrow, 1968.

Jones, Rhett S. "Community and Commentators: Black Theatre and Its Critics." *Black American Literature Forum* 14, no. 2 (Summer 1980): 69–76.

Joyner, Charles. *Shared Traditions: Southern History and Folk Culture.* Urbana: University of Illinois Press, 1999.

Kahn, Ashley. *A Love Supreme: The Making of John Coltrane's Classic Album.* London: Granta, 2002.

——. *The House That Trane Built: The Story of Impulse Records.* London: Granta, 2006.

Karenga, Maulana Ron. "Kawaida and Its Critics: A Sociohistorical Analysis." *Journal of Black Studies* 8 (1977): 125–48.

Keil, Charles. *Urban Blues.* Chicago: University of Chicago Press, 1966.

Kelley, Robin D. G. *Hammer and Hoe: Alabama Communists during the Great Depression.* Chapel Hill: University of North Carolina Press, 1990.

——. *Race Rebels: Culture, Politics, and the Black Working Class.* New York: Free Press, 1994.

——. "New Monastery: Monk and the Jazz Avant-Garde." *Black Music Research Journal* 19 (1999): 135–68.

Kenyatta, Jomo. *Facing Mount Kenya: The Tribal Life of Gikuyu.* London: Secker and Warburg, 1938.

King, Coretta Scott. *My Life with Martin Luther King, Jr.* Rev. ed. New York: Penguin, 1993.

King, Martin Luther, Jr. *Stride toward Freedom.* London: Gollancz, 1959.

——. *Strength to Love.* London: Hodder and Stoughton, 1964.

——. *Why We Can't Wait.* New York: Signet, 1964.

——. *Where Do We Go from Here: Chaos or Community?* New York: Bantam, 1967.

King, Mary. *Freedom Song: A Personal Story of the 1960s Civil Rights Movement.* New York: William Morrow, 1987.

King, Richard H. *Civil Rights and the Idea of Freedom.* 2nd ed. Athens: University of Georgia Press, 1996.

Kofsky, Frank. *Black Nationalism and the Revolution in Music.* New York: Pathfinder, 1970.

——. *Black Music, White Business: Illuminating the History and Political Economy of Jazz.* New York: Pathfinder, 1998.

Lawson, Steven F., and Charles Payne. *Debating the Civil Rights Movement, 1945–1968.* Lanham, Md.: Rowman and Littlefield, 1998.

Lears, T. J. Jackson. "The Concept of Cultural Hegemony: Problems and Possibilities." *American Historical Review* 90 (1985): 567–93.

Leeming, David. *James Baldwin: A Biography.* London: Michael Joseph, 1994.

Lemann, Nicholas. *The Promised Land: The Great Black Migration and How It Changed America.* New York: Knopf, 1991.

Lester, Julius. *Revolutionary Notes.* New York: Richard W. Baron, 1969.

——. *Search for the New Land: History as Subjective Experience.* London: Allison and Busby, 1971.

Levine, Lawrence W. *Black Culture and Black Consciousness: Afro-American Folk Thought from Slavery to Freedom.* Oxford: Oxford University Press, 1977.

——. "Jazz and American Culture." *Journal of American Folklore* 102 (1989): 6–22.

Lewis, David Levering. *King: A Biography.* 2nd ed. Chicago: University of Illinois Press, 1978.

——. *W. E. B. Du Bois: The Fight for Equality and the American Century, 1919–1963.* New York: Henry Holt, 2000.

Lewis, John, with Michael D'Orso. *Walking with the Wind: A Memoir of the Movement.* New York: Simon and Schuster, 1998.

Lieberman, Robbie. *"My Song Is My Weapon": People's Songs, American Communism, and the Politics of Culture, 1930–1950.* Urbana: University of Illinois Press, 1995.

Lincoln, C. Eric, and Lawrence H. Mamiya. *The Black Church in the African American Experience.* Durham, N.C.: Duke University Press, 1990.

Ling, Peter. "Local Leadership in the Early Civil Rights Movement: The South Carolina Citizenship Education Program of the Highlander Folk School." *Journal of American Studies* 29 (1995): 399–422.

——. "Spirituals, Freedom Songs, and *Lieux de Mémoire*: African-American Music and the Routes of Memory." *Prospects* 24 (1999): 213–30.

——. *Martin Luther King, Jr.* London: Routledge, 2002.

Ling, Peter, and Sharon Montieth, eds. *Gender in the Civil Rights Movement.* New York: Garland, 1999.

Litwack, Leon H. *Trouble in Mind: Black Southerners in the Age of Jim Crow.* New York: Alfred A. Knopf, 1998.

Lockwood, Lee. *Conversation with Eldridge Cleaver.* New York: Delta, 1970.

Lott, Eric. "Double V, Double-Time: Bebop's Politics of Style." *Callaloo* 36 (Summer 1988): 597–605.

——. *Love and Theft: Blackface Minstrelsy and the American Working Class.* New York: Oxford University Press, 1993.

Lynd, Staughton. *Living Inside Our Hope: A Steadfast Radical's Thoughts on Rebuilding the Movement.* Ithaca, N.Y.: Cornell University Press, 1997.

Lyon, Danny. *Memories of the Southern Civil Rights Movement.* Chapel Hill: University of North Carolina Press, 1992.

Malcolm X, with the assistance of Alex Haley. *The Autobiography of Malcolm X.* London: Hutchinson, 1966.

Mao Tse-Tung. *Quotations from Chairman Mao Tse-Tung*. New York: Bantam, 1967.

Marqusee, Mike. *Wicked Messenger: Bob Dylan and the 1960s*. New York: Seven Stories, 2005.

Marsh, Charles. *God's Long Summer: Stories of Faith and Civil Rights*. Princeton, N.J.: Princeton University Press, 1997.

Martinez, Gerald, Diana Martinez, and Andres Chavez. *What It Is . . . What It Was!: The Black Film Explosion of the '70s in Words and Pictures*. New York: Hyperion, 1998.

Maycock, James. "Seize the Time." *Guardian* (London), 21 August 1998, Section 2, 18–19.

Mayfield, Curtis. *Curtis/Live!* Chessington, UK: Castle Music CD, 1999.

McAdam, Doug. *Freedom Summer*. New York: Oxford University Press, 1988.

McAlister, Melani. *Epic Encounters: Culture, Media, and U.S. Interests in the Middle East, 1954–2000*. Berkeley: University of California Press, 2001.

McCormack, Donald J. "Stokely Carmichael and Pan-Africanism: Back to Black Power." *Journal of Politics* 35 (1973): 386–409.

McKissick, Floyd B. *Three-fifths of a Man*. London: Macmillan, 1969.

———. "The Way to a Black Ideology." *Black Scholar* 1, no. 2 (December 1969): 14–17.

McKnight, Gerald D. *The Last Crusade: Martin Luther King, Jr., the FBI, and the Poor People's Campaign*. Boulder, Colo.: Westview, 1998.

McMillen, Neil R. *Dark Journey: Black Mississippians in the Age of Jim Crow*. Chicago: University of Illinois Press, 1990.

Meier, August, and John H. Bracey Jr. "The NAACP as a Reform Movement, 1909–1965: 'To Reach the Conscience of America.'" *Journal of Southern History* 59 (1993): 3–30.

Meier, August, and Elliott Rudwick. *CORE: A Study in the Civil Rights Movement 1942–1968*. New York: Oxford University Press, 1973.

———. *Black History and the Historical Profession 1915–1980*. Urbana: University of Illinois Press, 1986.

Meier, August, Elliott Rudwick, and Francis L. Broderick, eds. *Black Protest Thought in the Twentieth Century*. 2nd ed. Indianapolis, Ind.: Bobbs-Merrill, 1971.

Meriwether, James H. *Proudly We Can Be Africans: Black Americans and Africa, 1935–1961*. Chapel Hill: University of North Carolina Press, 2002.

Michel, Gregg L. *Struggle for a Better South: The Southern Student Organizing Committee, 1964–1969*. New York: Palgrave, 2004.

Mills, Nicolaus. *Like a Holy Crusade: Mississippi 1964: The Turning of the Civil Rights Movement in America*. Chicago: Ivan R. Dee, 1992.

Mills, Sara. *Michel Foucault*. New York: Routledge, 2003.

Mingus, Charles. *Charles Mingus Presents Charles Mingus*. New York: Candid LP, 1960.

———. *Mingus Ah Um*. New York: Columbia CD reissue, 1998.

Minor, Ethel N., ed. *Stokely Speaks: Black Power Back to Pan-Africanism*. New York: Vintage, 1971.

Morrison, Toni, ed. *To Die for the People: Huey P. Newton Selected Writings and Speeches*. New York: Writers and Readers, 1972.

Murray, Charles Shaar. *Crosstown Traffic: Jimi Hendrix and Post-war Pop*. London: Faber and Faber, 1989.

Myrdal, Gunnar, with Richard Sterner and Arnold Rose. *An American Dilemma: The Negro Problem and Modern Democracy*. New York: Harper and Brothers, 1944.

Neal, Mark Anthony. *What the Music Said: Black Popular Music and Black Public Culture*. New York: Routledge, 1999.

Newton, Huey P., with J. Herman Blake. *Revolutionary Suicide*. London: Wildwood House, 1974.

Ngozi-Brown, Scot. "The US Organization, Maulana Karenga, and Conflict with the Black Panther Party." *Journal of Black Studies* 28 (1997): 157–70.

Novick, Peter. *That Noble Dream: The "Objectivity Question" and the American Historical Profession*. Cambridge: Cambridge University Press, 1988.

Nyerere, Julius. *Ujamaa: Essays on Socialism*. London: Oxford University Press, 1968.

O'Neal, John. "As a Weapon Is to Warfare . . ." *Callaloo* 11 (February–October 1981): 65–70.

Ongiri, Amy Abugo. "'Black Arts for a Black People!': The Cultural Politics of the Black Power Movement and the Search for a Black Aesthetic." Ph.D. diss., Cornell University, 2000.

Patton, Sharon F. *African-American Art*. Oxford: Oxford University Press, 1998.

Payne, Charles M. *I've Got the Light of Freedom: The Organizing Tradition and the Mississippi Freedom Struggle*. Berkeley: University of California Press, 1995.

Pearson, Hugh. *The Shadow of the Panther: Huey Newton and the Price of Black Power in America*. Reading, Mass.: Addison-Wesley, 1994.

Perlstein, Daniel. "Teaching Freedom: SNCC and the Creation of the Mississippi Freedom Schools." *History of Education Quarterly* 30, no. 3 (Autumn 1990): 297–324.

Perry, Bruce. *Malcolm: The Life of a Man Who Changed Black America*. Barrytown, N.Y.: Station Hill, 1991.

———, ed. *Malcolm X: The Last Speeches*. New York: Pathfinder, 1989.

Pinkney, Alphonso. *Red, Black, and Green: Black Nationalism in the United States*. Cambridge: Cambridge University Press, 1976.

Plummer, Brenda Gayle. *Rising Wind: Black Americans and U.S. Foreign Affairs, 1935–1960*. Chapel Hill: University of North Carolina Press, 1996.

Poitier, Sidney. *This Life*. London: Coronet, 1980.

———. *The Measure of a Man: A Spiritual Autobiography*. New York: HarperCollins, 2000.

Polsgrove, Carol. *Divided Minds: Intellectuals and the Civil Rights Movement*. New York: Norton, 2001.

Porter, Lewis. *John Coltrane: His Life and Music*. Ann Arbor: University of Michigan Press, 1998.

Powell, Richard J. *Black Art and Culture in the 20th Century*. London: Thames and Hudson, 1997.

Pruter, Robert. *Chicago Soul*. Urbana: University of Illinois Press, 1991.

Rabinow, Paul, ed. *The Foucault Reader*. New York: Random House, 1984. Reprint, New York: Penguin, 1991.

Radical Teacher 40 (Fall 1991).

Rampersad, Arnold. "Langston Hughes's Fine Clothes to the Jew." *Callaloo* 26 (Winter 1986): 144–58.

——. *Jackie Robinson: A Biography.* New York: Ballantine, 1997.

Ransby, Barbara. *Ella Baker and the Black Freedom Movement: A Radical Democratic Vision.* Chapel Hill: University of North Carolina Press, 2003.

Reitan, Ruth. *The Rise and Decline of an Alliance: Cuba and African American Leaders in the 1960s.* East Lansing: Michigan State University Press, 1999.

Rhea, Joseph Tilden. *Race Pride and the American Identity.* Cambridge, Mass.: Harvard University Press, 1997.

Rickford, John Russell, and Russell John Rickford. *Spoken Soul: The Story of Black English.* New York: John Wiley and Sons, 2000.

Roach, Max. *We Insist! Freedom Now Suite.* New York: Candid CD reissue, 1989.

Robeson, Paul. *Here I Stand.* London: Dennis Dobson, 1958.

Robinson, Jackie. *I Never Had It Made: An Autobiography.* New York: Ecco, 1995.

Rogers, Kim Lacy. *Righteous Lives: Narratives of the New Orleans Civil Rights Movement.* New York: New York University Press, 1993.

Rollins, Sonny. *Freedom Suite.* Berkeley: Riverside CD reissue, 1989.

Rosenthal, David H. "Jazz in the Ghetto: 1950–1970." *Popular Music* 7 (1987): 51–56.

Runcie, John. "The Black Culture Movement and the Black Community." *Journal of American Studies* 10 (1976): 185–214.

Said, Edward W. *Culture and Imperialism.* London: Vintage, 1993.

Sales, William W., Jr. *From Civil Rights to Black Liberation: Malcolm X and the Organization of Afro-American Unity.* Boston: South End, 1994.

Salvatore, Nick. "Reverend C. L. Franklin and Political Activity in Detroit, 1954–1970." Paper delivered at Southern Historical Association annual conference, Baltimore, 8 November 2002. Author's notes.

Sammons, Jeffrey T. "'Race' and Sport: A Critical, Historical Examination." *Journal of Sport History* 21 (1994): 203–78.

Sandage, Scott A. "A Marble House Divided: The Lincoln Memorial, the Civil Rights Movement, and the Politics of Memory, 1939–1963." *Journal of American History* 80 (1993): 135–67.

Sandarg, Robert. "Jean Genet and the Black Panther Party." *Journal of Black Studies* 16 (1986): 269–82.

Sanger, Kerran L. *When the Spirit Says Sing!: The Role of Freedom Songs in the Civil Rights Movement.* New York: Garland, 1995.

Santoro, Gene. *Myself When I Am Real: The Life and Music of Charles Mingus.* New York: Oxford University Press, 2000.

Saul, Scott. *Freedom Is, Freedom Ain't: Jazz and the Making of the Sixties.* Cambridge, Mass.: Harvard University Press, 2003.

Scheer, Robert, ed. *Eldridge Cleaver: Post-Prison Writings and Speeches.* New York: Random House, 1969.

Seale, Bobby. *Seize the Time: The Story of the Black Panther Party.* London: Arrow, 1970.

Senghor, Leopold. *On African Socialism.* New York: Praeger, 1964.

Sidran, Ben. *Black Talk: How the Music of Black America Created a Radical Alternative to the Values of Western Literary Tradition.* 2nd ed. Edinburgh: Payback, 1995.

Simone, Nina. *Nina Simone in Concert.* London: Polygram CD reissue, 1990.

Smethurst, James Edward. *The Black Arts Movement: Literary Nationalism in the 1960s and 1970s.* Chapel Hill: University of North Carolina Press, 2005.

Smith, Suzanne E. *Dancing in the Street: Motown and the Cultural Politics of Detroit.* Cambridge, Mass.: Harvard University Press, 1999.

Smitherman, Geneva. *Talkin and Testifyin: The Language of Black America.* Boston: Houghton Mifflin, 1977.

Stoper, Emily. *The Student Nonviolent Coordinating Committee: The Growth of Radicalism in a Civil Rights Organization.* New York: Carlson, 1989.

Storey, John, ed. *Cultural Theory and Popular Culture: A Reader.* 2nd ed. London: Prentice Hall, 1998.

Stowe, David W. "The Politics of Café Society." *Journal of American History* 84 (1998): 1384–1406.

Sullivan, Patricia. *Days of Hope: Race and Democracy in the New Deal Era.* Chapel Hill: University of North Carolina Press, 1996.

Sundquist, Eric J., ed. *The Oxford W. E. B. Du Bois Reader.* Oxford: Oxford University Press, 1996.

Theoharis, Jeanne F., and Komozi Woodard, eds. *Freedom North: Black Freedom Struggles Outside the South, 1940–1980.* New York: Palgrave, 2003.

Thomas, Lorenzo. "The Shadow World: New York's Umbra Workshop and Origins of the Black Arts Movement." *Callaloo* 4 (October 1978): 53–72.

Thompson, Kristin, and David Bordwell. *Film History: An Introduction.* 2nd ed. Boston: McGraw-Hill, 2003.

Tjerandsen, Carl. *Education for Citizenship: A Foundation's Experience.* Santa Cruz, Calif.: Emil Schwartzhaupt Foundation, 1980.

Torres, Sasha. *Black, White and in Color: Television and Black Civil Rights.* Princeton, N.J.: Princeton University Press, 2003.

Tuck, Stephen G. N. *Beyond Atlanta: The Struggle for Racial Equality in Georgia, 1940–1980.* Athens: University of Georgia Press, 2001.

Tyson, Timothy B. "Robert F. Williams, 'Black Power,' and the Roots of the African American Freedom Struggle." *Journal of American History* 85 (1998): 540–70.

———. *Radio Free Dixie: Robert F. Williams and the Roots of Black Power.* Chapel Hill: University of North Carolina Press, 1999.

U.S. House Committee on Internal Security, 91st Congress. "The Black Panther Party: Its Origin and Development as Reflected in Its Official Weekly Newspaper *The Black Panther Black Community News Service.*" Washington D.C., 6 October 1970.

Van Deburg, William L. *New Day in Babylon: The Black Power Movement and American Culture 1965–1975.* Chicago: University of Chicago Press, 1992.

———. *Black Camelot: African-American Culture Heroes in Their Times, 1960–1980.* Chicago: University of Chicago Press, 1997.

———, ed. *Modern Black Nationalism: From Marcus Garvey to Louis Farrakhan.* New York: New York University Press, 1997.

Various Artists. *Hitsville USA: The Motown Singles Collection, 1959–1971*. London: Universal CD, 1992.

Various Artists. *Voices of the Civil Rights Movement: Black American Freedom Songs 1960–1966*. Washington, D.C.: Smithsonian Folkways CD, 1997.

Verney, Kevern. *African Americans and U.S. Popular Culture*. New York: Routledge, 2003.

Vincent, Rickey. *Funk: The Music, the People, and the Rhythm of the One*. New York: St. Martin's, 1996.

Vincent, Theodore. *Black Power and the Garvey Movement*. New York: Ramparts, 1971.

Von Eschen, Penny M. *Race against Empire: Black Americans and Anticolonialism, 1937–1957*. Ithaca, N.Y.: Cornell University Press, 1997.

Walker, Clarence E. "You Can't Go Home Again: The Problem with Afrocentrism." *Prospects* 18 (1993): 535–43.

Walker, Jenny. "Black Violence and Nonviolence in the Civil Rights and Black Power Era." Ph.D. diss., Newcastle University, 2000.

Wallace, Michele. *Black Macho and the Myth of the Superwoman*. 2nd ed. London: Verso, 1990.

Ward, Brian. *Just My Soul Responding: Rhythm and Blues, Black Consciousness and Race Relations*. London: UCL Press, 1998.

———. *Radio and the Struggle for Civil Rights in the South*. Gainesville: University Press of Florida, 2004.

———, ed. *Media, Culture and the Modern African American Freedom Struggle*. Gainesville: University Press of Florida, 2001.

Ward, Brian, and Tony Badger, eds. *The Making of Martin Luther King and the Civil Rights Movement*. Basingstoke, England: Macmillan, 1996.

Ward, Brian, and Jenny Walker. "'Bringing the Races Closer'?: Black-Oriented Radio in the South and the Civil Rights Movement." In *Dixie Debates: Perspectives on Southern Cultures*, ed. Richard H. King and Helen Taylor, 130–49. New York: New York University Press, 1996.

Ward, Francis, and Val Gray. "The Black Artist—His Role in the Struggle." *Black Scholar* 2, no. 5 (January 1971): 23–32.

Warren, Nagueyalti. "Pan-African Cultural Movements: From Baraka to Karenga." *Journal of Negro History* 75 (1990): 16–28.

Washington, Booker T. *Up from Slavery*. New York: Dover, 1995.

Washington, James M., ed. *A Testament of Hope: The Essential Writings and Speeches of Martin Luther King, Jr.* New York: HarperCollins, 1986.

Watters, Pat. *Down to Now: Reflections on the Southern Civil Rights Movement*. Athens: University of Georgia Press, 1971.

Watts, Jerry Gafio. *Amiri Baraka: The Politics and Art of a Black Intellectual*. New York: New York University Press, 2001.

Weatherby, W. J. *James Baldwin: Artist on Fire*. London: Michael Joseph, 1989.

Weisbord, Robert G. *Ebony Kinship: Africa, Africans, and the Afro-American*. Westport, Conn.: Greenwood, 1973.

Weisbrot, Robert. *Freedom Bound: A History of America's Civil Rights Movement.* New York: Plume, 1990.

Werner, Craig. *A Change Is Gonna Come: Music, Race and the Soul of America.* New York: Plume, 1998.

West, Cornel. *Race Matters.* Boston: Beacon, 1993.

Wiener, Jonathan M. "Radical Historians and the Crisis in American History, 1959–1980." *Journal of American History* 76 (1989): 399–434.

Wilkins, Roy, with Tom Mathews. *Standing Fast: The Autobiography of Roy Wilkins.* New York: Penguin, 1982.

Williams, Mance. *Black Theatre in the 1960s and 1970s: A Historical-Critical Analysis of the Movement.* Westport, Conn.: Greenwood, 1985.

Williams, Robert F. *Negroes with Guns.* New ed. Detroit: Wayne State University Press, 1998.

———. "And God Lay Sleeping." Unpublished manuscript, in Tim Tyson's possession.

Woodard, Komozi. *A Nation within a Nation: Amiri Baraka LeRoi Jones and Black Power Politics.* Chapel Hill: University of North Carolina Press, 1999.

ya Salaam, Kalamu. "Enriching the Paper Trail: An Interview with Tom Dent." *African American Review* 22, no. 2 (Summer 1993): 327–44.

Young, Andrew. *An Easy Burden: The Civil Rights Movement and the Transformation of America.* New York: HarperCollins, 1996.

Young, Cynthia. "Havana Up in Harlem: LeRoi Jones, Harold Cruse and the Making of a Cultural Revolution." *Science and Society* 65, no. 1 (Spring 2001): 12–38.

Youth of the Rural Organizing and Cultural Center. *Minds Stayed on Freedom: The Civil Rights Struggle in the Rural South.* Boulder, Colo.: Westview, 1991.

Zinn, Howard. *Albany: A Study in National Responsibility.* Atlanta, Ga.: Southern Regional Council, 1962.

———. *SNCC: The New Abolitionists.* Boston: Beacon, 1964.

Index

Page numbers in italics refer to illustrations.

Joe Street is a senior lecturer in history at Northumbria University, Newcastle.

www.ingramcontent.com/pod-product-compliance
Lightning Source LLC
Chambersburg PA
CBHW021357090426
42742CB00009B/890